FREEDOM MADE FLESH

FREEDOM
MADE FLESH

The Mission of Christ and His Church

Ignacio Ellacuría

Translated by John Drury

ORBIS BOOKS
MARYKNOLL   NEW YORK

Originally published as *Teología política* by Ediciones del
Secretariado Social Interdiocesano, San Salvador, El Salvador.

Copyright © 1976 Orbis Books, Maryknoll, New York 10545

Library of Congress Catalog Card Number: 75-29759

Cloth: ISBN 0-88344-1403   Paper: ISBN 0-88344-1411

Manufactured in the United States of America

CONTENTS

Foreword

Latin America has often been pictured—or better, car-
icatured—as a sleeping man with a large *sombrero* on his head
relaxing in the sun. In Church circles, Latin America is seen as
the largest Catholic area of the world, but an area of backward-
ness in regards to culture, knowledge, and doctrinal formation.

This distorted picture has suddenly changed. The social
revolutions in Cuba and Peru have produced the beginnings of
alternate social systems. The changing reality of Latin America
has also produced a new type of theological thinking. Paulo
Freire and Helder Camara in north-east Brazil developed a new
educational theory based on their understanding of the reality
of Brazil. Freire's method of *conscientización* (consciousness raising) expressed in his books, above all in *Pedagogy of the Oppressed*,
has received world wide acclaim. After his exile from Brazil,
Freire even became a professor at Harvard!

Latin theologians, using the basic insight of *conscientización*, developed a new theological method called the
Theology of Liberation. Instead of starting from eternal truths,
which are then applied to the "world-life situation," the liberation theologians start with the reality or environment in which
the people are. This initial point illustrates the need for collaboration between the theologian and the social scientist. This
fruitful collaboration can be seen in the works of Juan Luis
Segundo, Gustavo Gutiérrez, José Míguez Bonino, and Rubem
Alves, to name only a few. The constant dialogue between
theologian and social scientist enables both to enrich their
understanding of the *total* person and total society.

The publication of Ignacio Ellacuría's book will introduce another theologian of liberation to the English-speaking world. This Basque Jesuit has lived and worked in the tiny Central American country of El Salvador for some twenty-five years. The "typical" Latin American theologian does not do his theologizing in an ivory tower; on the contrary, these theologians are ordinarily involved with student action groups, with the clergy who are dedicated to the integral development of people, and with groups of militant Christians. Ellacuría is no exception. He has been an active member of the various action orientated groups—clerical and lay—which have striven to develop a Christianity and Church lived out of the mandate of the Medellín Conference of 1968—pathfinder for the post-Vatican II Latin American Church.

The works of Ellacuría have been published mostly in local journals in Central America. A former student of Karl Rahner, he, perhaps more than anyone, has responded to the criticisms of Metz and others who fault Rahner's theology for its lack of "political" involvement. Ellacuría, while aware of the latest currents in European political theology, has chosen a different route than the critics of Rahner. He has tried to combine the insights of Rahner with those of the Theology of Liberation—a synthesis, which while theological in tone and content, is at the same time imbued with the reality of Central America.

"God's salvific communication and revelation are historical." The importance of this statement is one of the underlying themes which flow through his entire work. God is at work among his people here and now. The Church's role or mission is precisely "to proclaim the gospel message as the true salvation of human beings in history and beyond history."

On that broad canvas, Ellacuría skillfully paints the image of the Latin American Church as it emerges into an age of maturity. Its role is integrally united with liberation that is a political, religious, and Christian concept. This discussion of the role of "local churches" was one of the most discussed points of the

1974 Roman Synod. Ellacuría aligns himself clearly with the Third World Churches that are striving to express their "communion" with each other and with the Universal Church through a multiplicity of forms that respond to the local Churches' reality in time and place.

The last section of the book deals with a particular problem that confronts all Christians who find themselves in a revolutionary situation—"Violence and the Cross." As Ellacuría says, that phrase "probably provokes certain gut reactions even before it does anything else." Drawing upon the work of Lorenz and Freud in psychology, Ellacuría confronts violence from a theological and Christian viewpoint in the context of Latin America, which experiences, to use the phrase of Medellín, "institutionalized violence." The alternate Christian approaches to violence may be summarized by the names of Charles de Foucauld, Martin Luther King, and Camilo Torres. Ellacuría has tried "to provide a theoretical framework for concrete Christian action designed to combat the violence of injustice and the sin of violence."

For those of us who work or have worked in Latin America, this book hopefully speaks of our experiences and unifies them in a "systematic" way. For those who only "know about" Latin America, this book should serve as a helpful introduction to some of the Christian ferment which is bubbling there. To anyone it should serve as a model of the profession of faith of a dedicated Christian minister at work in the daily life of Latin America.

Lawrence A. Egan, M.M.

FREEDOM MADE FLESH

Introduction

1

Salvation History
and Salvation in History

One of the fundamental themes in present-day theology is the historicity of salvation. If this theme is not dealt with, the other themes in theology will not acquire their full import nor their full concrete thrust. For centuries now, due to a Greek philosophical mentality that is quite alien to the orientation of the Bible, a fundamental theme in theology has been the relationship of the supernatural to the natural. In other words, it has dealt with a theme formulated in terms of nature. On the one hand there was *the supernatural:* the trinitarian God revealed to us by divine favor and grace. On the other hand there was *the natural:* man as he appeared to be *in se* and once and for all. This problematic has had incalculable impact on theology, preaching, ascetics, and the Church's encounter with the world, so that by our own day it has deformed Christian praxis and undermined the relevance of our theology.

In the course of these pages I shall present reasons why that formulation of the problem should now be superseded, why it should be replaced by a more global presentation in terms of history: a history that includes but also goes beyond nature. This latter presentation should not be regarded as less theological than the older formulation as dealing with a dimension that

3

is only peripheral to the Christian faith. The newer formulation in terms of history is in fact more profound, more radically metaphysical. It is much more actual in the twofold sense of that term: i.e., in the Greek sense of "act" as reality in all its fulness, and in the temporal sense of "actual" as realization in the here-and-now present.

The initial formulation is simple enough: What does salvation history have to do with salvation in history? The term "salvation history" is a much more biblical and Christian way of expressing what classical theologians called "the supernatural." And the term "salvation in history" is a much more "actual" way of expressing what they called "nature."

The seeming parallelism of the two sets of terms is misleading, for the two formulations are not parallel at all. For one thing, history involves nature but subsumes it. I point this out here to show theologians who have been misshaped by the "nature" approach that the formulation in terms of history is more radical than their approach. Much more importantly, I bring it up here to point up the profound transformation that must take place in theology and the reflexive presentation of the faith if we are to move beyond a theological framework based on the duality of natural and supernatural, if we are to develop a theological framework based on salvation history and salvation in history. Thanks in part to Vatican II, people now tend to talk a great deal about salvation history. But there is reason to wonder how much conceptual seriousness they attribute to either term. In particular, one may wonder whether any serious effort has been made to spell out the implications of "salvation in history" for "salvation history," and vice versa.

It is political theology that has attempted to tackle the latter issue. But political theology is enveloped in such a cloud of prejudice and ignorance that there is good reason to believe its contribution has not been of much profit to us. For some it has been a rather ambiguous spur, for others it has been an equally ambiguous backward step. In these pages, therefore, I shall try to *do* political theology rather than to bandy the term about. My

aim is not to ape the latest European fashion in theology. Quite
aside from the theoretical reasons which demonstrate that we
must historicize salvation, that it is not a matter of merely being
fashionable, these pages are prompted by a real-life situation
and a real-life necessity. If a person does not sense and feel this
necessity, it is because he is not living his today in an "actual"
way. Let us consider this point briefly.

Secularization: A Determining Factor in Christian Activity Today

Here we shall not go into the whole theoretical problem of
secularization. We need only advert to the fact of secularization. If theologians were to claim that it is a superficial fact with
which theology need not concern itself, that would be the best
proof of the superficiality and ahistoricity of theology itself.
What is more, concern with this fact cannot take the form of a
special chapter or appendix in theology. The phenomenon of
secularization must be given more serious and comprehensive
consideration by theology. Any and every theological formulation must be reviewed and reconsidered in the light of the fact
that it is being addressed to an increasingly secular, or rather
secularized world. The difference between "secular" and "secularized" is very important. Proclamation of the faith to a world
that has always been secular is one thing; proclamation of the
faith to a world that is now undergoing secularization is quite
another thing. Today the world is being secularized in a positive sense; in other words, it is abandoning a religious form of
existence to don an areligious form of existence. That is the
world to which faith addresses itself today, the world in which
and from which we must systematically and theoretically
elaborate our faith.

Secularization is becoming more and more a fact. No one can
doubt that. The world is increasingly becoming a positive
value, and hence a pressure factor. Religious pressure—interior

and exterior, private and social—is more and more being re-placed by an increasingly interiorized secular pressure. It is not just that the world is becoming a larger factor in personal subjectivity and socialized objectivity. It is not just that it is exerting more and more attractive and configurative force over our lives. The world is also *worth more* and *valued more highly*. The higher valuation of the world is not only proper; it should also be promoted more earnestly as a historical sign of Christian salvation. The world cannot be equated with the flesh and viewed as the enemy of the soul. To be sure, the world as a social reality can be turned into a spectral soul world as well as an alienating enemy of social man; this is another theme that will come out clearly in the pages that follow. But this does not change the fact that the world, insofar as it is being shaped and turned into history by man, is also becoming more worthwhile; and that this greater value is more and more being subjectivized by a large portion of society.

At the same time the classic realm of "the religious," as something over against the world with its growing value, is *worth less* and is *valued less*. Here I am not referring to the Christian faith nor to the Church as a community of authentic Christian faith. I am referring to individual and collective religiosity. Whatever may be our judgment about the ultimate significance of the sociological distinction between faith and religion,[1] we can say that such a distinction is necessary from a Christian and theological point of view. It is particularly neces-sary from a sociological viewpoint insofar as it concerns a distinction between religiosity in psychological and cultural terms and Christian faith. (We should also maintain the distinc-tion between religion and Christian faith and, even more so, between religion and faith as we would use the term in refer-ence to the political mission of Jesus.)

To religiosity we would consign certain vitalist and emotionalist necessities as well as certain public and sacral manifestations whose connection with the Christian faith is highly debatable. (I am thinking, for example, of certain outpourings of piety by hippies and—for all their differences—the sumptuous sacral panoply of many manifestations involving the hierarchy of the Church.) For our purposes here, however, we need only underline the fact that the socio-cultural efficacy of "the religious" is diminishing in value and people's evaluation, and so is the force of "religious" motivations in prompting people to accept and live the faith. And that is quite aside from the fact that the religious element has often been turned into religiosity.[2]

Now if the growth of the *saeculum* (the temporalized world) and the decline of the sacral-religious realm are facts, it is obvious that only a secularized faith and theology have, or can have, complete meaning for an increasingly secularized world. It is undeniable that classical theology was formulated from within a societally religious world and for a societally religious world—in any case, for a world that is not ours today. It would be sad if we failed to see the implications of this sociological fact. We must not entertain the idea that classical theology can retain its value permanently even though it developed in a different sociological milieu. We must not imagine that such a milieu was the ideal situation for working at a theology, concluding that the proper thing to do is to keep on doing the same sort of theology in order to make that old religious world possible once again. It would be an impossible project, feasible only in a ghetto which ignored historical reality. And, in fact, it is not a desirable undertaking.

Faith and theology must take the world of today in all seriousness. In particular they must take the situation of the common people seriously and ponder its theological import. Only then will they be taken seriously and deserve people's interest. Let us note the fact that present-day theology frequently holds no interest even for those who are preparing for the priesthood. There is no simple explanation for the fact, and we certainly cannot place all the blame on the current expositions of theology; but the fact is significant nevertheless. We might hazard the opinion that the problem is not always what theology says but rather what is left unsaid. In other words, the problem is that it never manages to point up the secular dimension of its theological statements. Here I am not referring to the old debate over dogmatic theology versus kerygmatic theology, the final echoes of which I heard at Innsbruck. But even that debate indicates that the problem is intrinsic to the whole question of the relationship between faith and theology.

We cannot evade that question by maintaining that there is a scientific theology which should be cultivated in and for itself as a science, and also a theology that might serve the needs of pastoral activity. To say that theology can be a science is to make a "secular" affirmation, but such an affirmation belongs to a world that has long since passed away. Our secularized world cannot help but smile at it. The secularization of science inevitably entails the de-sciencing of theology. It is quite possible that certain elements of theological learning can be made scientific in a methodical way, but they would be scientific on a lower level and would represent a redoubt of the past in the present-day scientific model. By the same token, however, the fact that theology is not a science does not mean that it is nothing more than a learned catechism or that it derives its vigor from purely sociological reflections and activities. We should situate it on levels of intellectual reflection akin to those on which philosophical thinking operates.

This statement would seem to be quite traditional and to shed little light on the subject. It all depends, of course, on our conception of philosophy and its function. In the last analysis, philosophy is an intellectual treatment of real problems or, if you prefer, of the true reality of real-life problems. In other words, it is an intellectual treatment of the problems which reality, in all its totality and ultimateness, poses. Thus philosophical activity implies that we are living in reality with all the strength of our intelligence. It does not imply that we are engaged in some purely contemplative activity. Philosophical concepts must be historical and total, effective and real.

Not all who study theology should do so at the same level,

but each should do so at the maximum level of which he is capable. And the objective should be the same: to comprehend and transform reality from a Christian point of view, where transformation—and its conditions—is part of the transformation. The important thing, then, would be to show that a given theological affirmation is transforming, and in what sense it is, and that a given transformation demands a meaning—which may cost us much intellectual effort. In all likelihood this intellectual effort will not be shunned by people who see plainly that it is indispensable for a profound transformation. And this process should be abetted, as we shall see, by a specific orientation of theology. Such an orientation is what will be proposed in the following pages.

This task becomes more urgent if we consider those who are being initiated into theology. I personally do not believe that the fundamental element of a theological faculty or of a university is the students, that the primary task is to prepare professionals—including people whose consciousness has been raised. In my opinion, that is a bourgeois conception of what a theology department and a university are supposed to be. If it is a legitimate objective, it is a secondary, derivative one. The fundamental aim should be to be a critical and creative consciousness effectively at work in the service of the community. Consciousness implies science and scholarly knowledge, but it necessarily implies a knowledge "of" something, and we must pursue the consequences to the very end. It seems clear to me that the students can and should contribute to this function, serving especially as a stimulus.

In our present case, students are persistently asking about the problem which we have referred to as the problem of theology and faith. They are open advocates of a secularized world, and they are demanding a secularization of theology—not an outmoded form of secularization but a present-day version. Among students of theology we frequently find a fundamental problem. It is their own subjective version of an objective problem: i.e., the seeming duality of dimensions embodied in our talk about salvation history on the one hand and salvation in history on the other. On the one hand they feel they must participate in the world and help to transform it even more. On the other hand they feel they must proclaim the Christian faith.

Are these two tasks distinct? Are they connected by merely extrinsic motives: e.g., by a mandate of obedience, by purity of intention, by a process of humanization as mere prelude to evangelization? We must point up the intrinsic connection between a passion for the salvation of this world and a passion for proclaiming and fleshing out the Christian faith. Only then will we be able to open up a new pathway for those who are unwilling to mutilate either one of the two dimensions. To put it another way: Only a secular faith that is fully faith and fully secular, and hence only a theology with these same characteristics, can be acceptable today.

So the next question is this: What is the peculiar cast of present-day secularization? We have already indicated that it is an effort to redeem the catastrophic situation of humanity, of man in society. Secularization is a historical process, and the historical form it takes today can be given a name at least. It is "politicization."

Politicization appears on the scene as a historical process. It implies the transition from being-as-nature to being-as-history in the constitution of social man. History certainly erupts out of nature. The world becomes increasingly less "nature" and more "history," but the latter does not annul the former. Nature continues as a dynamic tension underlying history. At the same time, however, liberation from nature paves the way for a new totality, something that is both "new" and a "totality" in its own right. Nature is one totality, history is another totality of a distinct sort. History causes something new to break into nature: not only individual liberty but also collective or social liberty with its conditions—without which the former would be an abstract fiction.

Now this new totalization has a specific name: politicization.

The term is weighed down with obscure shades and colors. Secularization is a process of historicization, and today history is inevitably a political history. It might seem that I am playing with words but I am not, even though I do not have space here to explore each one of these stages in detail. Let me simply point to two facts. First of all, there is the sociological fact that the social, public, collective dimension is more than ever the dimension that forms the totality of human life in its concrete completeness; in this sense it is no exaggeration to say that the human individual is an abstraction. The second fact is more empirical in nature: More and more we find that authentically Christian vocations tend towards activity that is indiscriminately labeled political; at the same time we can readily see the sort of judgment passed against the present-day attitude of the Church by those who are concerned with maintaining the established order.

This is the problem on which we must focus our attention. And we must start from the fact of secularization, which in many instances takes the form of politicization, of trying to save human beings in their most concrete historical reality.

The Prejudice that Salvation Is Ahistorical

Inertia and fixation in the established order are not the only things which fight against this new formulation concerning the radical historicity of theology. There is also the continuing prejudice that salvation is ahistorical. Even though people may deny it with their words, it continues to be one of the most serious obstacles to truly living and reflecting on the faith.

The root of this prejudice is well known. To formulate it in Hegelian terms, it is rooted in the primacy of the principle of identity over the principle of contradiction. Some people try to blame this prejudice on Aristotle, when in fact it should be attributed to a Parmenidean and Platonic interpretation of Aristotle. This interpretation looks at man and social realities in terms of nature and substance. It sees man as part of the cosmos, as a natural being, except that his nature is more elevated or that he is part of nature in a freer way. Being is nature and nature is being, identical with itself in spite of its accidental and transitory mutations. At bottom nothing really happens, or the same thing happens all the time. So we get a static interpretation of nature and a naturalistic interpretation of man. At best, the unity of man, world, and history is broken up into an abstract scheme where man lives in a world moving through time. In other words, the world and history are turned into addenda extrinsic to man himself; and he himself is what he is *in se*, so that he need only act out what he already is. Both the structural implication of historical man in a historical world and the inherent dynamism entailed in this are completely lost.

This same prejudice toward making things abstract and static also tends to make man and God extrinsic to each other and to deny God's spending time in humanity precisely as history. God either spends his time with man in nature, or else in history in only a partial way. The whole problem of historical salvation is launched down a dead-end street. For two realities that are basically extrinsic to each other or—what comes down to the same thing—closed in upon themselves cannot come together in one and the same salvation. Hence the relationship between salvation history and salvation in history is also an extrinsic one.

A correct interpretation of this problem, one that was equally philosophical and theological, would be of great help and interest in getting us out of the gratuitous trap into which we have fallen. We cannot tackle that task here. I bring up the problem simply to show that theology may entail critical work that is difficult to execute. Making theology effective means making it real in the strongest sense of the term. But right now I should simply like to take a look at the historical character of salvation in order to show how little Christian foundation there is for an ahistorical view of it.

The Existence of a Salvation History

That there is a salvation history has never been denied. The problem is that it has not been taken seriously in the structuring of theology. Classical theology was too "scientific" to concern itself with the accidental and the changing, and it could not even verify the fact of salvation history because of its profound ignorance of the biblical data. Today salvation history is affirmed more explicitly, and attempts are made to turn it into the guiding thread of the new theology; but there still has not been much success in historicizing the message.

The classic text in this new approach is Cullmann's book on salvation in history.[3] It did much to introduce us once again to the historical dimension of the Christian faith. Going beyond Bultmann, Cullmann underlined the twofold historicity of salvation: 1) Salvation took place historically, that is, in a process; 2) this process can be verified with historical objectivity. Thus Cullmann got beyond the individual and personalist viewpoint with regard to the acceptance of the Christian message. He did not, however, lay sufficient stress on the total character of salvation, which would include its secular and political cast. (We shall return to Cullmann when we discuss the political mission of Jesus.)

Right now I should like to present a few ideas that point up the historical character of salvation.

God's word to man is a historical word. It is not a natural word, a word derived from the natural essence of the world and things. It is a historical word that breaks through into nature. This is obvious in the history of revelation, but it takes on its full import when the Revealer of the Father becomes history. As Hegel points out in another context (in the Introduction to his *History of Philosophy*), the real miracle is not the interruption of some law of nature; it is the irruption of history into nature, of personal liberty in the fixed course of nature. It is history much more than nature that is the proper locale of revelation and divine communication. This statement is of incalculable importance for theology and for Christian praxis. It is in history rather than in nature that we are going to call attention to the living God.

At the same time Christ, as the Revealer of the Father, is the Word for all human beings and for each individual, for all time and for right now. He is not some finished objective datum but a living word which implies, in its very being, the otherness of the listener in his or her own situation. Even if there had been no promise of the living presence of Jesus' Spirit, the historicity of revelation would be proven by the fact that it is directed to human beings living in historical situations that form their concrete reality.

So there is a history of revelation, and in more than one sense. There is a history of revelation, not only because revelation has been gradually given to mankind as it slowly fashions itself in history, but also because God's revelation continues to be given to us in our history. We can acknowledge that the deposit of faith is closed *as a system of possibilties*, as Zubiri does for example; but history is precisely the actualization of possibilities. Only the final end of history will actualize all of revelation; that which is revelation only as possibility is not yet actual revelation. The Christian and the theologian must turn their attention to the history that is being made by human beings if they wish to hear and heed the total, objective datum of revelation.

What does this divine word do? It saves. It may well be, as people like Zubiri have suggested, that salvation is not the most profound way of expressing what God is trying to do with mankind. But if we do not try to define it too completely and exactly, it may indeed serve as a good synthesis of God's activity with mankind. The important thing here, in any case, is to specify the historical character of this "salvation": Is salvation history a salvation in history or a salvation beyond and outside of history?

Salvation History as a Salvation in History

Salvation history is a salvation in history: This statement is the theme of this whole book. We cannot uncover its whole import until we turn our attention to history—specifically, to some of the basic steps in the history of revelation, and particularly its culminating moment: the historical life of Jesus.

At this point I simply want to frame the problem in general terms. If salvation is historical, then two things follow: 1) It will differ according to the time and place in which it is fleshed out; 2) it must be realized and brought about in the historical reality of human beings, in their total concrete reality. Hence one should not be scandalized to find that the Church is continually learning what its concrete mission is by taking fresh readings of revelation in the changing reality of human history; and that it proclaims salvation in different ways, depending on different situations. On the empirical level there may well be a great deal of opportunism in this, but that does not alter the fact that this is the only way for the Church to remain loyal to its mission. In the final analysis, God chose to proclaim and realize salvation through a human being in history who was the culmination of a long series of human beings in history. Moreover, this salvation is addressed to human beings in history, not to atemporal spirits.

It is in history, in its political history, that Israel learns to transcend the naturalistic idea of God and to comprehend his salvation in historical terms. One can say, in fact, that historical revelation was attained historically as an interpretation of historical reality itself. To put it another way, it was obtained in and through the concrete political situation of a people who gradually discovered a living God for living human beings. This point is brought out well by Auzou.[4] He shows us that the first Exodus was the pathway taken by the chosen people towards a profound experience of God as savior. Starting out from their socio-political experience, the Israelites struggled to realize a new interpretation of God and themselves in and through a new socio-political form. The same can be said of the so-called second Exodus where, on a higher level, the same experience is repeated so that it may eventually be transcended. The Christian pasch will transcend the political experience of the second Exodus even more, but it will not annul that experience by any means. Hence it is in the history of a people with concrete problems of a political nature that God's revelation and salvation take on flesh and blood. Moving from political experience to religious experience, they wait and look for Yahweh's revelation to interpret and resolve the problems of their nation as a public totality. God's revelation belonged to the chosen people. Membership in this people, which was the overall object of salvation, is the thing which permits each individual to hope for his own salvation. And the salvation of the individual relates to his or her life here and now. In and through this here-and-now salvation, the Israelites gradually come to learn about a higher salvation.

This approach is not without its hazards. The Jewish people were gradually coming to the point of identifying and equating the political realm and the religious realm. This would have annulled both their political life and their religious life. Yet we must remember that this was the way chosen by God to communicate himself to man and hence deserves our respect and attention. Further on in this book I shall try to show that it is in and through a new kind of political experience that a secularized world can obtain the experience of God as Savior. In the meantime, the pedagogical approach chosen by God for his chosen people should at least teach us not to be scandalized by people's efforts to find a political approach to faith. The curious thing is that Marx and the new rightist groups share this feeling of being scandalized, though of course in very different senses.

Let us consider for just a moment Marx's critical comments in his first thesis against Feuerbach. The theoretical, purely contemplative and interior approach is not the authentic and fully human approach. Feuerbach's flight into individualistic interiorization was due to the fact that the only form of praxis with which he was familiar was the ominous and rather base form practiced by the Jewish people. Marx recognizes the fact that Jewish religiosity was a political praxis, but it was an impure form of political praxis. As he sees it, Feuerbach was right in rejecting that praxis but wrong in thinking that anthropological purification could ever lay in abandoning any and all forms of political praxis. The Jewish approach was to be rejected because it was not transformative in itself, because it turned the work of transformation over to God in terms of reward and punishment. Jewish praxis was an alienation of praxis. We cannot flee from praxis, we must retrieve it in its specific immanent essence. We must abandon all reference to transcendence and an alienating God, immanently living, instead, the transforming praxis of nature and history. As Marx sees it, human plenitude or salvation lies in fashioning ourselves into a human society, a social humanity.

Much in these criticisms by Marx is valid, but we might well raise certain questions: Is Marx's interpretation of Jewish praxis correct? Does he correctly interpret the anthropological secularization of Christianity when he sees it purely and simply as a process of subjective interiorization? Is there no praxis for the full realization of man other than a closed immanent praxis? Marx certainly made clear the fact that man should not limit himself to contemplating and interpreting the world; that man must go on to transform it; that this transforming work is the principal ethical mission of man; that the inescapable objective of social activity is the construction of a human society and that this implies a social humanity; that if man does not realize this new humanity, no one else will do it for him; and that man's salvation or condemnation lies in the success of this work of realizing a new humanity. However, Marx did not make clear the fact that he saw Jewish religious politicization, Feuerbach's interiorization, and Marxist praxis as the sole and exclusive alternatives.

Post-Marxist theology has the task of seeking out a new

alternative in the task of making sure that salvation history will be salvation in history. Christians must admit that the socio-political version of the Jewish religion and that of their own political praxis are very primitive. They must insist that the presence of God in natural and historical reality is not the presence of a demiurge who miraculously rewards or punishes the religious behavior of individuals and nations. On the theoretical level they must seek a line of action that will transform the world and human society; then they must implement it in their praxis. It will serve as the essential sign, without which man's transcendent salvation cannot be rendered present. Christians must insist that history is the locale of God's revelation, and that this revelation is meant to show us here and now that God is revealing himself in history.

In short, Christianity must take seriously the thrust and import of the Word made flesh in history. God revealed himself in history, not directly but in a sign: humanity in history. There is no access to God except through this sign in history. Christians affirm that there is no communication with God the Father except through the sign of Jesus' humanity. One of the tasks of political theology is to elevate this affirmation into a transcendent, universal category. We must pick up once again the statement that Jesus has been constituted the Lord of history. History is the interval between his first and second coming. It is there that we must prepare the way of the Lord. Action in and on history, the salvation of social man in history, is the real pathway whereby God will ultimately deify man. It is not just that salvation history entails salvation in history as a corollary. Rather, the salvation of man in history is the one and only way in which salvation history can reach its culmination.

NOTES

1. See the remarks by Caffarena in *Metafísica transcendental* (Madrid, 1970), p. 13.

2. Here I cannot debate the issue raised by Danielou: i.e., that public religion is necessary if the Christian faith is not to be confined to a cultivated elite. The problem he poses is an interesting and relevant one, but his solution does not seem to be acceptable.

3. See Oscar Cullmann, *Salvation in History* (New York: Harper & Row, 1967).

4. See especially *De la servidumbre al servicio. Estudio del Libro del Exodo* (Madrid: Fax, 1969).

PART ONE

*The Political Character
of Jesus' Mission*

2

The Prophetic Mission
of Jesus

i.e., Jesus as Prophet.

To determine the nature and extent of salvation in history
within salvation history, we must center our reflection on Jesus
himself, who brings salvation history to its culmination. The
thrust and import of this culmination is certainly historical; in
other words, it comes from and moves towards something. At
the same time Jesus is clearly an indispensable key to the whole
process and somehow a definitive element in this coming from
and moving towards. Thus the prophecy of the Old Testament, for example, takes on its full ascendent import only in
terms of what Jesus himself represents. By the same token the
meaning of Jesus himself would escape us if we disregarded the
history of prophecy.

This is True

There is no lack of difficulties in trying to explore Jesus'
prophetic mission. A study of the political character of Jesus'
mission would certainly provide us with a sound orientation for
determining how much salvation in history plays a role in the
full picture of salvation history. But the political character of
his mission is already clouded and obscured in the New Testament version of his life. It continues to be obscured in the
course of centuries by both the classic and the less classic
readings of the New Testament. The classic readings suffer

from an ignorance of exegesis and history; the lesser readings suffer from a mere desire to continue what has been said before.

The political character of his mission is also obscured by the ahistorical cast of various traditional christologies, which do not take Jesus' historical life very seriously in trying to construct themselves. This brings us up against a preliminary problem that we must discuss a bit: What can a christology be? What should it be?

Problematic Character of Various Christologies

Theo-logical reflection on salvation in history clearly demands a christ-ology. Faith in Jesus is a decisive element in trying to understand salvation history, but this faith can and must, insofar as it is able, come into contact with the human logos. This converts faith in Jesus into a christology.

But what *logos* are we dealing with here? What approach of reason is the one which will enable faith to unfurl into the most complete intellectual comprehension? That is the issue we shall try to examine right now.

To answer these questions, we must begin with the fact that we find christology, distinct christologies in fact, in the New Testament itself. Present-day theology is discussing this whole issue, but we do well to recall it here. The New Testament does not simply record the faith of a primitive community in Jesus. It also transmits a process of reflection that was worked out by the primitive community or by one of its budding theologians, and that is theoretical and "logical" in varying degrees. This point cannot be overlooked because *logos* implies a situational reality which delimits approaches and selectively interprets events. This delimitation and its attendant interpretation is justified, and in the present case both can be regarded as inspired. But that does not mean that later christological reflection is to overlook the delimited and interpretive character of what might otherwise be regarded as unvarnished historical event.

The clearest proof of this is the fact that there are distinct christologies in the New Testament. Not only are events selected and systematicized in different ways, they are also reflected upon in different ways. These different reflections are not totally irreconcilable, of course, but that does not mean we can dismiss the differences lightly. Let me give just one example here that is closely related to our present theme. The christology of the gospel of circumcision is quite distinct from the christology of Paul's gospel message. Without going deeply into this much discussed issue, we can say that the former gospel pays more attention to the historical Jesus and to his social and historical repercussions. These repercussions are closely bound up with each other, needless to say. Paul's gospel, on the other hand, pays relatively little attention to the flesh-and-blood Jesus of history. It moves perhaps a bit too quickly to the Christ of faith. History is not to be identified with mere happening of course, but the sense and import of history cannot be indifferent to the visible, incarnate, real-life event that antecedes faith.

This difference is an important one. It indicates that the differing christological readings of the same historical Jesus are due in large part to the needs and situation of those who have faith in Jesus. Paul did not live together with Jesus, and this fact is worth noting. It is also worth noting that some Jewish Christians who did live with Jesus may have been a bit too close to him and may have failed to get beyond the material aspects of his behavior in history. That, too, would be a limitation. And the limitations of the various New Testament christologies must be overcome in a subsequent christology which takes them into account and then reworks them historically in a new reading that is framed historically.

This was not done by the Greek *logos*, which was indiscriminately used by many theologians as if it were the best or only possible *logos*. This is not to suggest that the Greek *logos* cannot make any contribution to christology. The earliest Councils demonstrate both the advantages and the limitations of the Greek *logos* in trying to work out a fresh elaboration of the Christian faith. Moreover, it can be maintained that the pre-ponderant use of a specific Greek *logos* was a fairly adequate response to a particular historical situation: i.e., where history was the concern of a small elite and was based on speculative contemplation rather than on any concern for the social trans-formation of a whole nation or people. That individualistic and intellectualist elite was interested in a theoretical and idealistic grasp of the Christian mystery. They worked out a historical response which embodied certain permanent achievements but which was not definitive, as in the Council of Chalcedon for example. But that does not mean that they spoke the most substantive word about christology or even that we cannot make further progress on the level of intellectual interpretation.

Today we need a new christology. Our major concern can-not be to quiet our intellectual unrest by somehow effecting a conceptual reconciliation between the oneness of Jesus' person and the duality of his nature. Today we must explore how Jesus realizes his salvific mission to man in a full and perfect way. This is not a purely functional emphasis, nor is it any less profound than the older framing of the question. If history is a more solidly metaphysical entity than nature, then our reflec-tions on history should be more profound than our reflections on nature and hence more operational.

Our new christology must give the history of the flesh-and-blood Jesus its full weight as revelation. Today it would be absolutely ridiculous to try to fashion a christology in which the historical realization of Jesus' life did not play a decisive role. The "mysteries of Jesus' life," which once were treated peripherally as part of ascetics, must be given their full import—provided, of course, that we explore exegetically and historically what the life of Jesus really was. We must move on to an historical *logos*, without which every other *logos* will remain speculative and idealistic.

This new historical *logos* must start from the fact, indisputable to the eye of faith, that the historical life of Jesus is the fullest revelation of the Christian God. It must also operate methodologically as a *logos* of history which subsumes and goes beyond the *logos* of nature—the latter often having neglected the being and reality of the former. Only a *logos* which takes into account the historical reality of Jesus can open the way for a total christology, a christology capable of dealing with the changing face of history. Only such a christology can reveal to us that there is salvation in history at the very roots of salvation history.

I do not propose to perform that task here. I mention all this to point up the limitations of the various classical christologies, to indicate that they can be superseded, and to justify the christological character of the perspectives presented in this book.

The Socio-public Dimension of Jesus' Prophecy

Sidestepping discussions about the character of Jesus' prophecy, which are not without relevance today, one can say that a very characteristic prophetic dimension is to be found in Jesus. The important thing for us to note here is that the people who lived with him situated him in the prophetic line. While their theological purposes might have differed greatly, the texts of Matthew 16:14 and Mark 8:27–33 clearly show that the people around Jesus placed him in the line of Elijah, Jeremiah, and John the Baptist. In short, they saw him as one of the great prophets. Without going into a detailed consideration of Old Testament prophecy, we can see that Jesus was viewed as living the life of a prophet by the people. Matthew and Mark may go beyond that to designate him as Messiah and Son of God, but that does not invalidate the historical process of which he is clearly a part. Jesus transcends prophecy, but from within the prophetic tradition. This is of incalculable importance. It is in and through the prophetic dimension that the people and Jesus' disciples move towards an understanding of who and what Jesus is in his ultimate reality. Hence one cannot grasp the ultimate reality of his life apart from his life as a prophet, nor can one explore it in all its depth if one does not pursue it to its ultimate reality.

The problem comes into sharper focus if we raise a basic christological question: When and how did Jesus acquire explicit consciousness of his divine sonship, of the ultimate character of his person? The christologies based on the Greek *logos* of nature, which did not go in for rigorous exegesis of the New Testament texts, gave *a priori* responses that were not very "historical."[1] We would suggest that Jesus gradually acquired full awareness of his personal being in and through the life in which it was fleshed out. If that is the case, we can assert that the revelation of the Father goes by way of Jesus' life and that we can arrive at that revelation only by following Jesus' life. Only by following his life and rendering it visible can we know who the Father is, proclaim it, and make it present to a world in history. There is no doubt that this new framing of the issue would shake fundamental theology to its foundations and give a very definite configuration to the pastoral activity of the Church. We must realize that the predominant role accorded to the sacramental sign is framed in the casual context of nature, whereas this new vision would give a predominant place to Jesus' prophetic word and life in the context of an historical *logos*.

So we must turn our attention to Jesus' life and what it really was, not so much for the sake of spiritual edification or for the purpose of establishing a psychological relationship with him but rather for the sake of its theological import. In this framework one of the most important pieces of data is Jesus' prophecy. John the Evangelist is not unaware of this approach, whereby one moves from prophecy to an affirmation of Jesus' divine sonship. He stresses the preparatory nature of John the Baptist's prophecy and the complete nature of Jesus' own prophecy: "Surely this must be the prophet that was to come into the world" (Jn 6:14; see also 4:19; 7:40; 9:17).

We can plainly see the features of Jesus' personality and life which made the people see him as one of the greatest prophets: He displays great freedom in the face of religious traditions and in the face of the established authorities who identify their establishment with correct religious tradition. He lives an austere life and boldly confronts earthly powers. He leads a public life that becomes a decisive moment in the concrete history of his people. The power of words and signs is displayed in an exceptional way. He becomes the definitive proclaimer of the kingdom, declaring it to be already present. He makes the living God present among men in a vital way, promulgating a new morality of the heart above and beyond all legalism.

Let us analyze the prophetic style of Jesus in more detail, since it has a major role in giving shape and form to the prophetic aspect of the Church. First and foremost, Jesus rejected moribund, ritualized religion. There is no doubt that he performed the basic religious practices of his people, because the interpreters of his life record his circumcision, his presence in the temple, his attendance at the synagogue, his observance of the Passover, and so on. At the same time, however, we must note that he clashed with certain practices that were considered to be of maximum importance by the legalists of his day: work on the Sabbath, hand washing, and so forth. From the personal practice of Jesus, as transmitted to us by primitive tradition, we cannot conclude that he denied or rejected the religious element in its entirety. Like the prophets, however, Jesus was not an official minister of the religious organization. He differentiated himself from them and stood over against the hierarchical apparatus. What is more, he combatted their way of establishing the relationship between God and man.

Jesus also nullified the carnal condition based on kinship with Abraham. In other words, he interiorized man's relationship with God (Jn 8:39): not in the sense of spiritualizing it but in the sense of making it a freely chosen subjectification, without which it would be a superficial, external fact. Man must freely appropriate what is there. Without this personal appropriation there is no properly human life at all. This point is brought out most clearly with respect to religious rites and the tendency to localize the encounter between God and man. He tells the Samaritan woman that God will be adored in spirit and in truth, not in one specific temple or another, because God is spirit. In other words, God is a totality present within all reality. The Jews enjoy the advantage of knowing in history who the living God is that we are to adore. But their localization and cultic manipulation of God is no advantage at all. For this same reason Jesus does not look with favor on long wordy prayers or mere words addressed to God. The important thing is to do the will of the Father.

He vigorously attacks the oppression exercised by religious authorities in the name of God. He is angered by the hypocrisy of those who equate God's commands with human traditions (Mt 15:1–20). He cites Isaiah to condemn merely external actions that do not come from the heart, and he explicitly urges people to get beyond ritualism and legalism. He attacks those who claim to hold the keys to the kingdom but refuse entrance to others (Lk 11:52); and also those who impose intolerable burdens on others and do not lift a finger to help them. Numerous passages could be cited in this connection.

In short, we find in his life and his mission a pronounced shift of religious emphasis to operative faith. In the new covenant and the new age, the important thing will be one's personal attitude, one's adhesion to him in faith and one's following of him in one's own life. On this personal relationship, where faith in him and following him are mutually interrelated, will depend Christian holiness. On it will depend the salvific presence of God in man and man's access to God. The revelation and, if you will, the revelation of God in man will depend completely on man's relationship with the one who proclaims himself to be the Way to God, the Truth of God, and the Life of God. There is no access to the Father except that exemplified by the life of Jesus. One of the basic formulations of this following of Jesus is to be found in the Sermon on the Mount,[2] which is not to be interpreted as a new law but rather as a principle of discipleship.[3] The yardstick of Christian living is not to be sought in some alleged supernatural grace whose presence eludes the objectivity of personal and social awareness; it is to be sought in the following of Jesus, which is a visible and verifiable reality. Our eye is not to be trained on some invisible supernatural element in our action or our person. It is to be trained on what is truly Christian: the following of Jesus fleshed out in our concrete lives rather than in the vague realm of pure intention.

This framing of the issue might seem to be purely religious at first glance. But as was the case with the prophets, it shows Jesus to be a public force stimulating people to undertake a thoroughgoing transformation of the public situation. Without going into the import of his purification of the temple, we can tell from the very placing of the scene in the Synoptic Gospels and John's Gospel that Jesus' new way of viewing man's relationship with God is going to bring him into collision with public religious authority. Even in Jesus' day the religion of Israel was one of the most decisive elements, if not the most decisive element, in giving configuration to public and private life. Any action upon this religious element could not help but be an action upon the public life of the nation. Even though Jesus' immediate emphasis was upon the socio-religious realm, he could not help but seriously interfere with the whole socio-political power structure.

The clearest proof of this is that those who dominated the religion of Israel, and hence the social configuration of the nation's life, saw Jesus as a dangerous enemy threatening their public preeminence even as they had viewed John the Baptist in the same light. In attacking their monopoly over faith in Yahweh and the necessity of their mediation in man's encounter with God, Jesus was undermining the power base of the priestly class. What is more, as we shall see later on, he was also jeopardizing the power balance existing between the nation and the Roman authorities; and it was within this balance of power that the Jewish authorities had to operate if they were to maintain the position they had managed to win. By purifying the temple for example, he threatened the source of their income.

Thus this first dimension which characterizes Jesus' prophecy would seem to contain a public aspect of major importance, and it should be recognized even by those who would like to reduce Jesus' activity to a purely religious dimension. The priestly class was not purely religious. In challenging its false religion, Jesus was already moving towards a public collision with the overall structure of his society. We must remember that the social realm is a structured one. To undermine one of its essential elements is to unbalance the whole structure. But there is much more involved in the prophetic activity of Jesus.

His denunciation is social as well as religious, hence completely in line with prophetic tradition. In his life he opposes not only the religious power structure but also the social power structure. His pitiless attack on the Scribes and Pharisees as usurpers of religious infallibility and hence of socio-religious power is the prelude to a denunciation of social power in a more specific sense. Without at all claiming to exhaust this theme, I want to mention Jesus' whole approach to the crucial problem of wealth versus poverty, and the reaction it produced: "The Pharisees, who loved money, heard all this and scoffed at him" (Lk 16:14).

In his preaching Jesus clearly places great stress on the theme of poverty and sets poverty over against wealth and riches. He does not just favor poverty as an ascetical counsel for those who would seek perfection. He puts poverty in dialectical opposition to riches. In other words, it is not a question of praising poverty in itself and condemning wealth in itself. It is the relationship between the two that interests him. He condemns wealth that makes people poor and praises poverty that points an accusing finger at the malignant reality of wealth.

The Sermon on the Mount, especially in Luke's formulation (Lk 6:20–26), is indicative here. It is a radical judgment, but it views poverty and wealth in relationship to each other. The poor are the lucky ones; the rich will not possess the kingdom of God because they already possess the consolation of wealth. The hungry will eat their fill while those who are now sated will know need. Those who are weeping now will find consolation whereas those who are smiling now will know pain and tears. Finally, those in power will hate and punish those who truly preach and live the Gospel whereas they will shower adulation on those who make a show of religion which really has nothing to do with the Gospel. The prophets are cited explicitly as an example: Your forefathers persecuted the true prophets and rewarded the false prophets.

It is a well known fact that Luke's formulation here and elsewhere is more radical than that of the other evangelists. For example, he does not leave any room for the evasive focus on poverty of spirit as Matthew does. Without getting into the differences of emphasis between the two and trying to reconcile them, let us simply note that Matthew's social denunciation is also quite vigorous. (The unfavorable reaction of some people to Passolini's film, *The Gospel of St. Matthew,* was not due to any falsification by him; it was due to their tendency to read the Gospel message in terms of sweetness and light.) What most interests us here, however, is the historical character of Luke's account. Luke's reading of the episode comes from within the context of a community where the problem of wealth versus poverty was obviously an important issue. This is evident, for example, from what Acts tells us about holding all things in common: Worldly goods were to be made available to people in terms of their need. Thus Luke interprets the Sermon on the Mount from within the concrete situation of the community. His reading of the incident is concretized in effective, real-life terms; it shuns any escape into purely interior, idealistic terms. That is the sort of interpretation that should be undertaken today, from within the context and historical situation of each individual ecclesial community.

So the theme of wealth versus poverty does not relate simply to individual ascesis. It is also a sociological theme, and as such it has something to do with man's access to God. Wealth is seen to be one of the greatest obstacles to the establishment of God's kingdom among men. As the history of salvation moves forward, it becomes more evident that poverty rather than wealth is the locus of God's revelation and salvation. In this sense, salvation history becomes more radical as it goes along. It starts with the message of the Old Testament prophets. Until the prophets appeared on the scene, material prosperity was viewed as a blessing from God. They pointed out that material wealth had now reached the point where it was trampling the defenseless poor and producing all sorts of oppression. They spoke out against it insofar as it was actually a cause of poverty, and this process of accusation reaches its culmination in the New Testament.

So the poverty of Jesus' life represents a fundamental theological value. It is not a matter of some merely psychological or affective response whereby the Christian desires to be poor with Christ in order to be more like him. The whole matter goes much deeper. Jesus' poverty has a socio-theological import of major importance. On the one hand it is both a precondition for, and a result of, his absolute freedom vis-à-vis the powers of this world; on the other hand it is the condition for access to the only kind of life in which God reveals himself.

Therein lies the importance of the repeated insistence on the poverty-wealth theme in the New Testament. This stress underlines the fact that this whole dimension, which is both individual and social in nature, is one of the essential elements in the Christian message. It has nothing to do with masochism or "class struggle." It has something to do with objective, real life. In the contest between poverty and wealth, it is evident that divine revelation lies in the former. It is in this light that we must consider the whole matter of sharing worldly goods in common, which was a clearcut though voluntary trend in the primitive Christian community. That trend had nothing to do with the establishment of communism, in the political sense of the term; it represents a fresh awareness and appreciation of the optimum conditions underlying the proclamation of the good news to human beings in history.

I would stress again that it does not involve an abstract commendation of poverty—as if permanent poverty and wretchedness were an indispensable precondition for accepting the Christian God. Nor does it involve an abstract condemnation of wealth—as if the use and enjoyment of material realities necessarily entailed the demise of Christian openness to the God of Jesus Christ. What is involved here is 1) a historical framing of the whole issue in the light of a very specific situation; 2) a dialectical relationship in which wealth causes and produces poverty, so that one is forced to choose between being with the oppressors or being with the oppressed. This framing of the whole issue does not annul the question of personal ascesis as a desirable practice, but it does specify the context in which it must be considered. It must be grounded on the theological and historical significance of Jesus' poverty, not on some alleged effective relationship with a historical Jesus who has now been transcended by the Christ of the resurrection.

The gospel message gives a series of reasons for giving historical and concrete preference to poverty—or if your prefer, to the poor—as the preferred locus of God's revelation. One could try to adduce reasons of his own, but it seems better to stay with the reasons presented by those who were closest to Jesus' own life. Without trying to give an exhaustive account of these reasons, I shall try to formulate some of them.

Luke considers wealth as dishonest (Lk 16:9) or even unjust. The Pharisees mock Jesus' description of it, and this prompts his own retort: "You are the people who impress your fellow-men with your righteousness; but God sees through you; for what sets itself up to be admired by men is detestable in the sight of God" (Lk 16:14–15). The point of his retort is clear from the immediate context. The Pharisees had laughed at his earlier statements about wealth and poverty because they "loved money" (Lk 16:14). They are not just people, even though they pose as such, because the wealth they love is an abomination in God's eyes. The gospel text allows no room for evasion here. One cannot say it is condemning unjust wealth. Rather it labels wealth itself as unjust, by virtue of its link with poverty.

This condemnation of wealth is not confined to its social dimension. It also has to do with wealth in relationship to God: "No servant can be the slave of two masters; for either he will hate the first and love the second, or he will be devoted to the first and think nothing of the second. You cannot serve God and Money" (Lk 16:13; see Mt 6:24). As Luke explains in another passage (12:15–21), wealth causes people to forget God's sovereignty. By virtue of its own inner dynamism, in other words, wealth tends to become an absolute value which forces people into idolatry. In many cases this idolatry does not take the form of denying the existence of God or divinizing wealth itself. It takes the form of viewing God in a distorted way so that he can be seen as the Lord of the wealthy, so that people may feel free to go about accumulating wealth in this world. There is no need to underline where that capitalist interpretation of Christianity, among both Catholics and Protestants, has led us in the course of history (see Max Weber's writings on the subject). If history itself did not prove that this was an anti-Christian interpretation, the words of Jesus himself certainly would: "The seed sown among thistles represents the man who hears the word, but worldly cares and the false glamour of wealth choke it, and it proves barren" (Mt 13:22).

Wealth makes it intrinsically difficult for God's word to reap its fruit in the Christian. This point is solidly established in the Gospel, particularly in two sets of passages: those which talk about the rich young man (Mt 19:16–22; Mk 10:17–31; Lk 18:18–30); and those which describe the scene of the Last Judgment (Mt 25) and Jesus' first preaching (Lk 4).

The incident dealing with the rich young man is clearly very important, and it is given detailed treatment in the Synoptic Gospels. The young man wishes "to gain eternal life." Jesus tells him to keep the commandments and enumerates a few. The young man insists that he already does that, but he feels that he does not yet possess authentic, eternal life. He asks Jesus what is still wanting in him. Jesus' reply varies slightly in each of the Synoptic versions. Matthew's introductory phrase, "If you wish to be perfect," has allowed people to get off the track and interpret the whole answer in a way that favors the rich. Mark and Luke, on the other hand, pick up the words of the young man and indicate that he indeed is lacking something—not to be perfect but to *have eternal life at all*. He must sell his goods, give to the poor, and then follow Jesus. At this response the young man became very sad and went off because "he was a man of great wealth" (Mk 10:22).

The scene has been falsified in many ascetic and spiritualistic interpretations. Eternal life is taken to be the life beyond, and it is falsely assumed that the keeping of the commandments will enable a person to attain that eternal life beyond. The text suggests clearly that the young man still lacks something in order to attain eternal life, but people wrongly interpret this to mean that he only lacks something for "perfection." Perfection, in fact, merely means full possession of eternal life, and we must take a completely different tack if we want to interpret this scene correctly.

The passage is dealing with the whole question of what is basically entailed in being a Christian, in following Christ.

Mere keeping of the commandments does not constitute Christianity. If a person merely keeps the commandments, he is not a Christian and he does not possess eternal life. The Christian is not an ethical creature engaged in keeping commandments. The Christian is someone who follows Christ's life out of faith and mirrors it in his own life. One of the inescapable conditions entailed in this following of Christ is the giving up of material wealth and the distribution of it to the poor. That is what following Christ entails. That is what it means to take up one's cross, a phrase which has Zealot overtones as we shall see later. Only those who are free of riches are in a position to follow Jesus and to continue his mission. Because of his wealth, the young man was not able to follow Jesus even though he was well disposed. Wealth did not prevent him from hearing the summons, but it did choke God's summons in the end.

This major encounter in Jesus' life and its import is corroborated by the words which the Synoptic evangelists attribute to him in this context. If a person does not renounce all his worldly goods, he cannot be Jesus' disciple. It is easier for a camel to pass through the eye of a needle than for a rich person to enter the kingdom of God (Matthew, Mark, and Luke). It is a Semitic idiom, to be sure, but it cannot be watered down to a meaningless phrase. At the very least it suggests that there is an almost insuperable contradiction between possessing wealth and gaining entrance to the kingdom.

The same theme could be handled from the opposite end, from the standpoint of poverty or the situation of the poor. Many incidents could be chosen from Jesus' life, but I shall focus on two very significant scenes: Matthew's description of the Last Judgment and Luke's description of Jesus' first preaching.

The importance of Matthew's text lies in the fact that it is framed in the context of the final, definitive judgment on mankind and, in a certain sense, on history itself: "When the Son of Man comes in his glory and all the angels with him, he will sit in state on his throne, with all the nations gathered before him. He will separate men into two groups . . ." (Mt 25:31–32). The text is a very familiar one. Here I should like to underline two features that are basic to our interpretation here. First, the judgment is framed in terms of a catalogue of items that are quite material in nature and that refer to the immediate needs of human beings: hunger, thirst, nakedness, and so forth. Second, man's response is identified with the person in need and with the Son of Man. The humblest human beings, as such, are Jesus' brothers. Action performed for them is action performed for him. And two facts aggravate the situation. First, there is nothing expressly supernatural or cultic or religious in the actions proposed. Second, there is no express indication as to why one should know that the Son of God lies hidden behind the Son of Man for whom one performs these actions. Those who denigrate the political mission of the Church as a "horizontalist" emphasis would do well to ponder the final judgment scene in the Gospel more often.

The other gospel text is that of Luke, and it deals with Jesus' initial preaching. It is important because it alludes to Isaiah, because Jesus seeks to tie his mission in with what he regards as the most radical element in prophecy: " 'The spirit of the Lord is upon me because he has anointed me; he has sent me to announce good news to the poor, to proclaim release for prisoners and recovery of sight for the blind, to let the broken victims go free, to proclaim the year of the Lord's favour. . . . Today,' he said, 'in your very hearing this text has come true' " (Lk 4:18–21).

The Isaian text expresses the prophet's mission in the context of a political mission. Even though Jesus transcends that particular context (Is 61:1–10; 62:1–12; 63:1–19), he clearly frames himself in the line of the prophets and in the political mission that is part of that line. The proclamation of the good news is primarily to the poor and the incarcerated; to them it announces liberation. The thrust and import of this liberation deserves extended treatment, and we shall treat it in detail in a later chapter. The important thing to note here is the way Jesus begins his preaching: He *begins* by associating his work with the *final* proclamation of definitive judgment. Between start and finish lies much teaching on the part of Jesus, but we must note the crucial character of these two groups of texts in determining the mission of Jesus and of those Christians who seek to follow him.

Jesus' activity in trying to satisfy people's material needs must be framed in the same line. Whatever the critical interpretation of these miracles may be, it is clear that the primitive community saw Jesus' satisfaction of man's concrete needs as a sign of the presence of the kingdom. So true was this that it sometimes led the crowd into erroneous interpretations of Jesus' prophetic character. This is evident in John's treatment of the miracle of the loaves. The action has sign value, but the sign is not interpreted correctly by the multitude. They start out on the right track, seeing Jesus as the true prophet who is supposed to come into the world (Jn 6:14). But then they turn off into a direction which Jesus refuses to take: "Jesus, aware that they meant to come and seize him to proclaim him king, withdrew again to the hills by himself" (Jn 6:15). We shall return to this passage when we consider the exact nature of Jesus' political mission.

So far we have pointed out two fundamental features of Jesus' prophecy: his new conception of the proper relationship between man and God; his new conception of the dialectical relationship existing between wealth and poverty insofar as it gives configuration to the kingdom and hence to the God-man relationship. These two features are substantial elements in his life and mission, and both bring him into conflict with the public authorities. His prophetic vocation, both insofar as it deals with the religious dimension and insofar as it touches upon the social dimension, causes interference with the public, collective structure and with the power system that gives configuration to society. By that very fact his mission can be seen to have not only a public character but also a necessarily political character. He clearly has no appreciation for any immediate political ambitions, but neither does he back away from his mission because it will necessarily have political implications. As the gospel accounts abundantly attest, there is a growing conflict between Jesus and the representatives of the power structure. The latter feel that their power and its underlying structure is being threatened seriously by Jesus. Jesus' more immediate struggle is with the socio-political level of power rather than with the state-government level of political power. This fact is of some importance in trying to determine the political character of Jesus' mission in greater detail. But it is also true that the dynamic interrelationship between the two political levels will necessarily bring him into conflict with the latter level as well. For the latter gives expression to the former, serving as its concrete support.

This moves us towards the heart of our theme here. What we have said so far suggests that there clearly was a political dimension to Jesus' activity. Yet people have constantly tried to evade the historical implications of the texts cited here. The New Testament, however, has much more to say about this whole problem, as we shall see now when we explore the messianism of Jesus.

The Political Dimension of Jesus' Messianism

It is easy enough to prove that there is a definite political import in Jesus' messianic mission. The real difficulty lies in trying to spell out the precise sense and scope of that political import. That is what I shall try to do now because it is one of the key factors in any attempt to show that salvation in history is a major part of salvation history.

The Political Context of Jesus' Activity

We must start from the fact that Jesus' whole life was spent amid an atmosphere of maximum politicization. The people of his nation were soaked in this atmosphere.[4] Here I shall try to point up a few basic facts that provide the context for our question here: What stance did Jesus adopt vis-à-vis a world that was highly politicized?

There is no little significance in the fact that Luke attempts to make the date of Jesus' birth coincide with that of the census. The dates are still debated, of course, but that only tends to emphasize the political import of Luke's attempt to tie the date of Jesus' birth in with a census designed to further direct tax collection. It was at this moment that Judea was incorporated directly into the Roman empire.[5] This new situation led to an uprising which was crushed by the Roman governor of Syria. According to Josephus, he crucified two thousand men. Indeed, throughout this period crucifixion had strictly political connotations, and this point should be borne in mind if we wish to avoid spiritualistic and ahistorical interpretations of that phenomenon. Leading this rebel movement in Galilee was a Zealot named Judas of Galilee, and it was during this period that the child Jesus was growing up. Undoubtedly all these happenings had an impact on the growing boy.

In the period from 15 A.D. to 26 A.D., four high priests were named in turn by Valerius Gratus. The last of these, Caiphas, would play a major role in the death of Jesus. This submissiveness of the priests to the Roman authorities, who commanded a view of the temple precincts from the Fortress Antonia, is one of the politico-religious features that gives form and substance to Jesus' own religious and public style of life. The lower levels of the priesthood were in closer contact with popular movements, but the upper levels were acting in connivance with the political and economic powers. Pontius Pilate was perpetually in conflict with the Jewish people. He committed various outrages against their religious beliefs and practices, regarding them as tokens of resistance to the total domination of Rome.[6] In his writings, Flavius Josephus describes the proliferating appearance of messianic figures, who proclaimed themselves to be the religious and political liberators of the nation. Their actions and beliefs eventually led to the great uprising that was crushed in 70 A.D. with the destruction of Jerusalem. At the same time various apocalyptic tendencies were widespread. They envisioned the imminent approach of the ultimate catastrophe which would usher in the kingdom of God.

The gospel accounts are not too explicit in underlining this politicized atmosphere, but they give more than enough hints as we shall see. Why didn't they call more attention to this atmosphere? Why did the earliest communities play it down? Why has the Church's reading and interpretation of the gospel account failed to take due account of the historical context of Jesus' life? It is not too difficult to find answers to these questions. The first chroniclers of Jesus' life did not want to interpret Jesus in such a way that he could be confused with the many messianic pretenders of his day. Moreover, they were writing to communities in which the Jewish element was meager or even subject to attack, and they did not want to present an image of Jesus which depicted him as clearly opposed to the Roman political world. Their interpretational limitation was dialectical because it was framed in the context of the immediate historical situation. Later interpreters would turn this purely methodological procedure into an absolute, failing to counterbalance it with the historical reality in which Jesus himself lived.

Despite all this, the Gospels do provide us with sufficient data to restore some precise historical perspective to the mission of Jesus. Without going into a full analysis of the historical situation, we can note some of the data contained in the Gospels: reference to the Galileans who were slain before the altar by Pilate and whose fate was reported directly to Jesus; the presence of Barrabas, who had committed murder during an uprising; the men crucified with Jesus are called *lestai* in Greek, and this is the technical term which Josephus uses to designate rebels against Roman authority.

In Jesus' day there were not only isolated incidents of political rebellion—these always being closely bound up with a religious interpretation of Jewish history. There were also various parties or schools of thought vis-à-vis the religious and political situation. Flavius Josephus talks about four such groups, referring to them as *hairesis* ("school of thought," "party," "sect"). At one extreme stood the Sadducees, who, as the New Testament suggests, held much economic power and professed a materialistic view of life. They were avowed collaborators of the Romans and proponents of a foreign style of life. At the other extreme stood the Essenes, about whom we now possess abundant documentation. They may be viewed as people who held the most spiritualistic interpretation, who withdrew from political activity and the world. While they passionately were awaiting the salvation of Israel, they were doing so in a way that could be considered a bit too passive and "supernaturally" oriented. Some figures of a public, prophetic cast may indeed have come from their environment—John the Baptist, for example—but this fact does not alter the general characterization of the group. A third movement was that of the Pharisees, a very rich and complex movement. Stating the matter in oversimplified terms, we could say that they stressed a religious emphasis which gave them great social influence over the nation. They promoted a theocratic restoration of God's kingdom, in which they would exercise a decisive leadership role.

Finally, there were the Zealots. In his *Antiquities of the Jews* (Book 18, Chapter 1), Josephus has this to say about them: "The fourth philosophical sect had been founded by Judas the Galilean. Its members generally associated themselves with the doctrine of the Pharisees, but they had an invincible love of liberty because they regarded God as their only master and lord. In their determination to call no one else their master, they showed indifference to the torture inflicted on their friends and relatives. Since many have borne witness to their resolute courage in enduring all these sufferings, I will say no more about them. My fear is not that my words about them would be doubted, but that I would give too faint a picture of their disdain for the sufferings they have endured. This folly began to take hold of our people during the procuratorship of Gessius Florus, whose excessive violence led to an uprising of the Zealots against the Romans."

The important point for us here is to recognize the existence of a rebel movement that took arms against the Roman authorities for religious reasons. It saw God as the only Lord of the Jewish nation. Hence the tax tributes, which recognized another temporal lord, were immoral denials of God. It is in this context that we should view the gospel proclamation that man cannot serve two masters. Without going into a host of historical questions that are very debatable,[7] we can underline one fact which Flavius Josephus brings out, i.e., that Judas the Galilean was an "intellectual," (*sophistēs* in Greek) who not only taught his people but also moved them to action; that he worked out his own interpretation of the contemporary movement in salvation history and fomented an armed uprising. The "philosophical sect" was not just a grouping of people who viewed events in a particular way; it was also a political party in some sense. And it was one of the conditioning factors around Jesus as well as one of the options that he continually had to confront, as we shall see later.

This highly politicized situation, in which there were at least four distinct politico-religious stances, was the situation in which Jesus found himself as he tried to determine his own proper mission and how to carry it out. To prescind from this context, which was the real-life, historical context of Jesus himself, is the best way to distort the whole sense and meaning of his life and to trample on the roots of a sound, complete christology.

The Political Condemnation of Jesus

If we want to get the political import of Jesus' mission into proper historical focus, we must start with the indisputable fact that Jesus was condemned for political reasons. As Brandon points out, the ironical fact is that Jesus of Nazareth was certainly crucified by the Romans as a rebel against their rule in Judea.[8] The Creed tells us this explicitly: He suffered under Pontius Pilate or was *crucified* under Pontius Pilate. The precise implications of this fact, of course, must be investigated.

Who promoted the death of Jesus is a matter of much debate. The evangelists stress that the main instigators were the Jews, making Pilate responsible only for the material execution itself. We need not discuss here how much theological interpretation and sociological opportunism is interlaced in their point of view. For even as they present the events to us, we can find enough data to determine the political character of Jesus' mission. We could carry this point even further if, for example, Brandon is right in saying that the Gospel of Mark was an apology of Jesus' life directed to Roman readers.[9] That may be possible, but it is not a critical point here. Looking at the matter from a Catholic viewpoint, we must accept the fact that the interpretative selection of the evangelists possesses a value that is backed up by the faith of the Church; hence their selection itself must be taken as the key to an interpretation. As we shall see, this means we end up with a less politicized Jesus; but it in no way obscures the authentic determination of the political character of his mission.

So the main fact is that Jesus was condemned to crucifixion for what were obviously political reasons. How much hypocrisy was involved is something we shall see. The mediation of the Jewish authorities in this condemnation is also evident.[10] It indicates that he was also condemned for religious reasons and thus supports our basic position: Jesus engaged in what was primarily religious activity; but it could not help appear to be political as well to those who held religious and political power. We have already pointed out that in Judea official religious power was certainly one of the decisive ingredients in the overall social power structure and hence a pillar of the political structure. But Jesus' final condemnation must be attributed to the Romans for reasons that were predominantly political.

Two things offer abundant proof of this. First of all, Jesus was crucified with two rebels (*lestai:* "guerrilla bandits" is one suggested translation), and crucifixion was a typical Roman punishment for Zealot rebels. Second, the *titulus* on the cross "states a purely political crime."[11] This remark comes from Oscar Cullmann, who is not at all inclined to give too much weight to the political factor in Jesus' mission.

The undeniable facts would indicate that Jesus was operating in a highly politicized atmosphere. He could objectively appear to be someone carrying out a political mission, and hence he ran the risk of suffering the attendant consequences. Yet this did not keep him from living his own style of life and acting as he saw fit.

He certainly appeared in that light to those of ill will, who saw him as a critical element undermining their domination over the people. He was indeed such a threat vis-à-vis the socio-religious power of the Scribes and Pharisees and vis-à-vis the socio-economic power of the priestly aristocracy and the Sadducees. The point is stressed well enough in the gospel accounts and need not be discussed in great detail here. The struggle between the two sides is bitter and open. Jesus' harshness towards the socio-religious leaders of the Jews matches that of the prophets in their most vehement diatribes. It is a fact that is all too quickly overlooked by certain segments of the Church.

Jesus also represented a political threat to the Roman authorities. The Jews made every effort to convince Pilate that Jesus was the enemy of Caesar, that he had sided with the Zealots in refusing to pay tribute to Caesar, and that he was inciting the people against Rome's authority. Jesus was taken in Gethsemane by a Roman cohort under the command of a tribune (Jn 18:3,12). In John's Gospel, Pilate seems to realize that there is something transcendent about Jesus' kingdom; but the fact remains that the inscription on the cross enunciates a political crime, whatever the reason for Pilate's decision to condemn him.

The most interesting thing, however, is that Jesus appeared in the same light to the people of good will around him. And the same applies to those who followed him at a greater distance. Those who followed him into the desert area and sought to proclaim him king (Jn 6:15) put Jesus in the Zealot line. Withdrawal to the desert was a common practice when the Zealots had to flee persecution or when they were preparing for an attack. Jesus, of course, did not accept their interpretation of him, but the people saw him as a possible king from within the context of their society and their messianic aspirations. The acclamations of the children in the temple contain a clear note of historical messianism (Mt 21:14–16). One need not go so far as to accept the recently proposed view that the phrase in Aramic was a cry of protest against Roman rule. One need only note the reaction of the priests and Scribes to realize that the phrase placed Jesus in the messianic line and thus threatened their power. It also endangered their safety since the Romans were looking down on them from the Fortress Antonia. The same can be said of his triumphal entry into Jerusalem, which certainly was one of the events that precipitated his death and which is recorded in all four gospel accounts. Matthew attempts to interpret the event in biblical terms. But even if one acknowledges that it ties in with a promise made to Jerusalem that her king would come in meekness and seated on a donkey, the fact remains that his reception by the crowd had clear messianic import. Now the messianism of the people, as we have noted, was strictly political in nature. John is very explicit in his comment: "The Pharisees said to one another, 'You see you are doing no good at all; why, all the world has gone after him' " (Jn 12:18). If his expulsion of the merchants from the temple is to be placed here as in the Synoptics (Mt 21:12–13; Mk 11:15b–17; Lk 19:45–46), rather than at the beginning of his public life where John places it (Jn 2:14–22), then even the most benign spiritualistic interpretation cannot deny Jesus' physical attack on the priestly cast and the profits it reaped from the purchases of average people.

At this point someone might object that Jesus' mission was wrongly interpreted by the simple people who saw him as the awaited Messiah. Hence our line of argument above has no real force. But one can answer this objection in at least two ways. The first response, which we shall go into immediately, is that even his most loyal followers saw him in the same light. The second response, even more forceful, is that Jesus gave the impression that he was the awaited Messiah. The Messiah had a clearly political dimension; Jesus tried to transcend this impression but did not evade it. This is a key point in our present study here: Despite the ambiguities surrounding his life style, Jesus chose that life style and no other. It is a theological datum of the greatest importance. Salvation history has an intimate relationship with salvation in history. The latter, as medium of full salvation, has an inescapable socio-political dimension. One may be able to go through this dimension and eventually get beyond it, but one cannot bypass it if salvation is to be effective and real.

Hence it is most significant that his closest followers saw him as a political figure. There is a clear indication that his initial group of followers took up with him for reasons of a messianic cast. To begin with, one of these was Simon the Zealot, who was probably called that for a reason (Lk 6:14 ff; Acts 1:13). As more than one commentator has noted, the word *kenana* is the Aramaic equivalent for the Greek word "zealot." Here is what Cullmann has to say: "This is the same person who is designated Simon *ho kananaios* in the parallel lists of Mark (3:18) and Matthew (10:4). These words are always mistranslated as 'Simon the Canaanite' (that is, from Canaan). Actually, however, *kananaios* has nothing whatever to do with the land of Canaan. It is simply a transcription of the Aramaic designation for Zealots. Zealot is the Greek word, from *zēlos*, zeal. . . . *Kananaios* comes from the Semitic noun *kana*, 'zeal.' *Kenana* is the Aramaic word for Zealot, just as *sicarius* is the Latin word for the same member of the Jewish resistance party."[12]

The same holds true for Judas Iscariot himself, whose affilia-
tion with Jesus and whose later desertion is psycho-
sociologically interpreted in terms of political messianism.
(The role attributed to Judas in the rock opera *Jesus Christ,
Superstar* is most interesting in this connection.) His name may
well be a Semitic translation of Latin *sicarii,* a term applied to
the Zealots because of the dagger (*sica*) they were wont to carry
under their mantle.[13] And then there is Peter, whose
psychological disposition is also that of a Zealot; his conception
of the Messiah will be examined later on. Cullmann has this to
say about his name: "In my book on Peter, I have indicated that
the designation 'Bar Jona,' applied to Peter in Matthew 16:17,
cannot with absolute certainty be translated 'son of John.' To
be sure, it is thus construed in John 1:42 and 21:15. But this
may well be a secondary explanation, for there is no documen-
tary evidence for Jona as an abbreviation for Johanan. Following R. Eisler I have mentioned in my book that according to an
old Hebrew lexicon (cited by G. Dalman) *barjona* is a word
borrowed from Accadian, meaning 'terrorist.' Thus we would
have here yet another designation for Zealot."[14]

The sons of Zebedee, the Boanerges or Sons of Thunder,
seem to be cast in the same mold. They want Jesus to call down
fire from heaven in order to establish the kingdom, and their
mother asks that they get the places of preference in that
kingdom. Finally, we have the testimony of Luke regarding the
demand of Jesus' followers after his resurrection. Even then his
most loyal supporters ask, "Lord, is this the time when you are
to establish once again the sovereignty of Israel?" (Acts 1:6).

Now if even his closest followers saw Jesus in this light, how
can one doubt that his condemnation by the Jews in power had
a clearly political character? His life certainly seemed to have
that cast. But what did Jesus himself think about all this? That
is the question we shall consider next.

NOTES

1. My point is sufficiently proved, I believe, if one reads some of the recent treatments and discussions of christology. Here is a sample list: Vogtle, "Exegetische Erwagungen über das Wissen und Selbstbewusstsein Jesu," in *Gott in Welt* (Freiburg: Herder, 1964), pp. 608–67; Rahner, "Dogmatische Erwagungen über das Wissen und Selbstbewusstsein Christi," now reprinted in *Theological Investigations*, vol. 5; the joint work of both on the term Jesus Christ in *Sacramentum Mundi*; volume 11 of *Concilium*, particularly the briefer notice by Gutwenger on the knowledge of Christ; and the comments of Schnackenburg on christology in *Mysterium Salutis*.

2. See Joachim Jeremias, *Palabras de Jesús* (Madrid: Fax, 1970); English edition, *The Parables of Jesus*, 2nd ed. (New York: Scribner's, 1963).

3. See Dietrich Bonhoeffer, *Nachfolge* (Munich: Kaiser Verlag, 1937); English edition, *The Cost Of Discipleship* (New York: Macmillan Paperback edition, 1963).

4. See S.G.F. Brandon, *Jesus and the Zealots* (New York: Scribner's 1967). His interpretation may be exaggerated at certain points, but his abundant data and bibliography are basic to any discussion of our theme here.

5. *Ibid.*, p. 26.

6. *Ibid.*, p. 69.

7. See *ibid.*, pp. 29 ff., and his full bibliography.

8. *Ibid.*, page 1.

9. See *ibid.*, Chapter 5.

10. See Werner Koch, *Der Prozess Jesu*, dtv.

11. Oscar Cullmann, *The State in the New Testament* (New York: Scribner's, 1956), p. 43.

12. *Ibid.*, p. 15.

13. *Ibid.*

14. *Ibid.*, pp. 16–17.

E. proposes a Christology based on the historical Jesus, in order to see salvation in history: He opposes a Logos of nature and a Logos of history = which seems to be a continuation of the salvation in history

Theme: an historical Logos = seeing Jesus a revealing + saving word by his message, teaching + actions; his life history. A focus on the historical Jesus. — and that as PROPHET

The socio–public dimension of Jesus life of his Prophecy include a) attack on Religion as pure formalism = religion is freedom + spirit sincerity b) his attack on wealth as causing poverty + identification of himself + the Kingdom with the poor.

E. then goes into the Political dimension of Jesus messianism: political death + etc

Criticism:
1) Whole thing based on the historical Jesus. — as Prophet. =

2) One cannot transfer the historical conditions + consciousness of history + ability to change it back into that Period + Jesus consciousness

3) Wealth + Poverty is treated ideologically — does not fit the date: should one embrace poverty as an ideal?

4) Jesus as political messiah = no one would make this the center for understanding him. Cf margin notes.

3

Jesus' Own Consciousness
of His Mission

Our subject matter in this chapter is Jesus' own growing awareness during his lifetime of the concrete path he was to take in carrying out his mission to reveal the Father and save human beings. It is gratuitous to assume *a priori* that Jesus did not learn to flesh out his mission in and through his experience in society and history. (By "fleshing out" we do not refer to some accidental determination but rather to the overall structuring of his mission.) Such an *a priori* assumption is grounded on very suspect christological principles, and it reduces our reading and interpretation of the New Testament to a fairytale approach. It is patent that the New Testament itself bears witness to Jesus' slow and hesitant growth in awareness, and it seems hardly plausible that it is presented as such for pedagogical reasons that Jesus himself or the evangelists deemed advisable. Even if that were the case, we would be justified for the same reasons in following the manner of presentation that Jesus himself followed according to the gospel accounts.

It seems much more reasonable, however, to think that the biographical and historical process of growth presented in the Gospels should be accepted with total theological radicalness. It indicates what Jesus was presenting objectively to those around him, and there is no persuasive reason for maintaining that it was not a real process of growth in his own human consciousness. Thus it is not a question of a feigned pedagogical approach but rather of a real biographical process.

The point of departure in this process was the politico-religious tradition which he received from his people and as it was interpreted in his concrete historical situation. That concrete situation, as we have noted above, was one of total politicization. From the Old Testament he possessed the promise of a new kingdom, which was intimately bound up with the historical destiny of his people. Jesus was grounded in this situation, operating out of his own specific intellectual structure, his own concrete human totality, his continuing advertence to the living God in prayerful retreat, his own observance of the surrounding social situation, and his own considered actions in the concrete. In and through the concrete experiences of his life Jesus came to learn how he was to understand the kingdom that he had come to proclaim and how access to this kingdom was to be provided. Reading the Old Testament and the historical experience of his people in the light of his concrete social situation, Jesus came to see the novel features of his own mission. The response he found in his living and preaching would teach him how to comprehend the ultimate pathways of his own mission. If people are not scandalized by the fact of God's incarnation, if they are willing to accept the possibility of such limitations being imposed on the Absolute, then they should not be scandalized if we pursue this fact to its ultimate consequences.

The Key Temptation of False Messianism

For our purposes here, the messianic consciousness of Jesus is a basic point of departure. When did he acquire this consciousness and how did he interpret it? It is a vast and much debated subject. Here we shall focus on those points that are vital to our present study.

The messianic consciousness of Jesus is spelled out by the evangelists when Jesus is baptized in the Jordan by John the Baptist.[1] For Mark, this episode represents the first epiphany of the Messiah-Son of God. Schlier perhaps places too much stress on the notion that in this revelation Jesus saw his path in history leading through death. He supports this view by relating the rending of the heavens in this scene with the rending of the temple veil at the time of Jesus' death. Matthew, according to Schlier, stresses Jesus' initial solidarity with sinners and with the pre-messianic approach proclaimed by John the Baptist: "This messianic king and Servant of God, as the voice of God proclaims him to be, is the righteous Servant of God who stands in solidarity with sinners and by his baptism already enters into his sufferings for them."[2] John the Evangelist, according to Schlier, points up the fact that the messianism of Jesus entails his shouldering of the sins of the world, and that Jesus now sees this task in a new and enlightened way, thanks to this special outpouring of the Spirit on him: "Finally, for the fourth evangelist, the baptismal event is the first epiphany of the Son, whose sonship appears in the gospel in ever new epiphanies of his glory through words and signs."[3] Schlier rightly notes that the pluralistic treatment of the four evangelists conveys to us the unified but pluralistic import of the baptismal happening itself. That happening manifests the hidden Messiah-Son of God, the just Servant of God who takes the place of sinners, the Lamb of God, and God's ever new Word. But perhaps Schlier does not give enough stress to the fact that this baptismal manifestation is not solely or even primarily for others, but for Jesus himself.

Though Schmid[4] may think otherwise, we are not propounding an adoptionist view when we interpret *"Today* I have begotten you" in strong terms. Such an interpretation does not imply that Jesus was the Son of God only from a certain point on in his life. It merely insists that he was becoming more fully aware of his true being through the course of his life. One of the major moments in this process was the moment of his baptism by John at the start of his public life. It was a manifestation of his self to himself and to others, a manifestation grounded in his messianic consciousness.

Having received this manifestation from above, Jesus will take a long stretch of time to reflect on the concrete meaning of his messianism, and hence of his missionary activity. The three Synoptic writers forcefully underline the fact that the great temptation faced by Jesus, both during his forty days in the desert and throughout the course of his life, was the temptation to interpret his messianism as most of his people interpreted messianism. If we see the temptation to false messianism as the key temptation in Jesus' life, we will be able to get a clear view of the political character of his mission and of the precise character of his own messianism—a messianism quite distinct and different from other messianisms of the past and present. But the very fact that this was the key temptation in Jesus' life proves once again that his mission did include a strictly political dimension.

The evangelists recount three temptations in the life of Jesus that are actually one and the same temptation. It was a real temptation in his life. If we try to interpret these temptations in pietistic terms, if we try to say that Jesus underwent them only to give us an example, then we are turning them into very superficial events indeed. Leaving aside the whole question of Jesus' impeccability, which may not even be well presented in the usual formulations, it seems obvious that the evangelists wanted to show us this at the very least: the thrust and import of Jesus' life vis-à-vis the messianic options which confronted him, and which existed as a real problem for him throughout his life.

The *first temptation* is the one in the desert, which is narrated in great detail by the Synoptics (Lk 4:1–13; Mt 4:1–11; Mk 1:12–13). We must remember that it deals with Jesus' first period of reflection after the baptismal manifestation by the Jordan. The gospel accounts should not lead us astray here, causing us to believe that Jesus fasted and prayed for forty days and only then was tempted. In all likelihood they present a summary account of the inner struggle that went on inside Jesus all during this period as he tried to ponder the import and proper style of his public mission.

Matthew presents the fundamental reality: "Jesus was then led away by the Spirit into the wilderness, to be tempted by the devil" (4:1). The three Synoptic writers stress that it is the Spirit who motivates or accompanies Jesus. It is not a matter of the devil trying to find out if Jesus truly is the Messiah. The important question is how Jesus himself will interpret messianism in the light of his own reading of the Old Testament.

The false messianism proposed to Jesus is symbolized in the stones being turned to bread so that people will follow him; in the dazzling theophany in the temple which will captivate people without producing any interiorization or real liberation; in the power and glory of the kingdoms of this world which have been handed over to the devil and which can be distributed as he pleases. Thus the basic import and content of the temptation is clear. It is an invitation to a messianism of great material achievements, of triumphal presence among bedazzled human beings, of a kingdom imposed on people by virtue of state power and glory. (It is worth noting that the evangelists seem to view worldly power and glory in diabolic terms. Luke, in particular, stresses that the kingdoms of this world have been handed over to the devil. It is not that they are diabolic in themselves, but in historical fact.)

To what extent have the followers of Jesus and the Church fallen prey to these temptations? That is a question to be tackled by studying history and analyzing our present concrete situation. It would seem that Vatican II opted for a response that is very much in line with that of Jesus himself.

The fact is that Jesus rejects this one temptation in its threefold form. He will have to distribute bread and food to those who are in need of it, but the primary feature of the new kingdom will be the word of God. A direct appeal to God, asking him to make himself miraculously present among human beings, is out of place, for it is human beings themselves who must make God present. And finally, any attempt to absolutize something other than God is a denial of the new kingdom. Even though Jesus will pay heed to the material needs of his fellow citizens, and also to their social and political problems, his predominant work will be to address these problems by revealing the Father in history. Keeping these two stances distinct will not be an easy task, but that is how Jesus will operate. He will follow this ambiguous pathway, refusing to turn his mission into pure politicization or pure privatization. It was not easy for him to renounce the tack of politicizing his own messianism, and that is why the evangelists refer to it as a temptation. At the end Luke notes that the devil left him for the time being once the temptation had failed.

The *second temptation* is reported by Mark. The episode is clearly messianic, and it is presented as such by the three Synoptic writers (Mk 8:27–33; Lk 9:18–22; Mt 16:13–23). Only Mark and Matthew point out the aspect of temptation in it, and we shall consider the episode here only insofar as it represents the temptation of false messianism.

Both Matthew and Mark locate the incident at Caesarea Philippi, a locale that is clearly subject to the influence of a foreign power and a foreign culture. Jesus asks his disciples what people are thinking about him. His disciples reply that they see him as one of the prophets resurrected: Elijah, Jeremiah, John the Baptist, or some other prophet. Then Jesus asks for the opinion of his own disciples, and the three Synoptic writers agree that it was Peter who spoke for them. Here is his reply in the three Synoptic versions: "You are the Messiah" (Mk 8:30); "God's Messiah" (Lk 9:20); "You are the Messiah, the Son of the Living God" (Mt 16:16). Aside from the fact that Jesus approves Peter's profession, the thing that strikes our attention here is the fact that Jesus orders his disciples not to tell others about this. We shall return to the whole matter of the messianic secret later. Here I should like to stress the fact that the messianism of Jesus is presented as a source of temptation.

Jesus tells Peter that he has been favored by a revelation from his heavenly Father. Yet, paradoxically enough, both Matthew and Mark tell us that Peter tried to give a political interpretation to Jesus' messianism. Jesus begins to replace the title "Messiah" with the epithet "Son of Man," and he begins to tell his disciples about his ultimate failure with the people and his approaching death. Peter does not understand this, and he tries to convince Jesus that his journey towards the kingdom cannot take that route. Jesus' reply to him is vehement: "Away with you, Satan; you are a stumbling block to me. You think as men think, not as God thinks" (Mt 16:23; see Mk 8:33).

Why does Jesus get so angry with Peter? The answer is to be found in the gospel text itself. Peter's words represent a stumbling block for Jesus and a source of temptation for himself and his disciples. And they are a real stumbling block and temptation, otherwise Jesus' indignation is not explicable in psychological and theological terms. Jesus himself, and also his disciples, gradually comes to see the true sense of his messianism, which of its very nature is ambiguous.

The *third temptation* takes place in the Mount of Olives. There can be no doubt that Jesus was severely tempted there, that he felt tempted down to the very core of his being. But what was the precise nature of the temptation? An overly pietistic and individualistic interpretation of this scene has caused us to forget some very pertinent facts. Only recently Jesus had entered Jerusalem in an atmosphere that clearly had messianic overtones. Then, according to the Synoptic writers, he had driven the merchants out of the temple by force. His confrontation with the religious powers had reached its peak. It would seem, then, that his withdrawal from the city to a secluded place must be viewed as a precaution taken by him against his enemies. What is more, in the texts that we shall examine below it is evident that his followers are armed and that they even put up armed resistance against the Romans and Jews who come to arrest Jesus. That is the real-life context of the episode.

Jesus, for his part, sees himself pursued relentlessly by his enemies. He has no doubt that death awaits him if he falls into their hands. But he has not yet fully come to appreciate the fact that his messianism must be interpreted in terms of apparent failure and ruin, and it is this realization that leads to his bloody sweat and agony in the garden. The thought runs through his mind of appealing to his Father for twelve legions of angels to restore him to his status as a triumphant Messiah. He does not make this appeal. He overcomes the temptation to flee and the temptation to reply to his enemies in their own violent way. If he is to be faithful to the kingdom, he has only one course open to him. He must be content with the tremendous political violence of his truth being sacrificed before the eyes of his enemies. It costs him a great deal to see this, but he finally does realize that it is here that the will of the Father lies.

These three temptations indicate that the purely political dimension was never far from Jesus' mind. He got beyond it, but it was the great temptation of his life. However, he did not go to the other extreme. He never gave up the political "bite" of his salvation message. If he had given it up, what finally happened would probably not have happened.

Jesus and the Zealots

If we set the political character of Jesus' mission over against the political activity of the Zealots, we will be able to get a clearer picture of Jesus' political mission and to interpret the real connection between his salvation message and history.

One can talk about a certain degree of sympathy and closeness between Jesus and the Zealots. This is not an explicit theme in the gospel accounts, but their silence is a positive one in this respect. In addressing the gentiles, it would have suited the evangelists very nicely to stress Jesus' condemnation of the Zealot revolutionary movement if there had been such a condemnation.

But there is much more than silence involved here. There is the fact, already noted, of the presence of Zealots among his closest disciples. Luke presents us with additional data. There is the comment of Gamaliel in Acts (5:37), which associates the case of the apostles with that of Theudas and Judas of Galilee; the two latter people were certainly participants in the Zealot movement. Later on in Acts (21:38), Paul is brought before a tribune who confuses him with an Egyptian who had instigated a Zealot rebellion. It is Luke who reports the fact (Lk 13:1) that people came to tell Jesus of the Galileans who had been slain by Pilate. Even though Luke uses the incident to advance his theological interpretation of the relationship between guilt and punishment, we can safely assume that those who came to Jesus wanted to warn him about Pilate's persecution since he too was considered to be a Galilean.

Moreover, the public attitude of Jesus bears resemblances to some of the attitudes of the Zealots. For example, he classes the publicans, the tax collectors, as sinners even though he does not cease to maintain close relations with some of them. He talks harshly and ironically about those in power who oppress other people and yet dare to pass themselves off as doers of good (Lk 22:35 ff). He fights indefatigably against the holders of religious power who oppress and despoil the people. He is persecuted by Herod, a lackey of Rome. Even though Herod does represent duly established authority, Jesus speaks harshly about him: "At that time a number of Pharisees came to him and said, 'You should leave this place and go on your way; Herod is out to kill you.' He replied, 'Go and tell that fox, "Listen, today and tomorrow I shall be casting out devils and working cures . . . " ' " (Lk 13:31–32).

On the Mount of Olives there is explicit reference to the use of the sword, and the sword symbolized participation in the Zealot movement. Luke attributes these words to Jesus: "Whoever has a purse had better take it with him, and his pack too; and if he has no sword, let him sell his cloak to buy one" (Lk 22:36). In that passage Jesus is contrasting his first sending out of his disciples with the present situation. Whereas he once sent them out without purse and provisions, he now urges them to provide for themselves. As Cullmann notes, he did really tell his disciples to get swords. In fact, some of his followers actually went so far as to use them. The overall interpretation of this passage is difficult, to be sure, because Jesus cuts the conversation short when his disciples tell him that they do have two swords. Whatever the correct interpretation of this passage may be, it is worth pondering how far the political activism of an apostle may go.

In the same gospel passage Jesus alludes to a text in the book of Isaiah (53:12): "He was counted among the outlaws." Jesus tells his disciples that he will fulfill that text, that he will be treated as an outlaw and crucified between two outlaws. In the context, "outlaws" refers to Zealots who were fighting and defending themselves with swords. Hence the reference to swords has its place in explaining subsequent events. At the same time, however, we note Jesus' explicit wish that the sword not be used in connection with him. Matthew reports this remark: "Put up your sword. All who take the sword die by the sword" (Mt 26:52). That is precisely what happens to Jesus and the apostles—not that they take up the sword but that they die violently. So the import of his remarks remains ambiguous and difficult to interpret, but I might suggest this interpretation. The use of violence by followers of Jesus is admissible, but Jesus himself is not going to take that tack. This does not mean that the Gospel is supposed to be proclaimed with the sword in the manner of a crusade. It means that sin must be resisted, even by violence, when sin itself is violence; and this violent resistance to sin may go as far as the shedding of blood. Jesus himself does not seem to sense any such vocation, and his violence will be of a different sort.

Finally, we have another passage that is clearly of a Zealot cast: his action against the merchants in the temple. There he clearly employs force, and he is obviously aided by the followers accompanying him. The curious thing is that his action is not directed against the profanation of the temple by the Romans, against which the Zealots repeatedly instigaged bloody uprisings. Jesus' action is directed against the religious and economic organization of the priestly aristocracy. In Jesus' action, therefore, there is less concern for political religiosity and more concern for man's authentic relationship with God in a temple profaned by commercialism.

All these events prove that Jesus was actively involved in the public life of his people and his nation. They also prove that there was a certain Zealot aura surrounding his behavior. On the other hand, it must be emphasized that *Jesus did not belong to the Zealot party and did not preach a properly Zealot line of conduct*.

Jesus shared their active expectation of the kingdom, but he understood the kingdom in a different sense and he envisioned the way to it differently. An activist hope in the kingdom—that is, active effort in this world and amid the historical realities of this world, accompanied by active hope rather than mere waiting—is what is shared by the two movements. But Jesus did not share the extremist religious nationalism of the Zealots. As time went on, he opened up more and more to a sense of universalism. At the start he felt called to save the children of Israel and he urged his disciples to restrict their activities to the chosen people; it is a datum of the utmost political import. But he gradually came to realize that the kingdom must be universal. In his preaching he favored the concept of the poor and poverty over the concept of the Jew and Jewishness. In other words he gave preference to a humanistic, social concept over a politico-religious concept. He ultimately took a stance in line with the universalism of the prophets and pushed that line of thinking further ahead.

Another point of essential difference between Jesus and the Zealots is that Jesus did not accept the immediatist religiosity of the Zealots. He rejected their overly simplistic religious formulation in which the kingdom of God in this world was equated with a political theocratic kingdom. In the theological realm this immediatist religiosity leads to an all too ready identification of the kingdom of God with a wordly political kingdom. In the socio-political realm it leads to a religious fanaticism which has very adverse effect on social and political coexistence as well as the secular life of God. The history of the Zealot movement and of fanatic religious uprisings bear clear witness to the erroneous nature of this interpretive identification. It is one thing to say that there is an intrinsic connection between the wordly kingdom and the kingdom of God, between salavation history and salvation in history. It is something very different to simply equate the two completely. Here the mystery of Christ's person in two distinct natures, which are not mixed on the one hand but totally and transcendentally unified on the other, offers a christological guideline that is of permanent value in any attempted interpretation.

Jesus' methods of action are not those of the Zealots either. For the latter, armed uprising in the tradition of the Maccabees was the decisive approach. For Jesus the decisive way was the denunciatory force of God's word. The latter approach was no less dangerous to the established order than that of the Zealots, as is evident from the fact that Jesus, too, ends up on a cross; but it probably was and is less effective in implanting justice on this earth. All one can say is that the following of Christ does not rule out other factors that may be more efficacious than its own work of inspiration and criticism.

Finally, there is an important difference between Jesus and the Zealot movement in two basic, interrelated points: namely, their understanding of the kingdom and the matter of tax payments. We shall return to these two points a bit further on. Here I should like to stress that Jesus' "religious" preaching went far beyond the religious content of the Zealot movement in every respect, at least insofar as we can tell from what we know about the latter.

These basic theoretical reasons are not the only basis we have for differentiating the position of Jesus from that of the Zealots. There are certain gospel texts in which Jesus seems to be making a discreet distinction between his stance and the stance of other people whose motivation might possibly be confused with his own. Here we shall follow Cullmann.[5] He notes that Jesus' exhortation not to stand up against evil (in the Sermon on the Mount) takes on special significance if we realize that Jesus continually had to face up to the Zealot ideal of opposing the Roman empire by force.[6] The same would apply to his remark about the violent: "Ever since the coming of John the Baptist the kingdom of Heaven has been subjected to violence and violent men are seizing it" (Mt 11:12). The follow-up verses in Matthew's Gospel talk of the law and the prophets prophesying up until the days of John the Baptist. Jesus seems to be suggesting that not prophesying is not the only thing that is going to be lacking; that there will also be a lack of force, so that the strong and violent will seize the kingdom.

Luke's version is a bit milder: "Until John, it was the Law and the prophets; since then, there is the good news of the kingdom of God, and everyone forces his way in" (Lk 16:16). Cullmann comments: "It has long been a matter of vigorous controversy whether the saying is to be construed 'in bonam partem' or 'in malam partem'—whether it contains praise or censure. Is the intention here to praise zeal for the Kingdom of God? Is indeed Jesus himself, as Albert Schweitzer thinks, to be reckoned among those who fought so impetuously to gain the Kingdom of God? I do not think the Greek expression will allow this interpretation. Much rather are we to think of people like the Zealot leader Judas."[7] Thus the question remains open, but that in itself is enough to indicate that the ascetic, spiritualistic interpretation of this "violence" is wholly unwarranted.

Another passage is in John's Gospel: "The sheep paid no heed to any who came before me, for these were all thieves and robbers" (10:8). Cullmann asks: "Are not the Zealot leaders in mind here, who led their followers to certain death at the hands

of the Romans? . . . It seems to me all but certain that the
Zealot leaders like Judas of Gamala are in mind here. Seen from
the outside, there must have been something common to
both."[8] Cullmann's interpretation corroborates the thesis I presented above, namely, that Jesus' activity was such that people
could confuse it with that of the Zealots. But I do not feel that
we must agree with Cullmann's view that Jesus was speaking
pejoratively about such people as Judas the Galilean. Jesus was
condemning mercenaries, people who undertook the work of
the kingdom for self-interested reasons and then left their followers in the lurch when danger came. That was not true of the
Zealots, and Flavius Josephus bears witness to their suicidal
courage in the face of torture and death. However primitive
their approach may have been, the Zealots were working for
the freedom of Israel and the recognition of Yahweh as the one
and only Lord. In their eyes, resistance to foreign domination
was a religious duty.[9] Josephus himself must admit as much:
"Despite all sorts of torture and bodily mutilation, aimed simply at getting them to recognize Caesar as Lord, they did not
manage to win over one person or even point anyone in that
direction. . . . What most surprised spectators, however, is
the fact that they could not even get children of a very tender
age to call Caesar their Lord."[10]

Jesus could not help but respect this fortitude and religious
authenticity. Yet he simply did not agree with the strictly
guerrilla methods utilized by the Zealots.[11] This fact does not
entail a Christian judgment on the guerrilla way of combatting
a specific instance of violence. It simply indicates that the latter
is a secular problem of technique which is not ultimately decided by religious reasons. Jesus preferred to take the approach
of a shepherd who would lay down his life for his own. But he
laid down his life in a physical and political way, in an active
way rather than by merely submitting to an expiatory death.

Another gospel text contains Jesus' comment to the women
who were weeping as they saw him on the way to crucifixion:
"Daughters of Jerusalem, do not weep for me; no, weep for

yourselves and your children. . . . For if these things are done when the wood is green, what will happen when it is dry? (Lk 23:28–30). Cullmann has this comment: "The saying of Jesus can have only the following meaning: If the Romans execute *me* as a Zealot, who am no Zealot and who have always warned against Zealotism, what will they do then to the true Zealots! For the Romans Jesus was in reality green wood, for he had indeed renounced Zealotism. Thus this saying of Jesus expresses exactly what I have endeavored to show here: 1) Throughout his entire ministry Jesus had to come to terms with Zealotism; 2) He renounced Zealotism, although he also assumed a critical attitude towards the Roman State; 3) He was condemned to death as a Zealot by the Romans."[12] And Cullmann finally concludes: "Jesus' whole ministry was in continuous contact with Zealotism. . . . This formed the background, so to speak, of his activity and . . . he was executed as a Zealot."[13]

It seems that Flavius Josephus also tends to view Jesus as a participant in the Zealot movement.[14] I agree with Cullmann that such was not the case, but I also feel that we may have to place even greater stress on the political character of Jesus' mission precisely insofar as it was an alternative to Zealotism. The crucifixion of Jesus as an apparent Zealot proves clearly how much his public life operated on a plane akin to that of the Zealots, even though it may have moved in a different direction. His repeated call to "take up one's cross" and follow him, which has been much abused in certain areas of Christian asceticism and has focused too narrowly on the individual, was a phrase of a Zealot cast, as Brandon has shown. Jesus' way of behaving before the public authorities could not help but lead to the cross—the punishment for political rebels.

This does not mean that there were not clear and obvious differences between Jesus and the Zealots—so much so, in fact, that Zealots as such could not be wholehearted followers of Jesus nor could the latter be wholehearted participants in the Zealot movement. It is certainly true that outsiders confused and equated the two movements, as did Jesus' own disciples before they had grasped the fullness of his message. It also seems true that Jesus felt tempted to view his mission in Zealot terms. But all this merely proves that there was a certain resemblance between the two movements in their denunciation of the real-life situation and in their proclamation of what the potential solution might be. And here I shall do no more than allude to a similar problem today in order to bring the problem of Jesus into sharper focus. Consider the many people who view the political activity of the Church as subversive activity of a communist sort. The similarity in the historical parallel is so obvious that it hardly needs detailed treatment.

At the same time, however, we cannot overlook the many texts in which Jesus presents an original position of his own which, as a whole, is radically distinct from that put forward by the Zealots. The gospel accounts and the whole proclamation of the good news in the New Testament offer sufficient proof of the fact. Here I have chosen to stress a partial but decisive aspect of Jesus' life, but this political aspect is not the whole story. My point in bringing it up is that if it is not included in Jesus' life—and how often it has not been—then we are following a mere caricature of Jesus' real life. But there is certainly much more: his call to personal conversion and to an interiorization of the kingdom; his reference to a universal Father will bring total definitive unity and liberation to all human beings; eschatological hope and love for strangers and enemies; his proclamation of peace, even though it be a costly and difficult peace. All these features, and many others, radically differentiate Jesus' message from the theocratic message of the Zealots.

To sum up, Jesus worked to transform a politicized religion into a political faith. He did not give up the idea of saving humanity, but he was interested in the full and total dimensions of human salvation. From salvation in history one must move on to a meta-historical salvation. Proclamation of this meta-historical salvation will help human beings to see what authentic salvation in history should be, just as authentic salvation in history will be the one and only valid sign, comprehensible to human beings, of what meta-historical salvation means.

Jesus and the State

There are two classic incidents which must be considered if we want to grasp the ultimate import of Jesus' political mission. One deals with the question of paying tribute to Caesar. The other is Jesus' discussion with Pilate concerning the nature of Jesus' kingdom. I don't think we can determine from these passages what Jesus' idea of the State was, but I do think they help us to grasp more exactly the sense and import of his mission. With this end in mind, I shall explore these passages here.

Tribute to Caesar

The import of the theme of tribute to Caesar is evidenced by its detailed treatment in the three Synoptic Gospels (Mk 12:13–17; Mt 22;15–22; Lk 20:20–26). Like the other two Synoptic writers, Matthew frames the incident in its full context. Pharisees and Herodians join together, trying to catch Jesus in what he says. Luke tells us that they are spies, posing as upright men, who want to hand Jesus over to the government authorities. The Sadducees do not appear explicitly in this incident, but all three Synoptics introduce them immediately afterwards. They pose another problem of a religious nature to Jesus. Whether they are present among the Herodians in our case here is not of decisive importance.

As our earlier analysis of the Zealots would suggest, the whole matter of paying tribute was both a religious and a political question. It was, if you will, *the* question which defined one's position vis-à-vis a basic issue, i.e., whether one sided with the Zealots or was a collaborationist. The fact that Luke refers to Jesus' questioners as "secret agents" is significant, especially when he also adds that they wanted to hand

Jesus over to the Roman procurator. It was in every way a political question, and it would later help to get Jesus condemned.

Jesus was caught in a very delicate situation. If he simply answered yes, asserting that one ought to pay tribute to Caesar, he would be setting himself over against the most authentic wing of Jewish religiousness, over against the rebel Jewish faction represented by the Zealots. If he simply answered no, asserting that one ought not pay tribute to Caesar, then he would be setting himself over against the authority of Rome, which was asserted precisely by the imposition of such taxes. It is clear that Jesus did not make a clearcut reply in favor of paying such taxes, for when he comes before Pilate he is accused of inciting the people, opposing tax payments to Caesar, and claiming to be the Messiah king. That such accusations may be false is of little consequence here. The point is that if Jesus' preaching and way of life had given the opposite impression, then there would have been no basis for accusations of this sort. Hence Jesus gave people reason to believe that he was an agitator in the Zealot line, that he opposed tax payments and claimed to be a political Messiah who would free his people from foreign domination.

Jesus' reply, therefore, must be set in its full context. A political trap had been set for him, and he certainly did not give an absolutely clearcut answer. His words were open to misinterpretation. The interpretation proposed below takes due account of both poles. It attempts to consider the complexity of Jesus' words and of the situation in which he finds himself.

His key response is: "Pay Caesar what is due to Caesar, and pay God what is due to God" (Lk 20:25). I would offer the following observations about this remark:

1) The phrase may have already been coined by others, specifically by the Zealots. One should give Caesar what is his, and God what is his. But the Zealots felt that the political sovereignty of Israel belonged to God, not to Caesar—a point into which Jesus does not enter. Now if that were the case, then the primary thrust of Jesus' response would be an attitude of

respect for the Zealot position. Jesus could not have been viewed as the Messiah by the people at large if he had openly proclaimed the obligation of paying tribute to Caesar. As Brandon puts it: "It was, indeed, a saying of which any Zealot would have approved, because, as we have seen, for the Zealot there was no doubt that God owned the land of Israel, not Caesar."[15]

2) The formal structure of the remark is not sufficiently clearcut to justify only one of the two interpretations. Indeed it is sufficiently ambiguous to prevent the spies from bringing a satisfactory answer back to their bosses. Jesus, in other words, does not play their game.

3) Moreover, the formal structure of his remark, apart from its historical and redactional context, is abstract and tautological. It says that everyone is to be given his due. The real problem begins when one tries to determine exactly what each one's due is.

4) Jesus' allusion to a coin inscribed with a likeness of Caesar helps to move his line of thinking foward. He wants to make the Zealots realize that there are affirmations of a political nature—or better, of a secular nature—which should not be directly tied up with the whole matter of the individual's and the nation's relationship with God. In other words, here Jesus' theology takes an important step beyond the religious interpretation of the Zealots. Jesus does not tackle the point directly and fully, but he seems to be suggesting that one could pay taxes and tributes without necessarily taking a religious stance. Needless to say, this does not imply that secular realities can insist on respect at any price; that on them one may pronounce only an ethical judgement, not a Christian evaluation. It simply recognizes the proper and rightful autonomy of secular realities, and it attempts to separate the proper political mission of the faith from a politicizing of the religious realm or, if you prefer, from a religiosizing of the political realm.

5) In concrete fact, the nationalist theocratic interpretation of the State is not the alternative Jesus proposes when faced with the problem of Roman domination. On the one hand, the nationalistic emphasis interests him relatively little; on the

other hand his real interest lies in what is happening to people whoever their oppressors and rulers may be.

6) Jesus' impression of political rulers is explicitated on another occasion: "You know that in the world the recognized rulers lord it over their subjects, and their great men make them feel the weight of authority. That is not the way with you . . . " (Mk 10:42–43).

7) On an analogous topic, tribute to the temple, Jesus indicates that it can be tolerated. Such payment was incumbent only on foreigners, and this tolerance enabled him to avoid involvement in unnecessary conflicts.

8) Jesus does affirm that one cannot give Caesar what belongs to God, even though he does not determine here what belongs to God. The kingdom of God is not to be understood in terms of such categories as tax payments. He evinces a tolerance of the State, if you will, insofar as it is a necessary means. But one cannot derive a Christian theory of the State from this passage since neither the nature of the State nor the matter of tax tribute is the direct subject of his reply.

Luke's closing remark about the incident is interesting: "Thus their attempt to catch him *out in public* failed, and, astonished by his reply, they fell silent" (Lk 20:26). This indicates clearly that he did not confirm the position of the Herodians. If he had wanted to do that, he certainly could have done so in explicit terms. The Synoptic writers report that Jesus was sincere, that he taught God's way sincerely and did not bow to superficial appearances. While the whole question of the legitimacy of tax payments might indeed be a moral question, Jesus' answer goes far beyond any captious morality.

A Kingdom Not of This World

It is before the political representative of Roman power that final judgment on Jesus' political mission is passed. Before the Sanhedrin the charge may have been predominantly religious in nature although, as we noted earlier, the root problem was a socio-political one. Before Pilate, however, the charge would have to be predominantly political. Jesus' accusers try to gather everything about his mission that might seem to be political in order to enlist Pilate's help in their task of getting rid of him. Without the help of Roman authority, it is unlikely that the Jewish leaders would have been able to liquidate Jesus so soon after he had been acclaimed by crowds of people. So let us examine this closing scene in Jesus' life.

The brunt of the accusation is found in Luke (23:2): agitating the people, forbidding tax payments, posing as the Messiah King. In John's Gospel he is accused of being a "criminal." The connotations of the term are absolutely political. It is equivalent to "Zealot," as the context itself reveals, for Jesus is accused of political subversion. Pilate himself clearly notices the political import and thrust of the accusation against Jesus, and he formulates it pointedly. According to all four gospel accounts, he asks Jesus: "Are you the king of the Jews?" At this point John the Evangelist adds an acute question by Jesus himself: "Is that your own idea, or have others suggested it to you?" (Jn 18:34). The point is well taken because the same term, Messiah King, could have very different meanings for a Jew and a Roman. Jesus' Jewish accusers take advantage of this very ambiguity, but Jesus himself does not. In the sense in which Pilate might have an interest, Jesus was not a king. In the sense of a messianic tradition, Jesus was a king; but there was a radical novelty in his kingship as opposed to the kind of kingship his people were expecting.

It is in this context that Jesus begins to explain the sense of his kingship and kingdom: "My kingdom does not belong to this world. If it did, my followers would be fighting to save me from arrest by the Jews. My kingly authority comes from elsewhere" (Jn 18:36). At once we notice that Jesus does not evade the ambiguity entailed in the use of the word "kingdom." If his kingdom really did not have anything at all to do with what a Roman procurator viewed as "kingdom," then Jesus would have withdrawn the term. He does not. He maintains the term insistently despite the misunderstandings which it may occasion. To put it in more modern terms: Jesus maintains some sort of political character in his mission even though the term "political" itself may lead to misunderstanding and equivocation. To withdraw the term would lead to even worse misunderstandings because there really is a political dimension to his mission. At the same time, however, Jesus is careful to distinguish his kingdom from others. His kingdom is not of this world. We must recall the pejorative connotation of the term "world" in John's Gospel. The differentiating element is the fact that Jesus' kingdom does not rely on soldiers. In other words, it does not have a governmental organization.

Upon further questioning from Pilate, Jesus describes his status and situation in positive terms: " 'King' is your word. My task is to bear witness to the truth. For this was I born; for this I came into the world, and all who are not deaf to truth listen to my voice" (Jn 18:37).

Here we come to the essence of his kingdom. He is to bear witness to the truth, and the term must be taken in its full implications: 1) The truth of which he speaks here is not some speculative, non-operational truth; it is an efficacious and total truth. It is the truth about the world—what it is, what it should be, and what is going to take place in it. 2) Jesus upholds the judicial and dominating character of his mission and truth, even vis-à-vis the world insofar as it gives configuration to human existence. 3) From within the context of this total truth one must be a proclaimer and doer of truth, seeking to gain dominion over evil. The world is already being judged, and Christian history should help to move this judgment along towards its consummation. 4) The effect and impact of this truth is liberty. It is a truth that sets human beings free. 5) One must belong to this truth in order to be able to hear it. One must do this truth in order to be able to receive it in full clarity and plenitude.

Pilate does not grasp this explanation, but he does glimpse that the accusation against Jesus does not have the crass political connotations that were suggested by the Jewish leaders. To get rid of Jesus, he sends him off to Herod; but the stratagem does not work.[16] He is once again confronted with the accused and comes to realize that he is not an agitator of the people (Lk

23:14). One interesting sidelight, mentioned only by Luke, is Jesus' silence regarding who would be the competent authority over him insofar as he is a Galilean. This is very much in line with his general attitude towards the authorities of his time.

To get out of the difficult situation, Pilate introduces the alternative of opting for Barrabas or Jesus. All four gospel accounts report this act, but the historicity of the incident is questioned by more than one exegete.[17] But whether the incident is based on historical fact or is introduced for apologetic reasons, its import is great in terms of an historical *logos*.

Barrabas certainly was a Zealot. He was a rebel *(stasiastos)* who had committed murder during an insurrection. It is he who will be preferred by the crowd over Jesus. Both Brandon and Cullmann see Barrabas in this light, and the fact that he and Jesus are placed on the same level indicates that the Romans felt they were dealing with the same sort of crime and punishment. Schlier, too, views Barrabas as a "messianic revolutionary."[18] In the gospel narrative, then, we may catch glimpses of an apologetic: 1) to show that the Romans did everything possible to save Jesus; 2) to exculpate Jesus from the charge of being a rebel in the style of Barrabas.

Behind this apologetic surface, however, we may discern even deeper levels. First of all, due weight should be given to the fact that the manipulations of the chief priests played an important role in the crowd's choice of Barrabas. This would suggest that Jesus' stance was more dangerous to their position than that of Barrabas; and their position rested, in large measure, upon their connivance with the Roman authorities. In short, Jesus represented a greater political threat to the existing structure of society and to its socio-political, religious organization. At one point Caiphas had noted (Jn 11:50) that it would be better for one man to die than for the whole nation to perish.

Yet it was the people who rejected Jesus. The gospel presentation may have theological reasons behind it, but perhaps we can discern another explanation of a sociological nature. The evangelists repeatedly stress the popularity of Jesus with the people. It is one of the reasons why the authorities do not dare to arrest him during the Pasch. How, then, are we to explain this sudden shift in favor of Barrabas? Perhaps we might conjecture that the political ambiguity of Jesus' position eventually came to disconcert the people, who saw Barrabas' position as more clearcut. The latter, after all, had actually fought against the Romans. Now if this conjecture is correct, then we have another, albeit indirect, indication of the rather special political character of Jesus' mission. John the Evangelist, however does stress that the cries for Jesus' condemnation came from the high priests and guards (Jn 19:6). So perhaps we should keep in mind what we said in an earlier paragraph when we try to propose any sociological interpretation, namely, that the ambiguity of Jesus' political mission was more of a threat to the dominant social figures in society than was the struggle of the Zealots against Roman political power.

The question is often asked: Why didn't Jesus protest and fight more openly and directly against Roman domination? It is a misguided question, I think. Jesus was less concerned with that problem than he was with the immediate socio-religious oppression he saw imposed on his people. Against this oppression he fought even to death.

Only at this point, when they see Pilate vacillating, do the Jews bring up what is clearly a religious accusation: that Jesus claims to be the Son of God. Even this accusation is political, however, since it was customary to divinize emperors and great rulers. Jesus is king in this world because he is Son of God. His right to reign in this world is based on his divine sonship. The priests see clearly that they will lose their theocratic religious dominion if Jesus' claim to a special relationship with God is vindicated. Even more upset now, Pilate tries to get Jesus to speak again; but Jesus remains silent. Only when Pilate tries to assert the absoluteness of his authority does Jesus answer him. Pilate asks: "Surely you know that I have authority to release you, and I have authority to crucify you?" Jesus' response, which is rather difficult to interpret, is: "You would have no authority at all over me . . . if it had not been granted you from above; and therefore the deeper guilt lies with the man who handed me over to you" (Jn 19:10–11).

The problem lies in trying to interpret "therefore" correctly. The authority granted from above and the man who handed Jesus over seem to stand over against one another. Jesus affirms that Pilate has no more authority than that conferred on him from above; if and when he goes beyond the bounds of that authority, he commits a despotic action. It might also imply that Jesus would not be in his hands now if his Father had not so arranged things; but this would not imply that it was the Father who handed Jesus into Pilate's power. Finally, the "therefore" links Pilate's responsibility with that of the Jews who handed Jesus over. Pilate, too, is committing sin because he is not wise enough to use the authority he has received from on high correctly; but the greater sin is that of the Jews who have handed Jesus over to him. The conclusion seems obvious: The death of Jesus is a Jewish-Roman matter; as such, it is both political and religious.

This is clearly shown by the final threat which the Jews pose to Pilate. Taking advantage of the objectively political appearance of Jesus' mission, they threaten Pilate: "If you let this man go, you are no friend to Caesar; any man who claims to be a king is defying Caesar" (Jn 19:12). It is clear, then, that Jesus maintained his status as a king right up to the end, even though the ambiguity surrounding this assertion led him to death. And he died by crucifixion, the usual punishment meted out to political prisoners of the Zealot type. Jesus could not overcome the surface appearance surrounding his affirmation of kingship. He seems to have realized where this would lead him, and yet he did not change it.

Here we are not going to draw all the theological consequences of the analysis we have made in this chapter. We shall consider those consequences in Part Three. But let us try to see where our investigation has led so far. We began by stressing the need to relate christology to an historical *logos*; only then is it possible for us to discover the ultimate import of Jesus' life as

[handwritten margin note:] SUMMARY

the real-life revelation of human salvation. Then we explored his prophetic behavior both as a religious critic and as a social critic. We saw that these two dimensions were unified and brought together in a higher political dimension.

Such an analysis, it seems, is very necessary if we are to take a fresh look at the life of Jesus and situate it in its real historical context. This does not mean that other types of analysis are thereby rendered null and void, for the real-life totality of Jesus' life would be impoverished if we rejected all other interpretations. Our stress on the political dimension of Jesus' life may have changed some people's thinking and disappointed others. But the data is there to be studied. While some specific points of exegesis may be considered problematic, the overall weight and coherence of the whole suggests that the fundamental analysis is not exaggerated.

In Part Three we shall look at this historical and exegetical analysis once again, attempting to provide a sound theological interpretation of it. Two basic points must be given serious reconsideration in the light of what we have discovered so far: 1) What is the exact import of Jesus' messianism? 2) What might the following of Jesus, the imitation of his life, mean in theological terms? These two questions do not exhaust the possible content of christology, nor even the possible contribution of an historical *logos* to christology. I do not propose to do any such thing. But these questions do, I think, provide a critical focus for the main question posed here: How is salvation history related to salvation in history? The facts and events of Jesus' life prove that such a relationship exists, and I shall try to explore their deeper theological meaning in the pages that follow.

NOTES

1. A brief treatment of this topic can be found in Heinrich Schlier, *The Relevance of the New Testament* (New York: Herder and Herder, 1968), pp. 239–48.

2. *Ibid.*, p. 243.

3. *Ibid.*, p. 247.

4. Josef Schmid, *Das Evangelium nach Lukas* (Regensburg: Pustet, 1955).

5. Oscar Cullmann, *The State in the New Testament* (New York: Scribner's, 1956), p. 18 ff. Cullmann bases his view on the support of such authors as N. A. Dahl, "The Parables of Growth," *Studia Theologica* 5, 1951, pp. 131–66; and H.G. Wood, "Interpreting This Time," *New Testament Studies* 2, pp. 262–66.

6. Cullmann, *ibid.*

7. *Ibid.*, pp. 20–21.

8. *Ibid.*, p. 22.

9. See S.G.F. Brandon, *Jesus and the Zealots* (New York: Scribner's, 1967), p. 56.

10. *Wars of the Jews*, VII, 416–419. Also see S.G.F. Brandon, *Jesus and the Zealots*, p. 57.

11. Brandon, *ibid.*, pp. 55 ff.

12. Cullmann, *The State in the New Testament*, p. 48.

13. *Ibid.*, p. 49.

14. Cullmann (*ibid.*, footnote 20) cites the following reference: A. Berendt, *Die zuegnisse von Christentum im slavischen "de bello Judaico" des Josephus*, 1906; cfr. A. Berendt and K. Grass, *Flavius Josephus vom judischen Kriege nach der slavischen Uebersetzung deutsch herausgegeben und mit dem griechischen Text vergiche*, 1924/27.

15. Brandon, *Jesus and the Zealots*, p. 347.

16. In general, the interconnection of the passion accounts is not easy to ascertain. But since we are more concerned with theology than with exegesis here, the constructed character of the gospel accounts actually helps us in our endeavor rather than hinders us.

17. Maurice Goguel (*Jesus*, 2nd ed. 1950, p. 382 ff.) is of the opinion that the scene is not historical. Cullmann (*The State in the New Testament*, pp. 47–48) recognizes great difficulties from a juridic standpoint but does not feel they are insuperable. Brandon (*Jesus and the Zealots*, pp. 258 ff.) rejects the historicity of the incident on the basis of its intrinsic improbability and on the silence of Josephus about any such custom.

18. M. Schlier, *Relevance*, p. 221.

In this Chapter, E. tries to define the political dimensions in Jesus' own conscious-ness. He treats Messianism — as a temp-tation which Jesus resisted by ~~not~~ accepting the popular interpretation, but he ~~remained~~ a political-messiah in a religious & transcendent way. (summary, p. 60)

E. then treats Jesus relationship to the Zealots. Not a Zealot, but parallels — rely on Cullmann.

E. then treats Jesus' relation to the Roman State — Tribute to Caesar — & the trial scene: Kingdom not of this world

All of this is based on interpretations of key pericopes in the Gospels. See Marginal remarks, p. 60.

summary — pp. 77 - 78

PART TWO

The Historicity
of the Church's Mission

If we do not take note of the essential historicity of the Church's mission in proclaiming the gospel message, then it is presumptuous or useless for us to examine the question of the Church's mission at all today. The slightest reflection will bring us to the realization that the Church's mission is historical, that this is an essential dimension of the whole question. Many misunderstandings in theory and practice arise from a denial of this dimension or an important evaluation of it.

God's salvific communication and revelation are historical. That is to say, they take place in history and they occur in an historical way. History is, by its very name, the locale for the communication and revelation of a God who is personal and who is the God of living human beings. This is not to deny that God somehow makes his presence felt also through nature; for one thing, nature itself comes to form a part of history. But it is in history that we find the privileged locale of divine revelation. We could deduce this notion from theoretical reasons, since God's communication with human beings necessarily has to be of a personal nature; but here it is enough to note the fact that this is how it has actually happened.

Now the communication of a living God in history means that this communication must be concerned with the history of human beings and that it must be so in a changing and progressive way. The two statements are interrelated. Without God's irruption into history, without his presence in the historical realm, we would know very little about him. But if his presence is to be found in the historical realm, then we must be open to this changing irruption which is history.

The proclamation of the gospel message, therefore, must possess the same historical character that revelation and salvation do. Otherwise something that is essentially historical would be turned into something natural. *And if the mission of proclaiming the gospel message possesses this same historical character as the message itself, then it must be carried out in history and in an historical way.* This, of course, implies that the history of salvation has something to do with salvation in history. It also implies that the salvation proclaimed by the Church in history must be proclaimed from within the history of salvation, not from some other context that is alien to it.

Not only must the Church proclaim salvation historically; it must also realize this salvation historically. Proclamation itself is a realization, and historical proclamation is an historical realization. But that does not end the matter. The Church, as the continuation of the principal sacrament which Jesus Christ is, must realize—that is, carry out and make real—what it proclaims. The proclamation and realization of salvation *goes on continually* today in Jesus Christ. What is more, the locale of this effectively continuing process is the body of the Church, which makes the invisible action of its head present and operative. To be the body of Christ means to be the locale of his presence and the mediating locus of his activity. And if the Church is supposed to realize Christ's salvation, the Church must do so in the history of salvation which it proclaims historically.

So it is the historicity of this task of truly proclaiming salvation that obliges us to continually review the mission of the Church in proclaiming and fleshing out the gospel message. This is especially true when we recognize, as Vatican II did very precisely (*Gaudium et spes*, no. 4), that the human race is in a new stage of its history. At such points humanity will be forced to ask pointed questions "about this present life and the life to come, and about the relationship of the one to the other" (*ibid.*), or, to put it in other words, about the relationship between salvation in history and salvation beyond history. Today that question confronts us as an extremely urgent one, entirely new in scope; and it confronts both the Church and those outside. It is a question which involves and concerns both the very being of the Church and its credibility, and it is in these terms that the true dimensions of the question can be estimated.

In restating and reconsidering the historicity of its mission, the Church is guided by perennial focal points. On the one hand it must listen in faith here and now to the ever new and vital word of God; on the other hand it must listen here and now to the world. Its listening must operate out of a certain time and place. Only then can the Church say how the sin of the world presents itself at a given point and how the hope of salvation presents itself in the same situation. It is the people of God, compelled to live within the framework of an ever changing world, who must proclaim and carry out a salvation that signifies Christian salvation. Proclamation, realization, and people of God are the three essential factors that compel us to give radical reconsideration to the mission of the Church.

The Christian is not a citizen of two worlds, but of one world in which the kingdom of God has appeared in an historical way. Hence there should be some evident confluence between that which is salvation history and that which is salvation in history. Confluence does not mean identity, but it rules out dissociation. What is more, salvation in history is the necessary mediating factor of salvation history. It is often stressed that Christianity proclaims the salvation of the whole person, not just of the soul in the next life. But that is not enough to say. We must also stress that the salvation of man in history, the full embodying of man's total reality in history, is the necessary means and medium for God's definitive self-revelation and self-communication. There are two fundamental mysteries which cannot be neglected if we are to interpret Christianity correctly: 1) the example of the Word made flesh, and the manifestation of his divinity in and through historically salvific actions; 2) the expectation of his second coming in full glory, for which the Church is to pave the way through its activity in the world.

The mediation of history is essential to the revelation of God. Hence there cannot help but be an intimate relationship between the fundamental yearnings of those who are trying to proclaim the kingdom of God and those who are trying to fashion the history of human beings. We must appreciate the full implications of this fact. It is not just that we must realize there is some relationship between the inner yearnings of the human individual and the Christian. There is more to it. We must also discover and point out the relationship between the basic yearnings of the people of God and the family of mankind. In other words, it is not enough to pose the problem in terms of personal, individual historicity; we must also pose it in terms of societal history. Social history does not annul personal historicity; it presupposes that history and brings it to its culmination. The convergence between the best impulses and thrusts of the world and the best thinking of the Church at any given point in time is not a matter of mere timeliness or opportunism. To phrase the matter in classical terms, there is a universal judgment into which all particular judgments will ultimately flow; and in the code of this universal judgment, what has been done for other human beings will apparently stand out more prominently than what has been done for Jesus Christ. Taken together, these two factors—the universality of judgment and the seemingly mundane cast of the governing code—put us on the right track in attempting to explain and explicitate the historicity of salvation.

Hence we should not be surprised to find that *liberty*, *justice*, *and love are simultaneously essential dimensions of the historical world today and of the proclamation of the gospel message.* Liberation can be viewed as a process of liberty, justice, and love. These three categories are explicitly biblical and explicitly secular. They may not be completely equivalent on the two planes, but they are intrinsically connected. They offer us the great possibility of working in a Christian way for the world and of properly incarnating—or secularizing—the Christian faith. They offer us the concrete possibility of unifying what is really one vocation, of working for the transformation of the world and simultaneously proclaiming the gospel message. On a more abstract level, they offer us the possibility of tackling one of the most classic themes of theology in a better way. What was once posed in terms of nature and grace may now be considered in terms of salvation history and salvation in history. The latter terms are much more biblical and existential. We may thus be able to tackle certain issues more effectively than we had been able to do in terms of nature.

In Chapters 4 and 5, I shall try to show how these three categories offer us an opportunity to give credibility to the Church's mission today. For its mission is to proclaim the gospel message as the salvation of human beings in history and beyond history.

4

The Church's Mission: Signs of its Credibility

In more and more places the Church is ceasing to live within the context of a cultural whole that for centuries has been known as Christendom. This fact is forcing the Church to adopt a more missionary outlook in the proclamation of the gospel message. The Church must make clear the credibility of its mission. If it does not take note of the profound historical change involved in moving from the context of Christendom to the context of a missionary Church, it will not proclaim and carry out salvation in a historical way. If it does, the Church will be returning to its primitive essence, to its pristine missionary origins.

Mission — because of the break-down of Xtendom

The Church as a Sacramental Sign of its Own Credibility

The invisible God is accessible only through the mediation of signs. The perfect sign is the man Jesus. He shows us in a historical way the need for mediation in the presentation of God to humankind and in man's gaining access to God. He also shows us what the historicization of this mediation can and should be. In continuing the work of Jesus Christ, therefore, we must seek out the specific kind of mediation that will signify

87

God and make him present in a sign way. If we were to presume to have some spiritualistic, individualistic, and merely interior access to God, we would be denying the condition of God's communication to man and the condition of man's access to God. We would be denying salvation history as God has communicated it to man. History, a specific history, is the living, personal mediation through which God draws near to man and man draws near to God.

Signs in History

The signs can be varied and different. But not every sign signifies God in the same degree—much less the God revealed in Jesus Christ. Nature, for example, can be a sign of God to some extent; but it is a diminished sign. If it is not taken up into history, it is more likely to remove us further from God than to bring us closer to the God revealed in Jesus Christ. In general, it should not be up to man arbitrarily to select signs that are to mediate God to us. For these signs should be constitutive ones, that is, signs which in and of themselves, rather than by arbitrary human designation, signify what they claim to signify. If the signs were to be chosen arbitrarily by man, then we would reduce God to human caprice. Neither can nature as such offer us signs that are intrinsically connected with the God of salvation; if that were the case, there would be no irruption of God into nature and we would end up naturalizing God. The signs must be historical signs, but taken or grasped from within salvation history. Insofar as they are part of salvation history and chosen by God himself, they necessarily go beyond human arbitrariness.

Salvation history tells us that the fundamental sign of God is history itself, but not all of history in the same way. It is primarily, though not exclusively, the history of the chosen people. It is lastly, though not definitively, history in the fullness of time that is Jesus Christ. And it is the Church insofar as it continues his life and mission in time.

Hence it is not nature and the natural order but rather history and the overall disposition of society that serve as the mediating corpus of God. This is a point of singular importance because it leads us to view the Church not as the defender of the natural order but rather as the orderer of societal realization. Nature would thus be a sign revealing and communicating God only insofar as it is an element of history and in the service of liberty in history. Such a view does not imply any falling into historicism, because the identification of nature with essence is a gratuitous one to begin with. History, insofar as it is the field of personal collective liberty, is the place where the free, personal, living God is made most present. Framed within history is the biography of Jesus, who offers us the indispensable sign-key. However much this key may scandalize those who have deduced the being of God from nature, the Church cannot cease to proclaim it as such ever and always.

It is in the same line that the Church must view its own character as a mediating sign. Only a Church at work in history can reveal and communicate the God of history to us effectively. Only in history will the Church find an adequate field to carry out its mission and make it credible. By making the saving mystery of Jesus Christ present and operative, the Church will make it possible for people to believe what the Church claims itself to be. In the days of Christendom as a total cultural complex, the Church made use of proofs of credibility that were extrinsic to the Church's basic being, e.g., socio-cultural supports, socio-economic supports, socio-political supports, and so forth. The Church will not need such external proofs when it strives wholeheartedly to be itself a sign, and only a sign, of the God who has revealed himself in history. The Church's being and life will prove the credibility of Jesus as the savior of humanity. Then people will be able to move gradually from one brand of credibility to another, from believing in Jesus as the savior of humanity and history to believing in him as the Lord, the prime revealer of the Father.

Possible Directions for the Church

The Church has adopted different approaches as it sought to increase in rationality vis-à-vis its own members, who wanted proofs of their faith, and vis-à-vis outsiders, to whom it wanted to prove the divine character of its own foundation. Using these different approaches, it sought to adapt itself to the needs of those who posed questions to it. As the era of the Church's dominance passed away and it was no longer natural for the Christian faith to serve as the social norm, the Church has sought to develop a fundamental apologetic that would make the Christian faith credible. Different fundamental theologies have arisen, all of them sharing one feature in common. They all were regarded as thresholds to faith, and hence to theology. This implied, to some extent at least, that the proof was external to faith itself. The world was divided into two, as it were, and then an attempt was made to bring all the divided parts together—with greater or lesser success.

Two fundamental approaches were used in all this. One started from objective signs of credibility based on nature, the other from objective signs of credibility based on subjectivity. The two approaches correspond to different situations, and they compel us to seek out another approach that will truly correspond to the new situation.

Let us consider these two approaches. The first appealed to nature as the secure locus of objectivity. The element of objectivity was grounded on the historically proven interruption of the laws of nature. Historical interruption of physical laws was said to prove the irruption of the supernatural into the picture. Underlying this approach was a certain specific way of understanding reason and nature, one that is highly debated and highly debatable. What is clearcut and undeniable here is an attempt to achieve the greatest possible independence from subjective attitudes and emotional reactions. This approach might be called a demonstrative apologetic of natural reason which, as such, is external to the process proper to that which one was trying to prove. A maximum of objectivity would seem to imply a maximum of exteriority. Nevertheless history, even though it was understood in an accidental way, did play an important role in this attempt to give credibility to the faith through a preliminary process of rationalizing, not the faith, but the act of faith.

The second appoach appealed to personal subjectivity as the fundamental reality. It pointed to subjectivity as the most real reality, as the basic fundament for verifying all other reality. By showing the openness of subjectivity to something above and beyond the immanent limitations of nature, and even of the world in its totality, it felt it had a solid basis for ultimately proving the coherent connection between the Christian message and personal or interpersonal subjectivity. The transcendentalizing of the process aimed at achieving a maximum of objectivity, but it also placed the fact of history outside the process itself. (This does not mean that taking note of the essential historicity of human subjectivity would in itself suffice to adequately interiorize the empirical process of history.) In this approach maximum objectivity was sought by a process in which personal subjectivity was transcendentalized. Inherent in this approach was the danger of reducing credibility and faith itself to subjective interiority—in the good sense of this term.

This is not the place to judge the value of these two approaches or the consequences they have had for pastoral activity connected with the Church's mission. I have alluded to them here only to show how the Church might be able to display its own credibility today. The answer seems to be that the Church must seek out those objective signs by taking historico-social reality as its starting point. This starting point gets beyond personal intersubjectivity on the one hand and the objectivism of nature on the other; and it gets beyond them by assuming them in a positive way. The danger of subjectivism is overcome by taking note of the objectivity of the subject, who is social in his actual realization in history. The danger of objectivism is overcome by taking due note of historicity, which includes within it personal intersubjectivity. Once again history shows up as the irreplaceable mediating factor of God, who freely chooses to reveal and communicate himself to human beings. Let me develop these ideas briefly.

The signs must correspond to the total reality of man, who is both nature and history. The objectivity of nature is an impoverished sign of the personal God who has revealed himself in salvation history. It has value insofar as it can offer support independent of all idealistic subjectivity; but it is alien to transforming praxis, to the historicity of reality, and to the personal immanence of God in human history. Subjectivity, too, is an impoverished sign of what God and man are in history. It has value insofar as it attempts to give an immanent base to God's presence among human beings; but it tends to conceive human transcendence in individual terms, and hence in itself it does not lead to praxis in societal life and history.

But if we start from historico-social reality, on the other hand, we can take up the values of the other two approaches without suffering from their limitations. The personal and communitarian reality of socio-historical man gets beyond the objectivity of nature and transcendental personal subjectivity. The reality of social man prevents the immanent link with the historical process from being watered down into idealistic subjectivity; and this same reality, insofar as it is personal and communitarian, rules out the static extrinsicism of natural objectivity. Moreover, the historical character of this new sign, which assumes the other signs and learns from them, obliges us to participate actively in a process which, in its very transformation, should continually be the mediation of a God who has already revealed himself, who is now communicating himself, and who will continue to communicate himself in the open-ended process of history. This history which is to be fashioned by human beings starts out from nature, to be sure, but only insofar as it is really and strictly historical is it the full and complete channel for God's revelation.

That, in fact, is how God has proceeded in salvation history. Salvation has been proclaimed to, and felt by, a people in the course of their real-life socio-political experience. Only in and through this communitarian, public praxis of salvation has it been possible to transmit something that gets beyond the salvation of this world. One might debate in theory whether fundamental theology should follow the same process in laying the foundations of theology that salvation history has followed in laying the historical foundations of salvation. But less open to debate is the fact that the proclamation of salvation today should follow the same process that it did on its initial appearance. What I am trying to point out here is what the Church ought to do in order to show itself to human beings today as the sign and body of Jesus Christ in proclaiming and carrying out salvation. I am not so much interested in trying to point out the pathway to be followed by theology in order to offer theoretical proof of the credibility of the faith.

The point of the argument

The point, then, is that the sign of credibility which the Church is should be fleshed out in historico-social praxis. Salvation must be proclaimed, but it must be proclaimed in a signifying way. And the nature of signs requires us to consider both what should be signified and to whom it is to be signified. What should be signified in this case is the total salvation of man in and through his intrinsic deification; and the addressee of this effort is the world of today, which is engaged in the salvation of the history that it bears on its shoulders. Thus salvation in history is the present-day sign of salvation history.

This historicity takes at least three forms: 1) historicity as real-life authenticity; 2) historicity as effectiveness in history; 3) historicity as hope in an eschatological future. Salvation must be historical in this threefold way. The whole salvation proclaimed by Jesus must be authentically proclaimed; it must be fleshed out in history, taking shape in the reality where it is already at work; it must be open to his second coming in a process of active preparation which transforms history and prepares for the final outburst of God's full glory. Thus salvation in history, some features of which we shall consider later, will be the mediation of salvation history in its totality. Salvation in history is not to be equated completely with salvation history; but the former is the body of the latter, its visible aspect, the thing which enables it to be operative.

In this task the Church is not just a historical sign of credibility. As Church, it is also the historical sign of the credibility of salvation history. But the Church itself is a historico-social reality and, as such, has an influence on the configuration of salvation in history. To be sure, the Church is not primarily an institution; it is rather the community of those who are animated by the same Spirit, who confess the same Lord and follow his life. But it is also a historico-social body which, as such, mediates salvation. Because the Spirit of Christ has *taken flesh* in it, the Church is subject to a series of institutional risks. It may, for example, shape its life after the "values" of surrounding society rather than after Christ. It may ally itself with the powers of this world in order to perdure as an institution. In seeking some vaunted common good, it may cooperate with a society or with certain classes which represent the objectification of collective, social sin or a sinful social situation; this may lead to the good of some people, but it will not lead to the overall common good. However, because it is the *Spirit of Christ* who has taken flesh in it, the Church goes on being the operative visibility of its Lord, the definitive locus of the promise.

Hence it is the Church that is guaranteed the authentic reading and interpretation of salvation history. It is above the danger of a wholly inner and subjectivist interpretation of salvation, and also above the danger of a wholly secularist and politicizing interpretation. Both dangers threaten it—the former as a collection of individuals who seek a direct relation with God outside the flux of history, the latter as the body of society. The overcoming of this two-edged danger is what makes possible a proper secular interpretation of the Christian faith. It enables the Church to determine what the Christian faith authentically is, independent of religiosity, and how the faith in its concrete incarnation is a transforming force for the total man. The Church speaks its total word in this world and from this world; in and from there it directs itself to the whole of reality, not just to one or more of its aspects. In itself and vis-à-vis the world, the Church ought to be the purest and most effective sign of the salvation which it proclaims.

Now if we bring these two things together—i.e., the essential historicity of salvation, and the necessity of mediating salvation in history itself through this fundamental sign of credibility called the Church—then we have a solid criterion for exploring and finding the proper incarnation of the sign. The sign cannot have such absolute value that it does not signify anything beyond itself. Nor can it be such that it does not intrinsically signify what it in fact is called upon to signify. The mission of the Church must move between these two extremes in order to avoid angelism on one side and secularism on the other: angelism in the form of religiosity, secularism in the form of horizontalist politicizing.

Today liberation, justice, and love offer the proper channel in which the Church can proclaim and carry out its salvific mission without falling into either angelism or secularism. They offer an adequate channel for mediating salvation in a historical way, and for allowing the Church to present itself as the sign par excellence of the God who saves the world.

Historico-social Liberation from Sin

There is a long tradition of spirituality in the Church which proposes contemplation and encounter with God in action. The important question here is this: What kind of action and activity? Is it to be action of an individualistic and spiritualistic cast? Or is it to be personal activity in history? And if it is the latter, we must determine the connection between this personal, historical action and man's encounter with God.

In the concrete, liberation is one of these activities, one of these historical processes in which man may encounter the living God who saves human beings.

Liberation as Essential to the Gospel Message

Today certain movements and ideologies present their message and their activity in terms of liberation. This fact should not frighten us away from proposing salvation as liberation today. Some may regard this as opportunistic, and others may be scandalized to see the Church present its message in these terms. But the fact remains that the tendency is not confined to grass-roots movements or avant-garde theologians. More and more the ecclesiastical hierarchy itself is proclaiming salvation in terms of the liberation of the oppressed. For example, the 1971 Synod of Bishops had this to say about God's salvific justice: "In the Old Testament God reveals Himself to us as liberator of the oppressed and defender of the poor, demanding from man faith in Him and justice toward man's neighbor." In all likelihood it was the conciliar message of the Third World bishops and the Medellín Conference that brought the term and reality of liberation into full focus in the Catholic Church. *Gaudium et spes* seemed to have some reservations about the term. While it talked about man's full and authentic liberation in positive terms (no. 10), it seemed to regard talk about his economic and social liberation as a form of atheism (no. 20). *Populorum progressio*, to be sure, did talk about the fashioning of a new world where man might lead a fully human life, free from bondage to other human beings and to a natural world that was not under adequate control. But it was the conciliar message of the Third World bishops and the Medellín Conference, together with the initiatives prompted by them, that led to a decisive change in Catholic thinking. People came to feel that development, even integral development, could not serve today as the mediating tool of salvation; that liberation would have to play the role instead. More recently the Church in Spain has adopted this same attitude, and this had led to increasing conflicts with the established authorities.

The *intraecclesial fact* is growing in importance. It must be taken seriously. It cannot be lightly disregarded as something opportunistic or scandalous. The fact that the Church has reread its message in the light of the present-day historical situation is not a flight of fancy but a sign of vitality. Thread-bare and overworked though the term may be, it is in the "signs of the times" that the revelation of God in history takes place. For the moment we may leave open the whole question of what meaning is to be attributed to this revelation. But at the very least one should admit that the varying situation in which the Church finds itself in history forces it to realize and carry out different possibilities. In other words, it historifies the message of revelation. As one Spanish thinker has noted, one may consider the deposit of revelation closed as a system of possibilities; but it is only in the process of historical realization that we shall find out what these systematic possibilities will lead to.

Thus the signs of the times compel us to draw out new and old possibilities from the hidden treasure in the deposit. While the actual fleshing out of these possibilities may be due in part to disparate movements and ideologies, this does not mean that the real-life possibility itself comes from them. Indeed one can assume that it is God himself who is speaking through these movements and ideologies, even though his voice may be distorted by them. If Caiphas did in fact prophesy, it should not surprise us to find that movements close to the people can also prophesy—though the Church may have to accept and purify this prophecy. By the same token we must not forget how much the world has learned from the Christian message. Certain truths which Christianity taught to the world may now be in circulation there even though the Church has come to neglect them. The world may remind the Church of these truths which the Church originally dispensed. And we must not forget that dialogue with the world is essential if the Christian message is to reach its full measure.

So the problem is not whether Christians and Marxists are talking about liberation today. The real question is this: What goes to make up Christian liberation, the authentic and complete liberation of which Vatican II spoke?

Not all liberation is Christian in its inspiration, thrust, objectives, and means. At the same time such liberation may be able to contribute substantive values to Christian liberation. Christian liberation is not set off as an alternative to other forms of liberation. As a Christian option, its purpose is not to replace other forms of liberation but to work within them as a transforming leaven.

What goes to make up Christian liberation can be deduced primarily from the sources and wellsprings of salvation history itself. Our reading and interpretation of these sources must be historical, however. That is, it must be framed in today's context even though its underlying impulse springs from salvation history and its demands. Without moving away from salvation history or dislocating it, we can make substantive statements about liberation that will be of great utility for Christian life in today's world. The term "liberation" itself is somewhat ambiguous, of course. Only in name is it similar to the secular and political liberation championed by oppressed classes and peoples and feared by oppressing classes and peoples. It is not to be equated with socio-political liberation. But Jesus himself insisted on maintaining his claim to kingship even though the term was open to ambiguity, because that is why he had come into the world. Hence the Church, too, must insist on its mission of liberation because that is why it was established. For Jesus' enemies, the title "king" was a political one; the word "liberation" is equally political in the eyes of the Church's enemies. As far as Jesus and the Church are concerned, these terms do move into the whole area of political and societal behavior and hence are political in that sense. But they are more than just political because they proclaim a salvation that runs through history but also goes above and beyond history.

We cannot work out a theology of liberation here, but I do want to indicate briefly how and why the concept of liberation plays a central role in both the Old Testament and the New Testament with regard to the interpretation and realization of salvation history. Although this whole topic is still under study, its fundamental lines are already surfacing in present-day biblical theology.

In the Old Testament it is quite evident that the chosen people learned the import of salvation and the meaning of a savior God in and through a political experience of liberation. One could say that this was the pedagogy chosen by God to reveal his true countenance to his chosen people. The Exodus experience is in fact an experience of political liberation. It concerns the Hebrew people as such, and it has to do with socio-political oppression that is also religious in a derivative sense. In this experience the Hebrew people begin to learn who God is and in what way he is God. The theology of the chosen people starts from there in trying to work out an understanding of their own being and history. One can scarcely overstress the importance of the Exodus in giving configuration to Yahweh's revelation to his people, nor the reality of socio-political experience in mediating the salvation demonstrated in the Exodus.

The same features can be found in the prophetic experience of the nation, which further develops God's manifestation to his people. It is with good reason that present-day pastors and theologians of liberation hearken back so insistently to the message of the prophets, for that message is an inexhaustible wellspring for achieving both secular and religious liberation. Advancing the religious experience of the chosen people, the prophets launch a vigorous attack on every kind of oppressor and oppression. They attack rulers, priests, unjust judges, and predatory power interests. They attack economic inequities and foreign imperialism. They do not do all this because they have lost their religious sense. They do so because they have attained a heightened awareness of man's closeness to God. Those who claim that the Church today is dedicating herself to socio-political tasks because it has lost the inner tension and thrust of the faith would do well to go back to the prophets and reconsider their judgment.

The prayer life of Israel embodied in the Psalms also high-lights the singular importance of liberation. This liberation is not confined to socio-political liberation. It touches upon every form of oppression. The Psalms talk about liberation from sin, sickness, and death; from enemies and persecutors; from the violent, the unjust, and the oppressor. In the Psalms we find a cry for liberation which seems to suggest that man in history is a being oppressed by all sorts of unjust domination and that God is the supreme liberator. One is struck by the number of times that liberation and salvation are equated, and by the new view of God that is attained in this process of salvific liberation. In its public and communitarian aspects, too, this prayer has a marked socio-political stress even though it is directed to God himself. It almost seems that the socio-political realm is the privileged locale for encountering God.

Even late in the history of the chosen people, when the history of revelation is far advanced, resistance to oppressive political power remains an essential feature of salvation history; and that would also include armed resistance. The books of the Maccabees recount the struggles of the chosen people against the Seleucids in an effort to attain a freedom that is both religious and political. From the beginning to the end of the history of the chosen people it is clear that there is an essential connection between their experience as a nation and their experience as the chosen people of God.

These points merely sketch some general features. A more detailed study of salvation history in the Old Testament would provide us with a wealth of material for working up a finished concept of Christian liberation and for establishing the connection between salvation history and salvation in history. It is not a matter of isolating selected texts in order to prove an *a priori* thesis. It is simply a matter of reading and interpreting the overall message of the Old Testament with due exegetical and dogmatic caution. If we do not do this from within the context of our own historical situation, there is a real danger that we may shortchange the revealed message and misinterpret the overall import of the New Testament. As St. Augustine put it, the New Testament makes the message of the Old Testament patent because the former is already latent in the latter.

Only an excessively pietistic and individualistic reading of *the New Testament* can account for our overlooking the essential interconnection between the two Testaments and the socio-political character of the New Testament itself. The New Testament does not annul the Old Testament; it goes beyond it and carries it higher. In trying to show this, we have often eliminated very positive values in the Old Testament. It is Luke who gives us the key to the proper way of interpreting their relationship. In his first public preaching (Lk 4:16–22), Jesus hearkens back to the prophetic tradition by citing a text from Isaiah: "The spirit of the Lord is upon me because he has anointed me. He has sent me to announce the good news to the poor, to proclaim release for prisoners and recovery of sight for the blind; to let the broken victims go free, to proclaim the year of the Lord's favour" (Lk 4:18–19). Jesus then goes on to say that these words are perfectly fulfilled in his person because he is the anointed messenger par excellence. The interrelationship of the Old and New Testaments is made clear in the fact that Jesus frames his public life in the prophetic line of the Isaiah text, for that prophetic tradition proclaims the yearning of the nation for restoration and liberation.

Today it cannot be doubted that Jesus' life had an essentially socio-political character. It was not limited to that, of course. But the fact remains that the overall incarnation of his message in the contemporary situation led him to a continuing collision with those in power who were oppressing his people; and he never evaded this confrontation. He fought against the socio-religious power of the priests and Pharisees. He fought against the existing socio-economic powers by stressing the dialectic of wealth versus poverty. And he fought indirectly against the power of the State which propped up this existing situation of injustice. It is this threefold fight which gave a political dimension to his activity and made it seem political in its aims; it ultimately caused him to be killed for political reasons. A Constantinian reading of the gospel message and Jesus' life has successfully obscured the fact that Jesus' public message came across as meddlesome to those who held power in a basically unjust situation. It seemed to represent interference in the political realm—which was really the objectification of a sinful condition. His proclamation of the good news in history led to his persecution by those in power. There could be no clearer proof of the fact that the salvation proclaimed by him explicitly steps into the reality of history. The socio-historical dimension of Jesus' message is clearly proven in the Sermon on the Mount, where those who enjoy power and possessions in this world are removed from the kingdom of God. They are not kept out of the kingdom because they are wealthy, sated, and happy now; they are kept out because they live in these circumstances while the majority of human beings are hungry, thirsty, and impoverished. Both his blessings and his maledictions are framed in this dialectical relationship.

Such is the understanding evinced by another New Testament text that stands close to the historical experience of Jesus himself: the Epistle of James. It tells us that a faith without deeds is a dead faith, that a faith which does not implement its teaching is an empty faith. And the implementation proposed in this epistle is a socio-political one which concentrates on socio-economic realities.

John and Paul amplify the concept of liberation greatly, stressing the goal towards which it leads. That goal is the freedom of the children of God in the fellowship of all human beings, who are brought together in and by one salvation process that is operative in history. They also stress the central place of the whole Christ, the creating Logos and Redeemer in the flesh, as the root source and principle of liberty; and the need for complete liberation from sin so that the glory of God may shine resplendently in those who have been justified by faith. These essential themes of the New Testament must be revived in all their force and historical relevance if we are to remain loyal to the gospel message and to our contemporary world. Christians cannot help but rejoice that liberation is a historical necessity today, for it is a theme that a person of faith has much to say about. In order to give theological foundation to the themes of progress and development, theology became more "divine" than Christian, more rational than biblical. If theology and pastoral concern want to proclaim Christian liberation, they need only immerse themselves in salvation history. Liberation is absolutely essential to the gospel message. Today, more than ever before, it is essential to the mission of the Church as well.

The Nature of Christian Liberation

The concept of liberation is a rich one in the biblical message and it is also extraordinarily complex. This fact itself proves that liberation occupies a central place in salvation history, and that salvation history is closely bound up with salvation in history even though the two are not identical. The biblical message talks about liberation from personal faults and their inner consequences for the individual. It talks about liberation from the objective forms of oppression that stem from the sins of human beings: sickness, premature death, poverty, devastation, and so forth. It talks about liberation from those in power on this earth who oppress and exploit the poor unjustly. It talks about liberation from imperial powers which impede the liberation of God's people.

A correct interpretation of all these varied forms of liberation must take due account of all the elements involved and then structure them properly. The general line of this structuring process is clear enough. On the one hand liberation in history signifies and realizes God's salvific promise to human beings. On the other hand God's promise of salvation to humankind impels human beings to liberation in history so that God's salvation may be made truly present on an ever new and higher plane. Thus there is constant interaction between the operative promise of God the Savior and the carrying out of this salvation in history. God shows his saving power in history, and in history the effectiveness of this divine promise is signified and made real.

Taking this as our keynote, we can say that in Christian liberation we find a distinctive interpretation of what man's salvific liberation (or salvation) is. Liberation is understood as salvation, and salvation is understood as liberation. It is precisely through the interaction of liberation and salvation that Christian liberation is able to evade two dangerous tendencies: 1) the tendency to view liberation as a purely immanent process; 2) the tendency to view liberation as a purely transcendental process. These two tendencies pose a constant threat to the mission of the Church in proclaiming the gospel message.

The distinctive character of Christian liberation is to be found in the fact that it entails *liberation from* something and *liberation for* something. All liberation is a process moving towards liberty; and liberty can only be attained through a process called liberation. This means that liberation is not prompted primarily by a negative thrust aimed at destroying something; it is prompted mainly by a positive thrust towards creating something. It is not animated by feelings of hatred and resentment, nor is it in its nature to use tools that are based on resentment and hatred. Its primary task is not to subvert and destroy, except when the forces that rule in fact are positively unjust rather than merely inadequate.

Insofar as the "liberation from" is concerned, Christianity passes judgment on that which is oppression and calls it sin. Indeed Christianity can only utter an explicit word about

Christian liberation vis-à-vis something which, in one way or another, presents itself as sin. While this might seem to be a limitation, it is in fact a radicalization. It will seem to be a limitation only to those who have a disembodied notion of sin, who see it as a purely spiritual fault that only indirectly affects the world of human beings. But just as one cannot know God directly, so one cannot offend him directly. Knowledge of God and transgressions against God are mediated through history. There is an historical objectification of sin, and it is absolutely necessary to maintain the distinction between personal sin and objectified sin.

In the concrete, anything that positively and unjustly stands in the way of human liberty is sin. It is sin because it prevents a human being from being a human being, depriving him or her of the liberty that properly belongs to a child of God. Sin is the formal exercise of an act of radical injustice. Recent documents of the magisterium amply spell out the connection existing between the destruction of humankind and the denial of God. By considering oppression from the standpoint of sin, the Christian radicalizes and absolutizes his or her condemnation. Sin is seen as the absolute negation and denial of the absolute in reality. Thus reference to sin does not imply flight from the world into subjectivist interiority or ahistorical transcendentalism. Instead it obliges one to turn towards the world in an even more radical way, because the transcendent and the absolute have now been injected into the very course of history itself.

By introducing the category of sin, the Christian is compelled to introduce the category of redemption as well. There is no salvation without redemption, no birth to a new life without a death. This death is for the sake of life, to be sure. The attendant pain and sorrow are suffused with the hope of resurrection. But it is still death, completely overturning everything that has been judged to be sin. The "developmentalists" of the last decade agreed that the quest was for a new man on a new earth. But they failed to engage in prophetic denunciation of the existing situation as a state of sin, and hence they evaded everything that is implied in Christian liberation.

The death-resurrection schema does not offer any theoretical problem to the Christian in terms of his or her personal life. It should not offer any such problems on the level of human collective life either. In the last analysis, this schema is the specifically Christian interpretation of history; and it is the same for both levels. In the face of personal, individual sin, one must undergo the death entailed in personal conversion. In the face of objectified societal sin, there must be a qualitative leap of redemptive death at the same level on which this sin is operative. One dies to sin. When the individual is bound up and identified with the sin, he or she dies to the old self in order to rise as a new human being. When the existing system is bound up and identified with sin, it dies to rise as a new, different system. No one who benefits in some way from this identification will be overjoyed to hear the doleful demands of liberation. That is why they stoned the prophets and crucified Jesus. But it is where sin abounds that redemption must also abound: both on the individual and the collective level. When the Christian frames his judgment in terms of sin, applying it not only to the individual but also to the world at large, he or she is not horizontalizing sin. On the contrary, the Christian is transcendentalizing what others want to maintain on a purely horizontal level, thus bringing it into relationship with God.

Insofar as the "liberation for" is concerned, Christianity offers the hope of a new kind of liberty and a new earth through the mediation of Jesus Christ, the one and only Lord and Savior. The human being is not just immersed in the redemptive process of liberation. The human being is also in the Church, which is the body of Christ and, as such, is animated by him. It is a process in which human beings and Jesus Christ meet and work together. In their flesh and their history, human beings transformed by their faith in Jesus Christ, endure and bear up with what is lacking in Christ's passion. But Christ himself also proclaims and promises liberty. Christian liberty is the transfiguration of human bondage in the free being of the Son of God. Christians are free because they are heirs to the promise made to all human beings. To be a human being in the historical incarnation of God's communication and revelation is to be a child of God by virtue of his sharing of his very own life. Where the bondage of sin abounded, there the grace of liberty abounded even more—surpassing sin, the law, and death. It is the free irruption of God into history that makes possible humanity's total liberation.

This Christian liberty affects the most personal life and being of individual human beings, but it does so in the full concrete web of history. If we acknowledge the reality of this concrete web of history, then any purely interior liberty is utopian, partial, and unhuman. Only in the liberty of all human beings is it possible for there to be total liberty for each and every individual. The Christian message proclaims a liberty which is not the liberty of a privileged few grounded on the bondage of the human majority. But neither is it the liberty of each individual as such, from which would result some alleged solidarity. The Christian message proclaims a social liberty, a liberty grounded on universal love. It requires a new human being. It requires the death of the human being insofar as the human being is enslaved to self and others. It calls for the formation of the universal man.

Christian liberty also calls for a new earth. There cannot be a new man without a new earth, and vice-versa. Human liberty cannot be real in the absence of those real conditions that would make it possible; and one can hardly expect real liberty to come from conditions that have so far created bondage. The existence of the new man is impossible in the absence of social structures that would be qualitatively new and that would truly establish a new earth. Christians realize that their filial liberty is a given, but they also realize that this liberty must be fleshed out and made real. In the last analysis it is liberty that best signifies the gratuitous nature of God's gift of love, the generosity of a God who had given himself to human beings in this world so that in this world they might know him as man's liberator and live accordingly.

It is not the intramural liberty of a world closed in upon itself. Christian liberation is simultaneously salvation in history and salvation above and beyond history. The liberator God, who transcends history, has been made present in history in a signifying way by man, and now man proclaims and affirms in history something that goes beyond history. History and that which lies beyond history are not identical, but they do mutually activate each other. The Christian affirms a "beyond," but this "beyond" is beyond *history*. The Christian maintains that one can go beyond history only if one makes every effort to ensure that history moves beyond itself. In history Christians see God incarnated in a historical way. In their yearning for man's complete liberation, they sense the presence of the living God who animates their activity. Hence it is within the context of history that the believer actively hopes and waits for God's definitive revelation in man.

The problem is ever the same. Where are we to look for transcendence and salvation? How are we to proclaim it to human beings? We must find the response to these questions in history and through liberative activity.

If people work within the world for the new future of history, and if they live on the basis of Christian promise and hope, then they are working for the definitive appearance of God as the absolute future of man (Rahner). One cannot existentially affirm the absolute character of the future that God is unless this future entails the surpassing of any intramundane future, however perfect it may seem. And we must affirm God, not only as the Absolute of individual experience, but also as the Absolute of historical experience itself. The latter includes the former, and the former is not total in itself because it includes the latter.

We would not know this—and conscious awareness is an essential element in history—if it had not been revealed to us in

Jesus Christ, the Word made flesh in the midst of human beings. The invisible reality of God can be traced in and through the visible reality of creatures; it can be recognized in and through the course of history. Hence it is possible for non-Christians to be working very actively for the coming of God when they are working for the creation of the new man. But insofar as they are outside the rim of revelation, it is problematical whether they can succeed fully in bringing about the fulfillment of man and the advent of God.

For this reason the Christian must move out into history as a Christian. The Christian must profess that Jesus, the Christ, is the Lord of history and at the same time work for the full realization of Christian salvation. The world is not going to believe the Christian, cannot believe the Christian, if Christians do not display in history their love for humanity, their hatred of sin, and their hope in action. Today Christ is in the hands of Christians and the Church. They must make him credible to a world that seems to be far away from him. Why doesn't the Church demonstrate from within itself that its message of salvation is operative through its work in history? Why doesn't it demonstrate by its deeds that its words and actions are indispensable in the process of liberation, so that the world may believe that the Lord whom the Church professes and signifies truly is the Savior of human beings? It is in history that the Church must be the sign of the gospel's credibility.

The work of Christian liberation opens up a privileged field of action for the Church in its work of proclaiming the gospel. At the present stage of history this liberation must be liberation from injustice and for love. The struggle against injustice and the effort to facilitate love are two signs of credibility that dovetail perfectly with the sign of credibility embodied in Christian liberation. Strictly speaking, there is only one historical process: It is one of liberation from injustice leading towards liberty in love. Only for the sake of ordered treatment have I separated liberation, justice, and love in these pages. Actually the three aspects must be considered together if we are to understand what Christian salvation truly is, that is, salvation in history leading us towards the fuller life of salvation history.

The Absolute Exigency of Justice

Liberation and the fight against injustice in all its forms are distinct aspects of one single historical process. The struggle against injustice is a basic feature of liberation, and the struggle to inculcate justice is a basic feature of liberty. So here we shall proceed to consider the matter further, attempting to get a bit more concrete.

In stressing that this whole process is a sign of credibility, I do not wish to give the impression that the Church must dedicate itself to liberation from injustice in this world simply and solely because it needs to do this as a sign of credibility. The Church dedicates itself to liberation because it is of the very essence of its mission, because it is an inescapable obligation in its service to the world. When it dedicates itself wholeheartedly to the full liberation of humankind, the Church is not simply engaging in good apologetics. It is performing its mission, carrying out its task to serve rather than be served. If the Church is to be credible to the world to which it has been sent, it need only be in fact what it is supposed to be by nature. It need only live out in history the being and life that it is supposed to be fashioning for itself. At each and every moment in history it must look for the sign-bearing role that will serve it adequately in fleshing out its true being in history, and that will enable the world to recognize its true character. So it must look for those signs that are intrinsically connected with its mission, that in and of themselves point up its intrinsic credibility. In all of its proclamations and activities it must demonstrate that it is here for the salvation of the world. And while it knows that the signs must be intrinsically credible, it must also remember that they have to be credible to a specific, concrete world. This means that they must also be intrinsically historical.

So it is a matter of service to the world, not service to itself. But the service which the world can and should demand from the Church is the kind of service which the Church, as Church, is able to give. Worldly powers cannot set limits on the service of the Church. The only limits on the Church in its service to the world are those limits which are intrinsic to its mission itself. It is senseless to worry about whether the Church is meddling in politics when it is carrying out its liberative mission. The only pertinent question from a Christian standpoint is whether it is departing from its mission or not. We must never forget that Jesus never abandoned his mission; and yet he was condemned by those in power for interfering in the autonomy of the temporal order.

The Struggle Against Injustice: A Christian Obligation

The existing situation of injustice is one of the essential features that gives definition to our present-day situation. *Gaudium et spes* (27, 29, 60, 63, 66, 67, 69, 71, 73, 79, 80, 81, 83, 85), *Populorum progressio,* and *Octogesima adveniens*—to mention only a few recent documents of the magisterium that are worldwide in their perspectives—point up both the radical and thorough nature of injustice in our world and the grave negation of God that it implies. The 1971 Synod of Bishops reiterates the same mournful analysis: "We see in the world a set of injustices that constitute *the nucleus of today's problems*" (my italics).

The passionate concern of the Church should not surprise anyone, even though it seems to disturb many public authorities. From the Christian standpoint, injustice must be defined as sin—as the sin of the world. Both the Old Testament and the New Testament are pervaded by a line of thought that sees injustice—both as deed and as situation—as something utterly intolerable. It is the great secular and religious sin which must be wiped out of the world. It is an objective, social fact which must be erased from history. It is a transgression which demands the death of *homo injustus* so that *homo justus* may be resurrected to new life. It is the denial of God himself, who is just by his very nature. Injustice negates the very heart and core of Christianity. By denying the universal brotherhood of God's children, it denies that God is the father of all human beings. It is both a dogmatic and an existential denial, because the existential affirmation of inequality and injustice gives the lie to any verbal profession of this basic Christian dogma. It is a denial of the first commandment insofar as that commandment was interpreted for us by Jesus Christ; for he made a basic link between it and the second commandment, saying that the two of them together summed up the whole law.

Injustice makes personal liberty impossible, and hence it prevents the most basic exercise of our personal reality and being. In that sense it is also the personal denial of God. It tends to blot out any hope of God revealing himself in history, thus placing a basic obstacle in the way of any attempt in history to prepare for the Lord's second coming. To be sure, it gives an impulse to history insofar as it prompts a reaction on the part of the oppressed, who try to create a history completely different from the existing one. But in and of itself injustice tends to blot out the justice of God among human beings; and it stimulates an antithetical dynamism that tends to jeopardize the buildup of a new society.

In its work of proclaiming and fleshing out the gospel message, the Church is called upon to take away the sin of the world and to communicate salvation. In one way or another, sin always operates through the personal will of man. But sin always takes on an objective form as well. This form is not just the fruit of personal sin or guilt. It is also objectified sin, which in turn stimulates new personal sins. The Church must pay heed to both forms of sin if it wants to carry out its mission completely. So it must engage in a relentless struggle against injustice and for justice.

The Struggle Against Injustice: A Sign of Credibility

How can a Church which had contributed so much towards the injustice and oppression of the world claim liberation and the struggle for justice as signs of its credibility? How is it possible that a Church whose essential vocation is to work for human liberation and against sin has so often turned into a force working against liberation and justice? What credibility does it deserve today when it tries to present itself to the world as the privileged locale of liberty and justice?

The answer to these questions is simple in theory. When the Church has been completely faithful to its mission, it has been a force for liberation and justice; when it has not been faithful to its mission, it has been just the opposite. Why is it that the Church can be unfaithful to its mission? That is a question which goes beyond our subject here. Let us be content with indicating how the Church can serve as a sign of the Gospel's credibility by engaging in the struggle for liberation and against injustice.

To become an effective sign of the gospel message, the Church must first recognize its contribution to the unjust oppression of human beings. That contribution is a fact. The Church has contributed to injustice by acts of commission and omission, abetting oppression to a greater or lesser degree. It must face this fact and acknowledge it. It is a fact within the Church itself, where respect for the human person and personal rights has often been subordinated to other inferior values, with the result that the institutional aspect has often stifled the primary and essential aspect of interpersonal communion and community. The Church's words have proclaimed one thing while its deeds have proclaimed something very different. As a result, it has gradually lost credibility in the eyes of many.

It is also a fact in the relations of the Church with the world.

There is no exaggeration in saying that the Church has some-times been more in the service of established (dis)order than in the service of establishing a new order. Indeed its failings in this area have been more frequent and serious than they ever should have been. The Church has often done more to serve the preservation of the natural order than to abet the social trans-formation of history. It has even gone so far as to take positive steps to reinforce an unjust order. And even when it has tried to soften the excesses of an unjust order, the Church has not gone far enough in facing up to its sinful character.

The Church, insofar as it is a penitential sign of permanent conversion, must recognize and acknowledge that it has not always been a radiant sign of God's justice and Christ's *kenosis:* that it has often been far removed from the lifestyle of the Lord; that the presence of Jesus has been distorted in the Church's own body. All of us who make up the Church must make this same admission. The Church's ability to undergo conversion would prove that the God of salvation is with it. If it acknowl-edged its sinfulness in penitential deeds rather than mere words, if it left behind its sinfulness and its complicity with sin, this would serve as a sign of its continuing hold on the power of holiness. Before launching out into the world, the Church must do penance precisely as Church. We must not think that sin resides only in the members of the Church. It resides in the Church herself, at least insofar as it is an institution and an institutional process. As such it should serve as a concrete sign of conformation to Christ, but it has frequently conformed itself more to the world of sin. If it does not effectively undergo this painful conversion, if it does not endure the humiliation of Good Friday, then it cannot expect the glory of resurrection or its acceptance by the world. For it will not be a satisfactory sign of the holiness of its Founder.

But that in itself is not enough. The Church must also take positive action in the fight against injustice. Its specific con-tribution lies in fighting injustice insofar as injustice is sin. The activity of the Church is directed against the sinfulness in

injustice. It opposes injustice insofar as this injustice is a negation of man and insofar as it causes man to negate God. The
Church must *denounce* injustice as a sin, that is, as an absolute
evil rather than a mere accident of history as history moves
towards its completion and perfection. The Church must denounce injustice publicly, incessantly, and forthrightly because the power of injustice operates publicly, incessantly, and
forthrightly. If it does not do this, the Church will be failing to
carry out an essential prophetic dimension of its mission.

The Church must also *announce*. First of all, it must announce
and proclaim that there is only one way to pass from sin to
resurrection and the new man, i.e., through dying to the present situation. In the last analysis, this calls for a radical conversion in history, for *metanoia* in the individual and revolution in
existing structures. To think that the Church should restrict its
activity to personal conversion, that this will eventually lead to
structural change, is to fail to realize that structures objectify
and condition personal, individual behavior. Personal conversion must have impact in the area of structural change if this
conversion is to attain its full objectification in history. At the
same time, however, the journey towards new structures will
not be a Christian journey if it is not plotted out and trodden by
human beings who have undergone personal conversion.

And the Church has more to do. It must support the struggle
of the oppressed from within as they seek to obtain their
liberation. It must not be deluded into thinking that the liberation of the oppressed will be achieved by the conversion of
those in power. Certainly the Church must strive for the liberation of all human beings to a universal liberty. But history and
the biblical image of the Servant of Yahweh show us that it is
the oppressed who will liberate the oppressor. The active nay-
saying of the oppressed is what will redeem the sin-laden
yea-saying of the oppressor. There is real interaction between
oppressor and oppressed, but the activity of the former tends to
maintain the state of oppression whereas that of the latter tends
to eliminate it rather than merely seek revenge. If the Church

identifies itself with the struggle of the oppressed, it will run head on into the oppressors who hold power. But only in this way can the Church serve as an irrefutable sign of the fact that it is dedicated to the establishment of justice no matter what the cost. If it continues to identify with those in power, and page after page of church history bear witness to this tendency, then it will be turned into a worldling. If it identifies with the oppressed, the world will reject it; but this rejection will be the clearest proof of its Christian character.

In acting thus, the Church will be following the purest strain of salvation history. That is what the prophets did; that is what Jesus himself did. If it follows in the footsteps of the prophets and Jesus, the Church will be forced to come into confrontation with those who hold power in this world. That is the implication behind Jesus' identification with those who are neediest. What one does for them, one does for Jesus himself. It is an active process of identification which seeks to solve their needs.

The help given to the oppressed must be active and effective. The Church has its own specific means and tools. With them it must flesh out in reality what it proclaims in words in order to prove that God's salvation is actually at work among human beings. The Church does not try to take the place of some other agency, for it realizes full well that the kingdom of God is not to be identified wholly with the kingdom of this world. The Church's activity does not consist in offering another possible technique among many. Its activity is rather that of the leaven in the mass of dough. Operating from within the context of God's kingdom, it works to make sure that man can truly be man, that the world of human beings will really be a human world. It works for the salvation of man, so that the Lord Jesus may truly reign over human beings and created things, so that they may be more truly human rather than something less than human.

Working for justice is the road to peace, to the individual's reconciliation with self, to the reconciliation of all human beings with each other, and to the reconciliation of history with nature. In doing this work, the Church will serve as the sign of

God the Creator and Redeemer. Operating in and through the painful process of history, it will move the world towards that grand finale when God will be all in all. It is an essential dictum of the Christian message that God's justice must operate in and through the hearts of men so that each individual may be the liberator of his fellow human beings and nature itself. But the justice of God cannot remain isolated in the heart of the individual. For man's heart is structured by the things and realities of history. The fact is that today one portion of humanity not only oppresses the rest of humanity but also is itself enslaved to nature. This gives new urgency and poignancy to Paul's statement that mankind and nature are groaning in the pangs of childbirth as they wait for liberation from the injustice that prevents them from being what they are truly meant to be.

Christian Love in the Liberation Process

When we talk about redemptive liberation and the fight against injustice, it might seem that we are forgetting the central place accorded to personal love in the Christian message. There is that danger, of course. But it would be even more dangerous to fashion a false, idealistic picture of Christian love, to picture it in ahistorical terms and place it outside the boundaries of liberation and the struggle for justice. So now we might pose this question: In what way should Christian love serve as a sign of credibility for the mission of the Church? How are we to picture this love in the concrete? Christian love cannot be reduced to an external addendum, or even to a final goal. In some essential way it must inform the whole outlook of the Christian and the whole process of history.

The Church as Sign of God's Love

God's love for mankind and mankind's love for God is an essential and distinctive tenet of Christianity. In the incarnate Son there is revealed the love of God the Father, who so loved the world that he gave up his only begotten Son. This is one of the essential points of the Christian message. Equally essential, however, is the conviction that God's love operates through human beings. These two basic dimensions meet and interact in the central mystery of the Incarnation, where the Son of God enters history and meets the human race. The Son of God becomes man so that human beings may attain their full stature as children of God. This fact is of fundamental importance in the Christian message. God, the distant one, draws near to humanity and lives with human beings so that he can communicate his presence. The primary instance of humanity in this case is Jesus himself. But Jesus has incorporated all human beings into himself, and it is the whole body of Christ that serves as the means whereby God may make himself present to humanity and humanity may draw closer to God. The humanization of the divine is the means indicated by revelation for the ultimate divinization of the human realm. There are two subtle ways in which we can deny the historical value of the Incarnation of the Word. We can disregard the means chosen by God completely, or we can overspiritualize it by divesting it of its historical substance.

The union of these two loves, God's love for man and man's love for God, is expressed most forcefully in the New Testament, particularly in the Johannine writings. John is explicitly concerned with the "signs" that proclaim Jesus' divinity. Their sign-bearing role is to be prolonged in a healthy balance between operative sacrament and evangelizing proclamation. John is the theologian of the Word-made-flesh and of the manifestation of the Father's love in him. Through the Word-made-flesh, eternal life—the eschatological dimension of salvation—is now made present among human beings in an ongoing process that will reach its culmination in the full revelation of God and the full divinization of the human world. This process implies and entails a confrontation with, and a judgment upon, the world; for in the world the powers of evil are objectified. The supreme command of God is expressed pointedly: "This is his command: to give our allegiance to his Son Jesus Christ and love one another as he commanded" (1 Jn 3:23). And this love must show itself in very concrete terms: "If a man has enough to live on, and yet when he sees his brother in need shuts up his heart against him, how can it be said that the divine love dwells in him?" (1 Jn 3:17).

These two brief texts will suffice to give direction to our reflections here. Love is in fact essential to the Christian message. But Christian love has a paradigmatic model: the life of Jesus himself. The love which Christianity proclaims, the love whereby Christians will be recognized as such and will make known the divinity of Jesus, must conform itself to the love which Jesus proclaimed and lived in his own life. This point deserves stress because Christian love, like Christian faith, has often been presented in terms of purely interior spirituality or external works of mercy. By selecting only certain features of Christian love, people have managed to deprive it of its effectiveness as an instrument of transformation. Only a realistic look at what love truly was in Jesus' own life will restore to Christian love its radical power of transformation. And only when it displays this radical transforming power in history will it be able to serve as a sign of the salvation that it proclaims. Is love stronger than hate in the task of transforming society? Is love stronger than the thirst for profit and the desire for private property in the task of transforming society? Can we even be sure that Christain love can do all this?

From the very start the life of Jesus makes it clear that Christian love must be fleshed out historically from within the context of the concrete situation in which human beings find themselves. Seen from the Christian standpoint, it is a situation of sin, injustice, and oppression; of egotism and concupiscence. Christian love is obliged to take on a particular cast; it must be a redeeming love fraught with sorrow and pain. The life of Jesus is the clearest proof of this. Jesus fought openly and harshly against the unjust powers of his day. His love had very specific features vis-à-vis the poor and lowly on the one hand, and the rich and powerful on the other hand. His struggle cost him his life. In this respect the real nature of Jesus' love has been distorted by an overly spiritualistic interpretation of the gospel message. According to this interpretation, Jesus himself did not kill; he handed himself up to death in order to fulfill his love for human beings. This presentation falsifies the reality. Of course Jesus did not actually kill. But there can be no doubt about his violent attitudes and his incessant combat against those who held power in his day. What is more, it is not historically accurate to say that he offered himself up as a victim for the sin of injustice and for the lack of love among human beings—except in the sense that he was the victim of injustice and of the lack of love among human beings. He fought against this sin, and he was punished as a result. Today's Christian and today's Church must not be scared away from their mission because they are going to be turned into victims by a world that cannot tolerate them. They need not make themselves silent victims. They will be made victims if they carry out their mission of bearing active witness to Christ's efficacious love.

The Demand for a Concrete Objectification of Love

The aim of the Church's mission is to see Christian love ignited in the hearts of all human beings and concretely objectified in history. This same aim should give form and shape to the means that are utilized to implant love. But we are dealing here with a concrete historical process, which can impose very stringent conditions on both the individual and society as a whole. That is certainly the case with us today. It is the cross that presides over Christian love as it goes to work in the process of redemption; and this cross is embodied in persons and in society as a whole.

The actual, concrete historical situation gives very specific and concrete features to the objectification of love in history. Today that situation is marked by great injustice and inequity in the distribution and enjoyment of the world's common resources, and by the fact that the vast majority of the world's people and nations are subject to unjust domination. The motivating force behind the process of transformation must continue to be the union of divine love and human love; hence there must be a continuing purification of our underlying motivation, of the goals pursued, and of the means chosen to attain our goal. There must be a continuing and ever new process of conversion to God, which will reveal man to us, and of conversion to man, which will reveal God to us.

Once the present setup of the world has been pinpointed as sin, however, Christian love must be framed as a struggle to eliminate sin from the world. To be sure, we cannot put the label "sin" on everything which the world displays or on all the actions of those who hold major responsibility for the state of the world. But the overall setup of the world today, as such, does give meaning and direction to some of these actions and features. The overall state and condition of our world today—alluded to in the preceding pages and in the documents of the magisterium—does represent the negation of God more than the affirmation of God. If we were to try to figure out who God is or what he will be to man in the future on the basis of the present state of our history, we would almost certainly come up with a caricature of him. Why? Because God's love is not only objectively affirmed but also really denied.

Moreover, real hatred of objectified sin can lead to an active rather than a merely passive clash with those who hold power by virtue of this sinful state. The battle to the death with sin cannot offer any possible limits to love as it engages in the struggle. But the possible identification of the human being with this sin complicates Christian activity to some extent. In the abstract one must seek the conversion of the unjust usurper of power and the restoration of his status as a child of God. But in the concrete one must take due account of the fact that in history the problem is more structural than personal, more tied up with class relationships than interpersonal relationships. In itself class confrontation is not interpersonal confrontation.

The distinction may seem to be subtle and risky, but it is real and necessary for all that. The classical moralists, who took such great pains to determine the formal nature of an action, could appreciate the clear difference between class struggle and interpersonal conflict. Today's moralists, who stress the danger that class struggle might hold for Christian love, could appreciate the enormous danger that the very existence of classes holds for the humanization of all human beings, who do belong to one class or another. Classes do not exist because there is a conflict; the conflict exists because there are classes.

However, it is not the conflict as such that ultimately determines Christian behavior. Over against sin resides and presides salvation. Redemptive liberation is matched and surpassed by the liberty of the children of God, injustice is matched and surpassed by the new justice of the kingdom, and the painful struggle is matched and surpassed by the hope for a better future. The Christian lives his objectification of love in history in the framework of faith and hope. If he does not pay due heed to this positive thrust and direction underlying his activity, there is a real danger that he will disfigure the objectification of his love and turn it into something that is offbase. He must pay due heed to the existing sinful situation and the struggle against it; he must also pay due heed to the future for which he hopes.

His faith and hope set limits on the potential objectifications of Christian love that are proclaimed and fleshed out by the Church and in the Church. In and of themselves Christianity and the Church do not have unique solutions or techniques for eliminating the objectified forms of sin in the world. There are laws, existing independently of the will of individual persons, which condition any potential solutions. Within the overall system, the solutions are conditioned by the very character of the system itself. This does not mean we are doomed to passivity. It means that we must devote adequate attention to the technical analysis of the situation and to possible solutions. There are whole areas where Christians do not have any distinctive or unique words to offer. For while the Church is the trustee of salvation history, it is not the sole trustee of salvation in history.

Faith and hope not only prohibit certain fields and ways of acting to the Church as such; they also specify the possiblities of Christian love by giving them clearer delimitation. (The case different with Christians insofar as they are individual human beings whose actions do not implicate the Church as such.) This fact is operative in two ways. First of all, even though one can see God's summons in the most diverse happenings and learn what salvation history is in the concrete from the most diverse ways of thinking, the primeval and decisive wellspring for comprehending and giving direction to salvation is the Church itself insofar as it is the living bearer of God's word. Secondly, the Church itself can never forget the fact that all its secular activity on behalf of salvation is conditioned by its own character as a sign.

Thus Christian hope impels the Church to engage in the active construction of the world, in a process that will really signify and lead towards the kingdom of God. This hope does set limits on the Church and its activity, as we just noted. But it also impels the Church to go beyond the active building up of the world, for in this work of building up the world it seeks also to move beyond the world. The Church seeks to move towards the kingdom of God, which is not to be identified wholly with the kingdom of this world any more than something signified is to be identified wholly with its sign. The sign and the thing signified are not wholly the same, even when they are intrinsically related to each other.

Active, operative hope leads towards the transcending of history, a history in which the second coming of the Lord is being prepared. God is the present future of history because he is the future present in history. It is not only sin that we must see in the world. We must also see the active presence of God. Operating out of this vision, Christians work for liberation from injustice and for the establishment of justice, seeing them as the condition for enjoying the universal fellowship of God's children. Jesus has come already, and he has overcome the world. But he cannot yet appear as the definitive Lord of history because sin is still present and because the glory of his resurrection has not yet been fleshed out in nature and history. As the Church moves pointedly towards the future, seeing it as the locale of God's manifestation among human beings, it is illuminated, motivated, and accompanied by the presence of the historical Jesus and the risen Christ.

So the Christian is and remains a non-conformist, ever challenging the particular historical forms in which salvation is supposedly being realized. The non-conformity and protest of Christians stems from the fact that they are seeking a more vital and fuller presence of God in history; they keep moving towards this fuller presence out of faith and hope. God must continue to draw nearer and nearer so that the world may have *more* life. This "more" does not negate or annul a full life here; it simply projects it further towards something beyond. In this dialectical tension between what they already possess but do not yet possess fully, Christians committed to the struggle must signify not only the aspect of death but also the aspect of resurrection. They must signify it and take delight in it. Their joy comes in part from their active effort to create a new earth. And behind it lies their hope in the active presence of the risen Jesus and their belief that the Lord of history, who has already overcome the world, is now accompanying his Church as it puts its hope to work in the course of its history in this world.

Conclusion

The Church's mission in proclaiming the gospel message is not restricted to the task that was spelled out in the preceding pages. There is no doubt that the most essential aspects of the Christian message could be expressed in terms of liberation, justice, and love—if we explored the full depths of these terms and combined them in the total reality that Jesus Christ repre-

sents for the salvation of humankind. But my treatment here
has necessarily been limited. I have focused on those apsects
that relate to the Church as a sign of credibility vis-à-vis a world
which is seeking salvation but which seriously doubts that the
salvation proclaimed by the Church is the salvation it really
needs. My feeling is that the focus and stress presented here is
necessary for the Church insofar as it is a sign. The Church as a
whole, in all of its activities, must be a sign of Jesus the Savior.
This obliges it to a twofold thrust in its acitivty: 1) It must do
what it really and truly signifies; 2) it must not rest content
with being a mere sign but rather move from being a visible sign
towards that which is more than just sign.

Today people talk about the socio-critical function of the
Church based upon its eschatological proviso. They also talk
about the Church as a locale of prophecy and of active hope
based on God's promise. The Church will carry out its mission
successfully only if it remains the loyal spouse of Jesus Christ.
Ever since the days of the Church Fathers, it has at times been
described as a harlot for leaving its spouse and turning into a
worldling. But Christ is with the Church because the covenant
is based on a promise rather than on a bilateral contract. It is
this ever-operative promise which guarantees that the Church
will keep carrying out the mission that has been entrusted to it.
The Church will be able to carry out its mission of signifying
and fleshing out the salvation of Jesus Christ only insofar as the
Church is preserved from the world and carries on the gospel
message—in short, only insofar as it is the holy Church. It is in
the world and in the service of the world, but it is not of the
world. It must continually undergo conversion and rehabilitation. It must be closer to the oppressed than to the oppressor
because it is the former who exemplify Jesus, the Servant of
Yahweh, who is saving the world in history.

Within the Church itself those who can best promote this
work of signifying salvation are those who possess the charism
of prophecy. The Church itself is prophetic, of course; but the
exercise of this prophetic function must be actualized in its

members. In a given instance this prophetic function may be fleshed out by any one of the sectors of the Church: the pope, the episcopal college, groups of bishops or priests, or groups of lay people. No sector of the Church enjoys exclusive rights over the charism of prophecy although the magisterium and the hierarchy do enjoy certain prerogatives in testing the validity of charisms.

It is even more important, however, that the Church as such make every effort to be the sign demanded by our times; and it must make this effort in all its activities. Its work as the leaven in the mass will be effective to the extent that its members wholeheartedly dedicate themselves to the task of expressing the totality of the Christian message and the full implications of Jesus' incarnation in the world. More directly the concern of lay people is the task of seeking positive secular forms that better objectify what the Church announces and proclaims. Annunciation and denunciation is also their concern, of course, insofar as they are members of the prophetic Church. But in the area of their direct contribution to the upbuilding of this world, they will sometimes find themselves obliged to opt for certain concrete steps, none of which can be equated with the basic, underlying option of the gospel message. In general it can be said that the mission which the individual is called upon to exercise in the Church will be conditioned by his or her personal vocation, charism, and place in the hierarchy. In these pages I have tried to show what is the basic mission of the Church today in proclaiming the gospel message. Within the framework of this fundamental mission, which is incumbent on the Church and all its members, it will be easier to find guidelines that will help the hierarchy and the laity to determine their own proper roles within the people of God as a whole.

Chapter begins with the statement out of an historical point of view that the Church must be a credible sign through its acts in history — to manifest the salvation of Jesus. I How — theologically — should Church display transcendence? (1) Liberation from sin (Historical-social) (2) fight against injustices (3) Dedication to Love

5

Liberation: Mission and Charism of the Latin American Church

Talk of liberation is in the air all over the world today, particularly in those regions which feel they are shackled by oppression. People talk about political liberation, social liberation, economic liberation, and so forth. The varied uses of the word suggest the wealth and depth of the term, but they also hinder its elaboration in any unified or unitary sense. Too many branches have sprouted on the tree of liberation, and their profusion now threatens the healthy growth of the trunk itself.

My purpose here is not to prune the tree by excising the superfluous branches. My purpose here is to explore and clarify the term insofar as that is possible by considering the vocation of the Latin American Church in present-day history. I shall suggest that the specific mission and charism of the Latin American Church can be tied up integrally with the basic concept of liberation. To say this is to explore the deeper recesses of the concept of liberation and to call for the radicalization of the Church's activity.

The linking of these two tasks lies at the very heart of this study. Liberation is both a political concept and a religious concept. At the very least it is certainly a Christian concept. We should not be frightened by the fact that it possesses both these features. Rather, we should be stimulated. Today the Church is clearly and openly turning its gaze to the world. At such a moment we cannot view the mission of the Church as something outside the boundaries of the political realm. The fact is that the world of humanity, as a formal totality, cannot help but be political. Hence the Church has only two alternatives. Either it does not turn fully to the world or else it must incarnate herself in the political realm. The reason for choosing the latter alternative is not that the political realm is a part of the overall social reality and hence deserves attention also. It is that the political realm, more than ever before, is an all-encompassing dimension which embraces what human beings are forced to put up with rather than what they can actively do. It is not simply that the political element touches upon every other dimension. Even more to the point is the fact that everything which is done or not done has some impact on the configuration of the political realm. And in turn the political realm—note that I am distinguishing "the political realm" from "politics" here—gives singular configuration to the shape of man's personal life. It is a grave mistake to think that one can lead a personal life outside the bounds of the political realm.

It is this link between the political realm and the totality of man—or man as a totality at least—that justifies the relating of Christianity to the political realm. And by Christianity I am referring to a whole way of living. In what specific way does Christianity, as opposed to other religions, view its relationship to the political realm? That is a question which deserves detailed consideration, but here I simply want to note the fact that the political realm and Christianity are necessarily related to each other. It would be an exaggeration to maintain that all theology, insofar as it is intellectual reflection on Christian faith and action, must be specifically political theology based on eschatology, the future, and hope.[1] But it is quite correct to maintain that theology and Christianity cannot be everything they are supposed to be unless they are willing to confront the totality embodied in the political realm.

These and other theoretical reasons justify the kind of reflection we are undertaking here. But the most potent justification is the concrete situation of Latin America and its peoples. The fundamental task incumbent on Latin Americans today vis-à-vis the political realm seems clear enough, however much people may dispute the most suitable ways to carry out this task in the concrete. The real question here is this: What can Christianity and the Christian contribute to the carrying out of this political task? Are there two distinct tasks here, one incumbent on the Latin American as a Christian and the other incumbent on the Latin American as such? What are we to say about this involvement in politics on the part of Christians and the Church, which is regarded as meddling by many? Is it correct to say that Christians, insofar as they constitute a Church, are improperly meddling when they concern themselves with the political situation? Is involvement in the political realm the same thing as involvement in politics?

Besides these questions, there are other things to consider. Some lay people and priests have felt obliged by their ecclesial vocation to become highly politicized. In some cases they seem to have gone to excess, impoverishing the Christian message on the one hand or relying on politics too much as a tool on the other. Neither in theory nor in practice do they seem to have managed to unify their action so that it is both fully Christian and fully political. The Latin American Church evinces a "guilty conscience" in this area. Those Christians who have undertaken political commitments feel obliged to do so out of respect for their Christian vocation; yet they cannot seem to figure out or establish the intrinsic relationship between their Christian mission and their worldly activity. But the same "guilty conscience" is evident in those who reject political commitment and involvement, because they cannot help but see links between Christianity and the exigencies of societal reality.

The road towards solving this whole problem complex would seem to lie in a thorough analysis of the mission and charism of the Latin American Church insofar as it is a living and distinct segment of the universal Church, and in a thorough Christian analysis of the concept of liberation. This concept seems at first glance to be political, and it is certainly used in different senses by different political groups. Has the Church acted here as it has often done in the past, maintaining allegiance to a political concept in vogue in order to bolster its power rather than to carry out its mission? What is the intrinsic relationship, if any, between the Church's mission and liberation? What sort of liberation can be viewed as a contemporary and pertinent embodiment of the Church's salvific mission? Can the concept of liberation offer a sound and adequate synthesis of what the secular activity and the Christian activity of Latin Americans should be?

These questions may help us to spell out a well-rounded concept of liberation and to give a sound orientation to the pastoral activity of the Church in the specifically Latin American situation. But if we are to answer these questions satisfactorily, we must first consider in what sense it is possible to talk about a charism and mission peculiar to the Latin American Church. Having done that, we should be able to show that a sound concept of liberation gives adequate expression to that charism and mission today. The historicity of salvation demands that the Church in Latin America be Latin American. If it turns its attention and energy to the Latin American situation, it should be able to figure out what its mission and charism is in the light of the gospel message. In the remaining pages of this chapter, I shall devote two sections to the historicity of salvation and its implications and two sections to the specific mission and charism of the Latin American Church.

Salvation History and Historical Salvation

There would be no need to start so far back if the thinking of
many segments of the Latin American Church were not dominated by a prejudice that causes the Church itself to remain in a
state of alienation. This prejudice, which is very operative but
not necessarily formulated in explicit terms, might be expressed as follows: The Church has always been the same, and
it will continue to be exactly the same in the present and the
future; moreover, it should be one and the same everywhere.
Underlying this prejudice is the assumption that social realities
are hard-and-fast realities rather than realities in history. Nature is regarded as a substance, and any change or mutation is
regarded as something fortuitous and accidental. This overall
outlook is clearly evident in the talking and thinking of many
ecclesiastics. Its seriousness can scarcely be overestimated because its impact extends from the structuring of the hierarchy
to the Church's understanding of its mission and the ordering
of ecclesial activities.

Faced with the prejudice, we must remind ourselves that not
even natural realities themselves should be conceived exclusively in terms of substance. In particular, historical realities
cannot retain their basic identity unless they continually undergo profound changes; for change and transformation are
essential to every historical reality. What this change entails
exactly may be open to debate. Some may agree with Hegel
that it involves the negation of every present moment; some
may agree with Bergson that it is a perduring evolutionary
search for ever new and more perfect forms; some may agree
with Zubiri that it involves a permanent process of creation in
which unforeseen possibilities are fleshed out in reality. It is not
easy to spell out the essence of historical reality, and people
may well debate the whole matter. But one can scarcely deny
that there are historical realities, that the Church is a reality in
history, and that change is an essential component of all histori-

cal realities. Here "essential" does not just mean "necessary." It also means that change takes place in historical realities on a deep and important level which involves both their totality and their basic unity. As Zubiri puts it in another context, the Church must always be the same and yet never quite the same.

One should not assume that this jeopardizes the unity or identity of the Church. Fear has caused theologians and ecclesiastics to forget the historical character of the Church and of its salvific mission. Theologians have forgotten the profoundly historical character of the biblical message and have focused their thinking around concepts such as nature and substance that were inherited from Greek thought. Ecclesiastical leaders have identified the unity of the Church with an imperial form of organization that was more concerned about structure than about interpersonal communion.

Today people commonly talk about salvation history, and about Christianity as salvation history. Some people, to be sure, do wonder whether Christianity really is a religion of salvation purely and simply. They feel that the peculiar character of Christianity lies in the fact that it has gone beyond the classic framework of salvation peculiar to most religions; that it is to be viewed more in terms of "deification."[2] Leaving that whole question aside, we can certainly say that the category of salvation does have an important place in the Christian message and in Christian activity. There certainly is a salvation history, and Vatican II based its dogmatic thinking on this theme to a large extent. But if we accept the importance of salvation history, then obviously we must accept the fact that Christian salvation is a historical salvation. Let us consider these two points in a bit more detail.

God's word to man is a historical Word of salvation. It is certainly a word concerning salvation throughout its history; but when this revealed word reaches its culmination in the Word, then it takes on a very specific name, i.e., Jesus the Savior. The name of God for us, his being-with-us and his being-for-us, is embodied in the name of Jesus; and its purport and function is embodied in the word "Savior." Christianity affirms that man is in need of salvation, and that the salvation needed by man cannot be attained apart from Jesus. At this point we are not yet going to try to spell out the thrust and import of this salvation offered by the Father in and through his Son. But in the very fact of saying that the salvation of mankind is to be found only in the incarnate God, we are already offering an interpretation of man and alluding to something that transcends man. This transcending, however, does not imply separation; instead it implies the shouldering of the totality that man is. At this point we glimpse the necessity of interpreting this salvation in dialectical terms; for while it is the salvation of man, it is not from man. In other words, this salvation subjectivizes the work of salvation in a locus that is superior to man; at the same time, however, it incorporates everything that man is as an object of salvation and draws it into the overall process, so that it can truly be the salvation of a person.

This supreme Word of salvation is historical, not only as salvation but also as word. It is not simply a natural word, a word that is deduced from the natural essence of the world and existing things. This view would strip time of the personal and theological dimensions of revelation. In fact, however, the historical singularity of Jesus as the Word of God uncovers the ultimate meaning of every prior divine word and definitively sets in motion the essential historicity of the whole process. By so doing, it allows for a truly metahistorical dimension in which the transcendence of both the natural and the personal realm is rendered present. Thus the message and promise of Christianity cannot be deduced *a priori* from the nature of man or the world; it must be related to an irruption that is both free and historical.

The Word of salvation is historical in another sense as well. Jesus, the Christ, is a word for all human beings; but he is also a word for each individual human being. He is the word for all time, but he is also the word for here and now. He is the latter, not because each individual assimilates what is meant for all or because the here and now is simply a moment in a process that remains ever the same, but because he is a Word that is a person and because his Word is a personal one. It is a personal Word because this word is spoken to a given individual. All other voices are voices crying in the wilderness. Jesus the Word and the words of Jesus have not been spoken or heard once for all time and all people. They are heard and nurtured and fulfilled in a journey through history that is shaped by the historical situation. Rather than talking about a history of dogmas, we should talk about a history of revelation—although the two terms cannot be used in the same way. The human being who hears the word is always a distinct and different human being; and the personal word that he or she hears personally is not something that is simply received but rather something that is shared between two persons. Because of its profoundly historical character, then, revelation always gives more and more of itself—to paraphrase the happy expression of Zubiri.

Now if that is the case, then the fundamental question to ask in any attempt to discover the mission and charism of the Latin American Church would be this: What will Christian revelation offer when it issues its summons to the Latin American as someone distinct from the European and the North American? What will this revelation say to the Latin American? What will it say in the Latin American? Our answer to these questions will determine the ability of Christanity to face up to the Latin American situation and say something worthwhile. It will also specify the Christian identity of the Latin American.

But it is not just that there is a salvation history. There is also the fact that salvation must be historical. This implies two things: 1) Salvation will differ with the time and place in which it is fleshed out; 2) it must be fleshed out in history, in human beings who live in history. Salvation cannot be defined in univocal terms. Nor can it be defined as if man were a spirit without history, a spirit who is not incarnated in history. Nor can it be defined as if salvation in the "hereafter" were not supposed to be signified and signalized in the "here and now."

The historicity of salvation could be deduced from the historicity of revelation itself. If revelation has a history and if salvation has been proclaimed in a historical way, that is due to the fact that man himself is historical and it is his salvation that is being sought. It seems preferable, however, not to focus on a deductive process when one is trying to pay heed to the biblical message. Here I do not intend to present all the data of the Bible in order to prove the historicity of salvation. But I do want to highlight some of the more noteworthy points in order to lead into a discussion of the historical character of salvation.

Israel comprehended its salvation on the basis of its own liberation in history. The revelation of God's word was embodied in its own history as a people, a people with concrete problems of a predominantly political cast. It was the salvation of a people, rather than of isolated individuals. This salvation had much to do with liberation from the nation's political enemies. They were the enemies of Yahweh because they were the enemies of his people. At this stage of salvation history people moved from political experience to religious experience. They hoped and expected that religion would interpret and resolve political problems—that is, problems which were those of the nation as a public totality. The individual belonged to the people of Israel, the people being the overall object of salvation. Through membership in this people, the individual could hope for his or her own salvation in the here and now situation. To be sure, there were religious projections associated with this notion of salvation; and on the whole they were imperfect and ambiguous. Indeed, as we shall see, mere aping of these same projections would be tantamount to denying salvation history itself.

Personal problems did not lie outside this process of salvation. Salvation was liberation from one's personal sorrows, one's personal sins, and—to some extent—from death itself. All this was seen in the light of the relationship between man and God, but it had immediate repercussions of a profane and public nature. Israel needed the categories of guilt and sin in order to interpret the reality surrounding it. But even though sin suggested an immediate reference to God, it was also a category that evaluated the human world on every level —private and public, personal and structural. As we shall see later, it was a category that transformed the interpretation of history and of political activity.

So politicized was salvation in the eyes of the Israelite nation that in the early stages it was not able to differentiate the religious realm and the political realm satisfactorily. Israel thought that its salvation would be attained historically by virtue of its historical relationship to Yahweh as his special people. If it remained faithful to the covenant in the course of history, its reward would be complete political triumph over other nations; and this would pave the way for a definitive material well-being for all.

The level of interpretation rises with the advent of the prophets. The nation's religious thinking is purified and deepened by a more religious idea of God and a more personal conception of the God-man relationship. But this continues to have real repercussions on the politico-religious interpretation of Israel's history and salvation. There certainly is a surpassing of earlier religious experience, but this surpassing does not entail erasing the note of politicization or forgetting the relationship between the religious and moral deportment of the nation on the one hand and its destiny in history on the other. Even Jeremiah, whose early chapters seem to focus mainly on the more religious sin of idolatry, never ceases to be a political prophet. He threatens the nation with political punishments for their sins, and he also puts much stress on those sins which we today would call social sins. These sins, and Jeremiah's denunciation of them, clearly have political import.

To indicate the shift of the prophets towards the more spiritualistic interpretation of the New Testament, one can look to a singular text in Jeremiah for support:

The days are now coming, says the Lord,
when I will make a righteous Branch
spring from David's line,
a king who shall rule wisely,
maintaining law and justice in the land.
In his days Judah shall be kept safe,
and Israel shall live undisturbed.
This is the name to be given to him:
The Lord is our Righteousness.

(Jer 23:5—6)

It is an important passage because it reiterates the classic scheme: the need for salvation, since uprightness and justice are not practiced and hence there is no security or peace; the hope of a historical salvation for a historical people; the promise of a savior whose name is "The Lord is our Righteousness." This saving Lord will bring justice to the earth, and his presence among men must be viewed as the presence of God and of righteousness. Only then will there be peace and security among human individuals and nations.

The term "righteousness" (or "justice") is extraordinarily complex in the prophetic tradition. In essence, however, it is the opposite of the injustice that is committed against human beings—particularly against the weak and powerless. This notion gradually paves the way for the New Testament conception of justification. We cannot show here how there is clearly no justification without justice or righteousness, so I shall simply mention the fact that in its use it can be illegitimately restricted in two ways. It can be interpreted in such a way that the religious dimension is reduced to a purely interior and spiritualistic one of direct relationship to God, and to a purely individual dimension in which salvation and condemnation apply solely to the individual as an isolated entity.

Granting that the word "spiritualization" itself is ambiguous and does not adequately describe the underlying reality, we still cannot deny that the religiosity of the Old Testament is somehow "spiritualized" in the faith of the New Testament. Nor can we deny that this was due in part to the fact that Israel suffered political downfall, so that the religious realm was "depoliticized" to some extent. In some sense one can talk about a negation of the Jewish religious experience. But in fact this negation is not an abolution of that experience; it is rather a surpassing of it. The Jewish religious experience was not reduced to nothingness by the Christian faith; instead it was preserved and surpassed. The Jewish religious experience did not avoid the danger of using God for the sake of temporal welfare and political domination. It hardly managed to get beyond a purely social and political realization. While it related the temporal realm to Yahweh, it did so in an inadequate and purely extrinsic way. Hence it could be denied and annulled "atheistically," and it deserved to be. And that applies as well to God's causal intervention as it was interpreted by popular Judaism.

Does this mean that the New Testament proposes that individuals are to be religious while the political realm is to be atheistic? Is there no relationship between the political realm and the Christian realm? Or is the only proper relationship between them to be found in a theocratic State?

An affirmative answer to these questions would seem to be implied in Marx's theses on Feuerbach. While we may disagree with him, his remarks can help us to figure out the proper relationship between the political realm and the Christian realm; and this is a basic problem in trying to determine the mission and charism of the Latin American Church.

In his first thesis Marx accuses Feuerbach of regarding the theoretical approach, the purely contemplative and interior approach, as the authentically human approach. According to Marx, Feuerbach retreats back towards purely contemplative interiorization because he views praxis solely in terms of its "sordid manifestation in Judaism." Marx recognizes that Jewish religiosity is a political praxis, but he sees it as a shabby form of political praxis. To that extent Feuerbach is right in rejecting it. But Feuerbach is wrong in thinking that anthropological purification is to be attained by abandoning praxis in every form. Jewish praxis is to be rejected because it was not transforming in itself, because it left transformation directly to God in terms of reward or punishment for man's religious or moral acts which did not effect the transformation of social reality. Jewish praxis led to an alienated praxis. Man should not flee from praxis, however. Instead human beings must rehabilitate praxis in terms of its own immanent essence. They should abandon all transcendent reference to God and live out the immanent praxis that will transform nature and history. True human fulfillment is to be found in fashioning a truly human society, a societal humanity.

Here some questions are very much in order. Is Feuerbach's interpretation of Jewish praxis correct? Is it correct to interpret Christianity as a process of interiorization? Is no other praxis possible except the completely immanent praxis proposed by Marx? It is certainly true that Marx made certain truths clear. Man must not confine himself to interpreting and contemplating the world; he must go on to the important task of transforming it. The principal ethical mission of man does lie in this effort of transformation. The inescapable goal of human action is indeed to fashion a truly human society, a humanity that will live as a social community. If man does not flesh out this new humanity, no one else is going to do it for him. And man's salvation or condemnation does lie in the success or failure of his effort to fashion this new humanity. But just as Marx sees an alternative to Jewish praxis on the one hand and Feuerbach's Christian interiorization on the other, so today's Christian is entitled and even obliged to look for a fourth alternative—one that gets beyond Jewish politicization, purely contemplative interiorization, *and* the purely immanent praxis envisioned by Marx.

The Christian must admit that the social version of Jewish religiosity and the religious version of its political activity are primitive. The Christian must assert that the presence of the divine in the reality of nature and society is not that of a demiurge who miraculously rewards or punishes the religious behavior of human beings and nations. The Christian must realize that activity which transforms the world and society and which is rooted in Christian inspiration is the essential and constitutive sign which alone makes man's salvation and divinization real and present. Christians have tended to view the spiritualizing of the Old Testament as a process of Platonizing, and the process of supernaturalizing as a process of extra-naturalizing. Thus they have tended to disregard two basic and central tenets of Christianity: 1) Only in the humanity of Christ are we to find access to the Father; only thus does the Father reveal himself to human beings and only thus can people be brothers and sisters, children of God. 2) The risen Christ is to be fashioned by the continuing historical incarnation of his redemptive action as Lord of history.

To get beyond the other alternatives cited above, we must look to the deeply Christian category of "sign." The humanity of Christ is the sign of his superhumanness, the worldly aspect of the Church is the sign of its otherworldliness. As the bearer of salvation, the Church must be the sign that makes salvation present and effective in a historical way. The sign leads us beyond itself, but without the sign there is no beyond for us. The sign both is and is not what it signifies. And in our present context the sign cannot be something arbitrary or whimsical. By its very nature it should lead us towards that which it claims to signify, as is evident from the historical example of Christ himself. The sign enables and obliges us to transform the worldly realm because it is only in this realm that we can find the sign at all. It obliges us to look for that sign which will truly call our attention to that which God has revealed in Jesus Christ. It obliges us not to rest content within the sign itself; for if it truly is the sign established by Christ in his historical revelation, it will drive us beyond itself. If Christian activity is framed in terms of a sign, then we will be able to get beyond naturalism and extra-naturalism, secularism and mere pietism.

Indeed we will be able to get beyond all sorts of schizophrenia and contradictory significations that now mar the witness of Christians in the world.

A Latin American Church in Latin America

We have noted that Christianity is a salvation history, that salvation is meant to be historical, that the Church is the bearer of this historical salvation, and that the Church must flesh out its sign function in history even as its founder became incarnate in history. Now if all that is true, then the Church in Latin America must necessarily be Latin American.[3] The Church must operate in history and in a historical way. It must, in other words, communicate the presence and summons of God's historical word to each and every human being in a real-life way. This process of historicization means that the Church must be incarnated in time and place, and in the set of conditions which each place exerts on a given time. By that I mean that not all of us who live in the same age necessarily live in the same time frame.

It might seem that there is no need to stress the importance of localization and temporalization since Vatican II and Pope Paul VI have urgently recommended these two approaches. But the actual reality of this incarnation in the liturgical, theological, and administrative realms of the Church prevents us from entertaining any illusions about the matter. There is no profound acceptance of the historicity of salvation. Nor is there any real acceptance of its most direct and immediate corollary, namely, the differences in mission and charism to be attributed to different local and regional churches. Hence we are compelled to emphasize certain ideas which justify the distinctive incarnation of the Church in Latin America and which provide a basis for determining what the exact nature of that distinctive incarnation might be.

If faith were merely the acceptance of a fixed deposit of

dogma by some universal human being, then the only accom-
modation or adaptation required would consist in the correct
translation of certain texts whose distinctive history and language had somehow been forgotten in the past. But that is not
what faith is. There is no universal human being; nor is the
deposit of dogma formed by items of intellectual content which
are learned, accepted, and then simply transmitted. Faith is a
personal relationship, which takes its start from a personal God
and is personally addressed to a person who is conditioned by
his time and place, his people, and his history. The original
communication took place at a specific point in history, but this
communication continues on as a living, personal reality
through the mediation of the Church.

In and through this faith, salvation is communicated. The
divine word accepted by faith is what saves; but it saves insofar
as it is received and accepted, not by mankind in general, but by
this specific human being. God's word saves only insofar as it
has been historicized; and it can be historicized and brought to
its fulfillment only in the concrete reality of the living human
individual. The universality of salvation and God's word
should not be taken to mean that it touches only that which is
common to all human beings. It is not universal by a process of
abstraction; it is universal by a process of concretization. Its full
totality becomes real only in the salvation of the whole human
being and of all human beings. The authentic universality of
salvation will be achieved only when it fully takes in all the
historical variation and variety of concrete human lives.

It is up to the Church to perpetuate this universal salvation in
a way that fits in with this authentic universality. The Church
may not entertain the notion that the catholic universality of its
mission consists in the ahistorical repetition of the same salvific
scheme over and over again to all the human beings who exist
and live in history. To do so would be to disown the historical
character of salvation and the salvific character of the Church.
To paraphrase a classic dictum of theology, one can say
that outside the Church there is no salvation, but only what

has been taken up by the Church can be saved within it.

The fulness of salvation that is proper to the Church requires a full-fledged incarnation in the radical historical variety that is lived by human populations. By the same token, the Church will attain its salvific plenitude only when every human being is saved in his or her totality. It is this totality, in the twofold sense of universality and plenitude, that will offer the Church the means for its full-fledged growth. It is not a matter of quantity or numbers, of the saved being few or many. It is a matter of plenitude, of a plenitude that is qualitatively historical and qualitative in an historical way. The distinct and different modes of human existence must be assumed and saved by that which carries on the salvation of Jesus Christ, i.e., by the Church. Christ himself will not attain his full measure as Savior until all the different kinds of salvation needed by human beings and their historically different situations are integrated into him. Until this happens, Christ's incarnation, redemption, and resurrection will not attain their full measure.

On this journey towards the qualitative plenitude of salvation in the Church, full-fledged Christian incarnation in specific privileged locales will challenge and contradict spurious forms of incarnation that are not in line with the gospel message. The Church is ever in danger of being turned into a worldling, of distorting the obligation of incarnation in such a way that it ends up aping the sinfulness and alienation evident in the world's mode of existence. Within the Church we must recognize and accept the diversity of its members, the charisms of different individuals, and the diversity of the local churches. By virtue of their distinctive forms of incarnation in specific situations, these local churches are called upon to live the plenitude of the gospel message in distinct ways. We see some acknowledgement of this fact insofar as the distinct vocations of various religious orders are recognized; but this recognition must be broadened to cover all the sectors of the Church that live Christianity in their own distinctive ways.

Such would be the case with the ecclesial sector which we

call Latin American. It is Latin American, not only because it lives in Latin America, but also because it seeks to respond wholeheartedly to the distinctive sociological reality of Latin America. It makes perfect sense to ask what is the peculiar mission and charism of the Latin American Church as opposed to that of the Church in other areas of the world.

Charism of the Latin American Church

In this section I shall try to describe Latin America as a salvific category, that is to say, as a distinctive reality which must be saved in a distinctive and specific way by the gospel message and which can contribute to the plenitude of Christian salvation in its own qualitative way. It is not just a geographic reality. Proper use of the term cannot be based solely on the fact that one belongs to a designated geographical region. Geographic location is one condition, but it is not the thing that gives formal identity to the reality called Latin America. It is no easy matter to provide a sound sociological description of the Latin American reality, but a solid theological interpretation of Latin America depends on such a description. So I shall attempt it, knowing full well that I am not telling the whole story but rather speaking from a specific point of view.

From that viewpoint it must be said that Latin America should not be viewed as a shadowy imitation of the Western world, but rather as an integral part of the Third World. Quite obviously Latin America's mode of existence in the Third World is not the same as that of other areas such as India or Vietnam; and life in South America is not exactly the same as life in Central America. What is more, basic elements of occidental culture do seem to form part of the culture of Latin America itself. That does not invalidate our basic assumption here, however, because the historical individuality of Latin America is clear enough and is still in the process of formation.

This fact permits us to posit a definite future as an element that gives configuration to the Latin American present. That future cannot be mere imitation of the developed countries, of the United States in particular. It must be Latin America's own future, shaped by Latin Americans and by the proper available means. If our tools are mere imitations, then our future will be a mere imitation also; this holds true particularly in the field of education. And if we do not have a clear idea of our own distinctive future, we will not be capable of fashioning suitable tools of our own.

Operating from an ecclesial viewpoint we can indicate some characteristics of this future, mainly because the impact of Christianity continues to be significant with respect to the sociological reality of Latin America. At the very least we can talk about a Christian predisposition in Latin America, although we must also admit that Latin American Christianity must be purified in many ways if it is to play a profound role in shaping the future of Latin America.

A reconversion of the Church to the Third World, to those features of the Third World that are clearly evident in Latin America, would simultaneously help to purify the Church and make a significant contribution to the future of Latin America. Much of the intraecclesial tension evident in Latin America today is due to the resistance of ecclesial structures to the notion that we must fashion a Church here which will correspond and respond to the social reality in which the Church lives its life. This resistance prompts even greater insistence from others that the Church become a Church of the poor, a Church of the Third World, with all the consequences that option would entail.

The fact is that the reality of Latin America demands some such effort at conversion if the Church is to be an effective aid in the creation and realization of the future of Latin America. From the standpoint of the gospel message it is indisputable that a turning towards the poor would purify the Church. And it would be easy to show that a purified Church is absolutely necessary if it is to provide the full measure of salvation that is properly its own, and if it is to fully carry out its mission in giving shape to the future of Latin America.

The Church has a universal vocation of salvation, but its most proper locale is the world of the poor. This does not mean that there must be poor people for the Church to exist or to be holy—a thesis which is shared by certain Marxists and certain lackeys of capital (more than capitalism) including some Christians. But if there are poor people around, then the Church cannot be holy or salvific unless it lives in, with, and for the poor. But the poor are not just the mission of the Church. They are also its salvation and the locus of Christ the Savior's presence. By the same token, it is true both in terms of past history and the present day that those who stand at the other end of the spectrum represent the locus of the Church's perdition. Only by incarnating itself in the reality of the Third World and serving the most needy can the Church hope to purify itself, renew its life, and recover the true impulse of the gospel message. If it does this, it will immediately turn into a sign of contradiction and suffer persecution; and this will prove that the Church is the authentic bearer of the word and promise of its founder.

Is it not true that this decisive turning towards the poor is the mission of the Church in Latin America, and of the Latin American Church within the universal Church? In Latin America "the poor" are not a fringe group; they are the majority. In a real sense they define what Latin America is: poor in health, poor in education, poor in living standard, poor in having a say in their own destiny. By virtue of the universal vocation of the Gospel and by virtue of the historical summons specific to the region in which the Latin American Church lives, it must be the Church of the poor. If it were to be that in truth, then it would give impetus to a new historical form of Christianity that should be transmitted to the universal Church. And this new form will be transmitted, if it acquires the necessary drive and tension.

The fundamental, specific charism of a given Church cannot

be determined in the abstract. We should not be surprised that local churches have their own specific charisms when we realize that localization is essential to the Church. The determination of a community's specific charism cannot be made in the abstract; it must be figured out on the basis of real-life experience and history. This follows from the fact that the Church itself is historical, as is the salvation proclaimed by it and realized in it. But if localization is not to turn the Church into a worldling, if its real-life awareness is to remain authentically Christian, then it must meet a prior condition; it must first turn towards the poor. The perennial message of the Gospel must be heard and heeded in its natural locale, that is, in a Church incarnated in the world of the poor. That world is lit up by the gospel message, and the good news becomes light and life from within the context of that world. If this is realized adequately, then there will inevitably appear charisms of a more individual character, charisms that are prophetic, or hierarchical, or theological, or whatever.

Such charisms are already finding their voice in Latin America on all these levels. The reason is to be found in the fact that Latin America, as a member of the Third World, is speaking out on problems that are very much related to the specific nature and thrust of the Christan message. These problems have to do with such issues as the oppressive power of money, the greedy quest for profit, the desire to possess money and enjoy its benefits, the disparagement of the human person, and the existence of inhumane living conditions. What Latin America seems to need most is the very thing that is the most authentic strain in the gospel message: the denunciation of wealth and greed, the liberation of the oppressed from injustice in all its forms, respect for the human person as a child of God, the formation of a worldwide community of human beings, and the transcending of human history.

Thus Latin America represents a historic challenge to the possibilities of Christianity. Why? Because the seed of the Christian faith has been sown there, because it offers the best opportunity for calling attention to Christian values, and because it obliges the Church to be what it truly is or else to stop posing as the word of salvation. The full and integral salvation of the Third World, of the world of the poor, is a great historical challenge. Responding to this challenge should be regarded as the fundamental charism of the Latin American Church. The Johannine writer centered God's commandment around this point: "To give our allegiance to his Son Jesus Christ and love one another as he commanded" (1 Jn 3:23). This commandment must be carried out in history, and it is peculiarly incumbent on the Latin American Church. There are two inseparable aspects to this commandment. Faith alone is not enough; love and the works of love alone are not enough. Urged on by the social reality in which it lives and in which it should incarnate herself, the Latin American Church is at a point in history where it can and must respond to the charism that is truly its own and that exists here and now.

Church Mission and Latin American Tasks

For obvious historical reasons the Latin American Church is faced with the obligation and possibility of giving a total incarnation to the Christian message of salvation. As we noted earlier, this total incarnation cannot help but present itself in secular and political terms. The question is not whether the Church should be a political force or not, whether it should clash with other political forces; for the Church should never go out in search of political power. What is involved here is the Church's fidelity to its own mission. It must foster the full, integral salvation of man—and that entails a political dimension. Precisely because the Church is the bearer of Christian salvation, it cannot fail to offer its service to the task that confronts Latin America.

But that raises certain questions. The Church in Latin America has a specific mission, and Latin America itself faces an urgent task. Are the two things distinct and different from one another? Will the people of the Church find themselves left on the sidelines as Latin America undertakes its task of radical transformation?

The answer to these questions is to be found, I think, in the concept of liberation, which is both political and Christian at the same time. All complete liberation is political, and all authentic liberation is Christian. In the following reflections I shall try to show the dual political and Christian character of liberation, and to indicate how they can be brought together.[4] It is not a matter of discussing the question in abstract terms, because the problem itself is certainly not abstract and because these reflections were not intended to represent a theoretical discussion but rather to provide a program of action.[5]

Liberation differs from other possible alternatives in its radical nature. Radicalized Christians latch on to the concept of liberation while other Christians shun it or try to soften its impact. Politicians in power tend to prefer other terms—"development," for example—while opposition politicians lean towards "liberation" or equivalent terms. (It all depends, of course, on the relationship that exists between the party in power and the party out of power. Sometimes the opposition is the "loyal" opposition.)

Is there a sound theoretical and theological basis for the radicality of the concept of liberation? Leaving aside the whole area of social theory, we can certainly say that there is a solid basis for its radicality from the standpoint of Christian theology. Why? Because any Christian judgment about the prevailing situation in Latin America must be guided and dominated by the category of sin, and because the redemption of sin in Christianity is governed by a distinctive schema involving death and redemptive bloodshed. But before I examine the negative, critical aspect of liberation and its positive, constructive aspect, I think we must consider the specific and peculiar sinful character of the structure that now prevails in Latin America.

The judgments made by the Medellín Conference and other authoritative sources are quite clearcut. While the precise sinful character of the Latin American situation may have to be worked out more fully, the basic Christian evaluation cannot be other than it is. The existing situation does not allow the vast majority to exist as full-fledged persons or to live as human beings. They are crushed by the weight of basic needs that cry out for alleviation. An institutionalized system of injustice actively impedes the establishment of fellowship among human beings. Modelled on the consumer society of the capitalist world, it poses obstacles to solidarity and Christian transcendence. The world and society, which are supposed to serve as the medium of God's presence among human beings, deny the very essence of God as love and as the touchstone for every other reality. Instead of making visible the incarnated image of Christ, the existing situation is a permanent denial of that image. From a Christian standpoint there is only one word for such a situation: It is sin.

Some people will claim that some of these negative features are not due to the specific will of persons as such; that they should be regarded as natural deficiencies which can be cured by integral development rather than as sin which must be redeemed by liberation. This viewpoint is not valid, however. It is valid insofar as it exculpates individuals as such from guilt. It is not valid insofar as it denies the character of sin that applies to the structure as such. The existing structure negates and denies the Christian way of life. It is not just that it does not signify in a visible way what Christianity is as God's presence among men; it positively and actively makes it impossible for people to lead a Christian life. Historically speaking, we cannot simply talk about defects or deficiencies; we must regard the situation as one of sin. To do otherwise would be to wallow in abstractions that would lead us into serious mistakes in trying to formulate solutions. Moreover, if we forget the important place of the category of sin in any Christian interpretation of personal and societal reality, we will greatly impoverish the

Christian message and relativize man and society. It is said that
we have lost our consciousness of sin, but the problem goes
deeper than that. We have also lost our knowledge of what sin is
to begin with. We must get beyond the partial notion of sin as a
merely individual violation of some law. We must recover the
social dimension of sin as the annulment of God's presence
among human beings and the domination of evil which pro-
hibits the freedom of God's children.

Once we have recovered our knowledge of what sin really is,
we must heighten people's awareness of it and promote Christian confrontation with everything that is sin. This confrontation operates in the dialectic of death and resurrection. Only
those who die will live; only those who deny themselves can
follow Christ. There is no way to Christian resurrection except
through the redemption that finds expression in death on the
cross. If people reject the label of sin, the reason is that they are
trying to evade the necessary consequences of a recognition of
the reality of sin. They are trying to evade the necessity of
dying to the present situation in order to fashion a new, more
authentically Christian situation. They are looking for placebos
so that they will not have to face the harsh reality of Christian
solutions. We should not forget that the negative, dialectical
philosophy transmitted to Marx by Hegel is comprehended by
the German theologian in terms of the New Testament dialectic which maintains that only negation leads one to a higher,
surpassing affirmation. Insofar as this negation has been interpreted in purely individual and ascetic terms, in terms of
intention rather than incarnate implementation, it is clearly an
impoverishment of the Christian message. And this impoverishment has forced people to work out a political secularism outside the boundaries of Christian life.

Liberation takes the historical signification of Jesus of
Nazareth with full and radical seriousness. It accepts the archetypal idea of death and resurrection with all its implications.
It accepts the presupposition that salvation must necessarily
take the form of incarnation, granting the presence of sin in

history. But it does not rest content with this archetypal idea, which might just as well be inferred from a philosophical analysis of historical reality. It also turns its attention to the concrete image of Christ in the concrete circumstances of his earthly life in history. Its aim, of course, is not mere imitation but rather an authentic following of Christ; but this does not prevent it from giving transcendent value to his individual figure in history in the whole matter of determining what integral salvation is meant to be. It does not presume that one can know God and his plans for history apart from the one who is the Word of God. Instead it believes that this Word, for whom all things were created, had to be an incarnate Word so that what was originally nature could move through death and resurrection towards personal plenitude.

In this Christian vision of liberation we must have both features: death and resurrection. The latter presupposes the former. But if the former is truly Christian, it is sustained and guided by the hope of a resurrection that has already begun here and now. There is no resurrection without death. Without the sorrow-laden disappearance of the existing structure of sin, we cannot enter a new earth as new human beings. And since this whole treatment here is aimed at praxis, I should like to highlight some possible ways of dying to sin and of rising to new life. For both the negative and the positive aspect must be operative in a spiraling process that leads us further and further on.

The first question that the Latin American Church must ask itself is this: What are the sins that must be eradicated from Latin America? There can be no salvation without the eradication of sin; and if it is to be pardoned, sin must be wiped out. Like Christ, the Church is here to take away the sin of the world, not just certain individual sins. The Latin American Church, in its unity and its diversity, must engage in a profound and ongoing examination of conscience on the local, regional, and continental level. It will not be able to do this unless it first makes an earnest effort to bring back before its eyes the full image and message of its founder; unless it first commits itself wholeheartedly and primarily to the service of the world of the poor. To abet this examination of conscience in Central America, one can propose certain basic and critical topics that surface when one observes our concrete situation from the standpoint of basic Christian categories.

It is not easy to provide a systematic presentation of the sins evident in Latin America, to focus on one radical sin from which all the others flow. Any such attempt would require a wealth of studies—sociological, psychological, historical, philosophical, and theological—which lie far beyond the scope of my treatment here. So I shall content myself with an ordered enumeration of the more blatant problems.

From a biblical perspective it may well be that the root sin is to be found in an overall way of life, a civilization, that is grounded on the twin notions of profit and private property. It is not that wealth and private property are evil in themselves. They are necessary to some extent, given the imperfect state of the world and human beings right now. But the very fact that our way of life is grounded on, and conditioned by, the quest for profit and for more and more private property represents a serious form of idolatry. It produces a whole series of pernicious consequences that give shape to consumer society. Perhaps never before in history has it been so easy to appreciate the full import and perduring value of the Bible's persistent denunciation of riches and greed for riches. The very existence of the Third World, which is an obvious corollary of the existence of the other two worlds, and the different standards of living to be found in any particular nation are decisive proof that a national or international society based on the notion of profit represents a negation of both God and man. It might seem that I am making too much of a concession to Marxism in stressing the role of private property in the unjust configuration of society. But I would reject that accusation for several reasons. First, I am not talking solely about private property; I am also talking about the greedy quest for profit. Second, my

judgment against them is based on the fact that they are fundamental items in the present structuring of society. Third,
wealth is one of the central concerns of the Bible itself when it
tries to pass judgment on human beings and society itself.
Fourth, the reality of Latin America itself offers sufficient
proof of the radical nature of this sin insofar as it is subject to
internal pressure from the powerful and external pressure from
foreign economic interests. Fifth, Marxism itself has come to
rest in a form of private property; though it might claim to be a
national form of ownership, it is no less private and restricted
vis-à-vis other nations.

One consequence of this basic sin, at least to some extent, is
the situation of objective injustice and institutionalized violence. This situation has been highlighted and stressed often
enough. Its existence is scarcely denied by anyone, except
perhaps by selfish interests. It need hardly be pointed out that
the Bible sees it as one of the most serious sins of all, one which
greatly inflames the wrath of God. Under this heading we
would have to list the innumerable forms of oppression suffered
by the vast majority of the Latin American people. A small
minority holds the reins of economic power, and uses this to
expropriate for itself all the other forms of power. The conditions of life are inhumane; most people suffer from hunger,
insecurity, poverty, and lack of education. It is not simply that
we have an unjust situation marked by inequities in the distribution and sharing of goods that should belong to all; it is that
this situation is actively fostered or, at the very least, allowed to
continue without any effort being made to change it.

To make sure that this basic situation does not change in
character, the communications media are manipulated. They
are used primarily to give the people a false image of reality, to
inculcate a set of values that will prop up the consumer society
that has generated the existing state of dehumanization. The
communications media represent the hypocritical conscience of
the ruling class in society, obscuring or deforming the real state
of affairs. How much oppression is embodied in what the

communications media say or keep silent about! How oppressive they are when they are kept in the hands of those who hold power in a consumer society!

And then there are the excesses evident in the holding and use of political power. Power is kept out of the hands of the people. The main goal is to defend the established order, and even torture is permissible to achieve that goal. Pressure from other nations and from external interest groups also helps to keep most people from developing maturity, personal awareness, and the autonomy implied in true personal liberty.

The list could go on and on. There is no room for hope or for a transcendent vision. The materialism of consumerism and the oppressive weight of life's basic necessities make it impossible for people to get beyond mere immanence. Human beings are forced to live on something less than a truly human level by the weight of artificially created needs (consumerism) or by the weight of real societal needs that go unfulfilled. The same basic framework continues to operate, proving that the oppression resulting from unfulfilled basic needs is due in large measure to the multiplication of artificial consumerist needs.

These are some of the sins of the world in which the Church lives. But we cannot overlook the sins of the Church itself, which is supposed to save the world from its sin. Just as the world and society are supposed to serve as the mediating channel of God, so the Church is supposed to be the supreme sign of Christ's redemptive presence among human beings. The sin of the world resides in the fact that it, the supposed medium of God, distorts his presence. The sin of the Church resides in the fact that it does not adequately carry out its irreplaceable mission as the sign of Christ, the sign that is supposed to make his presence real and effective. At the insistence of Deschamps, Vatican I affirmed that the Church is a sign by its very nature; that it bears indisputable witness to the divine mission of Jesus Christ and is supposed to prove its credibility. It is time for us to spell out the import of that teaching, to stress the fact that the presence of the Church should offer a natural and ready motive for drawing closer to the divinity of Christ. Our stress today should be on testimony rather than on apologetics. We should spell out why the Church must make itself truly present in the world of the poor in order to carry out its sign function and to follow Jesus of Nazareth. In a visible and real-life way, he served as the sign of his own divine sonship.

The Church can never cease to be an efficacious sign of Jesus' divinity. For that very reason, however, everything within it that obscures its fundamental mission and denigrates its basic vocation takes on the formal character of sin. Does the Latin American Church fully measure up to that mission, particularly, with regard to the poor and the oppressed? Not always, and in some places it does the job less satisfactorily than in other places. It is here that our collective examination of conscience takes on greatest urgency. It is in this connection that we must give careful consideration to two basic aspects that are directly related to the liberative mission of the Church: 1) its real and authentic self-awareness and self-understanding; 2) its understanding of its mission.

The Church in Latin America sees itself as a locus of salvation, as it must. But the notion of salvation that underlies the thinking of most people in the Church is that of the eternal salvation of the individual, which is guaranteed and to a certain extent effected by the ecclesiastical organization. To be sure, the polar opposite of this view is also to be found in the same Church. Some people see salvation in purely temporal terms and deny any role to the organizational Church as such. But the very existence of this view proves the prevalence and weight of the prevailing individualistic view.

Without going into a detailed study of the consequences of the prevailing view, we can readily see some of the more important consequences of such a view of salvation. There is an almost exclusive emphasis on internal, individual sins, and an almost total neglect of the social dimension of historical sins which politically condition the behavior of individuals and the transcendent import of their actions. The authentic following of Christ is devalued and stress is laid on sacramental grace. As a result, people completely lose sight of the historical visibility of grace and the visible configuration of one's life in accordance with the historical life of Jesus of Nazareth. The Christian dimension of temporal activity is not explored. There is greater concern for the organizational setup of the Church, for its institutional and sociological form, than for persons and interpersonal community.

Insofar as the Church's understanding of its mission is concerned, dedication to the poor does not stand out as the principal task; nor can it be said that the Church articulates its mission as that of liberating human beings from every form of oppression. The Church in Latin America has been, and continues to be, excessively concerned with wealth and power and overly caught up in service to the privileged sectors of society. This cannot help but have grave consequences for its function as a sign of Christ, and for its evangelical liberty and effectiveness. It is not just that the Latin American Church runs the risk of turning into a worldling, of becoming salt without savor and leaven that does not uplift the mass. The bad thing is that this approach may be viewed as an inescapable means for carrying out the task of evangelization; that the Church may feel it has to use power, wealth, and pressure tactics in order to come out triumphant in the task of evangelization. That the Church finds it necessary to get involved in secular tasks, particularly in education, is scarcely a new phenomenon. But secular tasks have their own inner dynamic, and this dynamic is conditioned by the dynamism of the world that was so strongly condemned in the New Testament. Hence it has often happened that the secular dynamism has won out over the dynamism of the gospel message. Today another secular and political task is proposed in connection with the mission of the Church. This time, however, it must be guided and motivated by a non-worldly dynamism, by the Christian dynamism of poverty, service, and liberation rather than by the worldly dynamism of wealth, power, and oppression. As I have already suggested, the whole dynamic of the Third World must be interwoven with the dynamic of Christianity. This does not mean that they are to be equated outright, but it does mean that they are parallel. They can give impetus to each other, and they can even be brought together in the dialectical synthesis of sign and signified.

It is the category of sin that provides us with the key for justifying the activity of the Church in the secular realm. In its overall orientation today, the secular realm as a political totality can be clearly diagnosed in evangelical terms as sin. The mission of the Church is to take away the sin of the world. The Church must call things what they are and propose pathways to redemption. And the Church must do the same with respect to itself.

But it is not enough for the Church to dedicate itself to taking away the sin of the world. Christian salvation does not consist in the absence of sin but rather in the fulness of life. The Latin American Church must work to promote the creation of a new man on a new earth as the eschatological sign of something that is yet to come but is already present and operative. The Church must not rest content with prophetic and apocalyptic denunciation. Admittedly it can never give up this work of denunciation. It must always adopt a critical attitude towards any human achievement, precisely because it sees the character of any achievement as a sign and medium of something that is not merely and purely human. The Church can never forget that it must contribute to the destruction of the objective structures of sin, to the destruction of objectified sin. But the Church is also obliged to help fashion the new man and the new structures which will make his existence possible. It is not the Church's specific job to create the actual technical models. Its task is rather to work out the true meaning and import of their creation and utilization. The Church is not the mass, but the leaven in the mass.

What might this meaning be in terms of the reality of Latin America? It can be expressed in terms of liberation and liberty.

Liberation must be preached and turned into a reality be-

Liberation
is from
SIN

cause it is, in the last analysis, a liberation from sin. It must be proclaimed insofar as the sinful character of certain structures and behavior patterns becomes evident. But liberation must also be turned into a reality. The Church, itself a sign, must work for the full liberty of human beings as the sign that foreshadows and makes possible the liberty of the children of God. First of all, this liberation must be from every form of injustice and from everything that can be regarded as unjust oppression that demeans man's dignity and fulfillment. It must also be liberation from the pangs of basic human needs. It must be liberation from the objective shackles of hunger, sickness, ignorance, and helplessness, and from the artificially created subjective shackles of a consumer society. In short, it must be liberation from nature that is designed to further the creation of the human person.

Given the existing situation, there can be no liberty without liberation. But the Church must work for liberation with its gaze focused on liberty. In other words, its work on behalf of the elimination of dire needs and oppression will serve as a backdrop for its struggle to affirm the values of human fulfillment and personal community as signs of man's full control over himself. It is to this end that the Church's efforts on behalf of the humanization and personalization of man are directed. In the last analysis it is liberty that defines the being of the human person, even though it may not serve as a complete or formal definition. On a different plane, it also defines the essence of the Christian. The Christian is one who is free from the law, which oppresses man from without; the Christian is one who is free from the concupiscence that oppresses man from within. And the Christian is one who is free from the total and permanent oppression of death. Only in this way does the Christian achieve full liberation from sin in a new divinization which makes total liberty possible.

In this work of liberation there is no doubt that the Latin American Church can to some extent be in accord with various movements that have similar aims. This fact may create confusion for some people, even for people of good will. But if people consider the most positive aspect of the problem—that is, the liberty that one is trying to make possible—no confusion is really possible, at least for people of good will. Two features of the Church's commitment can be highlighted as differentiating ones: its attention to the strictly personal dimension of liberty, and its attention to the transcendent dimension of the Christian's activity in the world.

In its work of salvation the Church has frequently exaggerated the individual dimension, the element of personal responsibility regardless of what structures or circumstances prevailed. That was one of the reasons why the Church did not see why it ought to interfere with structures themselves. It did not see them as a direct object of its salvific activity. All it asked of them was that they allow it to act freely upon individuals or that they facilitate its efforts with human souls. Only slowly and belatedly did the Church come to pay close theological and sociological attention to the importance of structures. It began to pay sociological attention to them when it noted the importance of structures in giving shape and configuration to the personal life of the individual. It began to pay theological attention to them when it realized that structures serve as a sign medium which either abet or hinder what we might call the "presentability" of God.

This new awareness of the role of structures helped the Church to realize that it must work for the transformation of structures. But this awareness has not caused the Church to forget the indispensable role of persons and interpersonal community in this same process of social change. It has learned the importance of structures. But it continues to teach the point that structural changes, without a corresponding conversion in individuals, cannot really facilitate the rise of the new man whom we are seeking. There is no sense debating here which should come first, for the two types of transformation are obviously tied together. The point is that individual persons, too, must undergo conversion. Through the process of death

and resurrection they are supposed to attain the liberty proclaimed in the Sermon on the Mount, so that the new world can
come into existence. Human persons are the ones who are
meant to find their fulfillment in God so that they do not fall
back into the molds of the old man as they attempt to fashion
new structures. It is the human person who is supposed to
attain conversion, salvation, and fulfillment in and with structures. One of the great dangers facing the renewed Church is
that it forget this.

The second differentiating feature mentioned above is the
transcendent dimension of secular activity. Once again we find
that the Church has only gradually come to its present view of
the matter, and that is no accident. For a long time it has
worked exclusively on behalf of the transcendent dimension. It
has paid attention to the temporal thrust of the spiritual realm
and to the importance of the whole man, but only in terms of
the hereafter. The Church has not devoted sufficient attention
to the necessity of fleshing out salvation here and now and
embodying the hereafter in the here-and-now sign. The
Church is now growing more and more acutely aware of the
necessity of mediating and signifying the totality of salvation in
the sign-bearing visibility of activity in this world. The Church
is the one who most truly possesses and implements a particular
kind of knowledge. It knows that reality is not exhausted by its
temporal, worldly dimension; that human activity does not
terminate in the immanence of this world and history. The
liberty which the Church tries to procure by its efforts does not
terminate in the here and now; it is fleshed out here and now so
that its full measure may be attained in the hereafter. In some
transcendent way the eschatological future is already present in
our activity today; it makes room for the here-and-now presence of the risen Christ among men, and he is the ultimate
exemplar and pillar of the hope that underlies our activity.

The Church will not carry out this mission on behalf of
liberty if it does not promote the fullness of liberty within itself.
It must be clearly evident in the Church itself that liberty is

possible for human beings. The Church must begin to liberate itself so that it will be obvious that it is free of all worldliness; free of the trappings of wealth, honor, and power; free of avarice, fear, and servile attitudes; free of structures that configure its hierarchy and its methods of government along the lines of the most dictatorial States. The Church must encourage within its own boundaries the fullest measure of liberty possible, since that is what the New Testament sought to proclaim. The Church must foster and encourage a maturity motivated by love and liberty rather than by fear. It must promote a maximum of personal relationships and a minimum of institutional relationships. It must always place the value and worth of the person above that of the institution.

Today the phenomemon of secularization in all its various forms is of grave concern to all the churches. One typical form of the phenomenon in Latin America is political. People in the church feel more and more obliged by the critical societal situation to become political. This has its dangers, but in all likelihood it represents a historical necessity and a historic opportunity. As a prophetic community and a eschatological sign, the Church is essentially political. Why? Because the objectified character of the public community is nothing else but the social and political body of human beings united together. As such, this body expresses and signifies the fulness of man as a being with others even as it structures and conditions the personal behavior patterns and the total development of the individual. What is more, Christian salvation is proffered in the framework of the people of God. This framework of a people necessarily possesses a public and political character. It is a kingdom in the world even though it is not of this world.

More and more it is becoming clear that secular activity is an obligatory praxis for Christian faith. Once liberation is viewed as Christian liberation, it seems that there is no real difficulty in establishing a link between the obligation to live the Christian faith and the obligation to live a life of activity in the world. Christian liberation, which is a redemptive liberation, is an interpretation and a praxis that is both fully secular and fully Christian. And it is this in a singular way within the context of the reality of Latin America. To see it in this light seems to be the particular charism of the Latin American Church. To carry out this liberation in a fully Christian sense seems to be the particular mission of the Latin American Church. For its own good and the good of the universal Church, the Church in Latin America must be truly Latin American with all the consequences that entails.

NOTES

1. See *Diskussion zur "politische Theologie,"* edited by Helmut Peukert (Mainz: Grunewald-Kaiser, 1969). The theology of liberation can find support in a preliminary analysis of what we are to understand by "political theology," but it does not depend on the latter. It is being worked out in terms of Latin America, and it is independent of political theology as the term is often used. Furthermore, it should be remembered that political theology owes its impetus to the Third World.

2. It is Zubiri who objects to calling Christianity a salvation religion. He sees man's deification as the essential and formal element of Christianity.

3. Here we take for granted as a basic socio-historical presupposition the fact that Latin America is a differentiated and yet unified reality. Obviously many different cultures coexist in Latin America. The context should make clear which Latin America I am talking about here.

4. The theology of liberation is now in the process of formation. It is focusing attention on, and raising questions about, many major theological concepts: collective sin, redemption, resurrection, salvation, the Third World as the Servant of Yahweh, secularization, nature and person, eschatological hope, sign and transcendence, politics and Christianity, prophetic denunciation, revolution and violence, the new man and the new earth, and so forth.

5. The reflections in this book were prepared for a conference on joint pastoral action.

*The Question of the Chapter, p. 130 —
is what is the connection between liberation +
the Church's salvific mission; relation between "secular"
activity and Christian activity*

Points made:

- Salvation is universal; ie — ① it will take different forms in concrete history, and ② must be fleshed out in human lives (134)

- history of meaning of salvation in OT & NT
- Salvation in history summary — p. 140
- The Church immersed in the concrete salvation p. 142
- Poverty & the relation of Xtianity & the Church to it pp. 146-147

- <u>Liberation and Sin</u>
- sin the central concept for understanding man Xtian manner LA & Church's Role there (p. 149, 158) Discussion of the nature of sin & the Xtian reaction to it — death & Resurrection Personal & Social sin — death & life through death (ie social structures that are sinful must be changed)

PART THREE

Violence and the Cross

The very juxtaposition of the two terms, "violence" and "the cross," gives rise to a whole series of questions. Indeed it probably provokes certain reactions even before it does anything else. Some will regard the juxtaposition as a sacrilegious profanation of everything that the Christian cross is; others will regard it as a demeaning sacralization of all that revolutionary violence is supposed to be. Each of these reactions implies a specific interpretation of violence and of the cross. Obvious as these interpretations may seem, they are not really so clearcut at all. In like manner, the questions based on these initial reactions, with all the overtones and undertones involved, presuppose some prior agreement on the basic connotations of the terms themselves.

People pose questions and offer answers concerning the relationship between violence and the cross. Are they the same thing? Do they have any relationship to each other? Is the relationship one of complete opposition between the two?

Faced with the whole issue of violence, an issue that is so topical today in both theory and praxis, we must seek logical clarification to avoid falling into fallacies and ethical clarification to avoid falling into hypocrisy. Only then will we be in a position to undertake a theological study of what violence is in human life and thought.

But what is to be understood as violence? Some people, with some reason, would like to reduce violence to that which is commonly regarded as physical violence unleashed by a human being. But aside from the case of torture in all its varying forms, physical violence shows up most clearly in nature itself and hence should be referred directly to God. This suggests that physical violence, even that unleashed by a human being, does not acquire its specific character as violence from the fact that it is a violating force but rather from some other factor that deserves to be studied more carefully and closely.

Where are we to find this other factor or feature that gives violence its peculiar character and that is not immediately obvious to us? Will we not find it in other forms of human behavior which embody unlawful exercises of power and which therefore seek to mask the character of violence that they contain? And what could be worse than the violence of impotent power, which still has sufficient force to do violence and yet hide the fact that it is violence? It silences its victims in all sorts of ways, accusing them of being the perpetrators of violence and creating a climate of public opinion that totally conditions the judgment of others.

Thus there is urgent need for some logical clarification that will enable us to pinpoint the formal and specific feature of violence in the various forms of apparent violence that we encounter today. But there is also an urgent need for an ethical unmasking of those forms of behavior which hide their real violence behind the protective shield of seemingly legal attitudes and which tend to forget the violent nature of their own origin and of the ways they use to maintain their present power. We cannot rest content with an analysis of political power. We must also consider economic power, social power, religious power, and so forth.

6

Violence and Aggressiveness: Basic Viewpoints

What standpoint will serve as the most satisfactory starting point for an honest and enlightened examination of the problem of violence? The answer to that question seems clear enough. While violence is present in human life everywhere in the world, there is no doubt that it is in the Third World that it appears with the greatest sense of urgency today. Indeed it is in the context of the Third World that violence has surfaced as a theological concern. By the same token, those who do not have a realistic notion of the true nature of the Third World are in danger of misunderstanding what violence really is. It is not that violence is exclusive to the Third World, but that violence shows its true scope and outlines only in the context of the Third World. Hence it is in that context that violence reveals its true nature. It is in the Third World that violence fully displays what is only hinted at in other areas of the world.

We can, of course, find violence if we look elsewhere. We can look at the phenomenon of capitalistic violence in nineteenth-century Europe, of racial and political violence in Nazi Germany and Stalin's Russia, of all the various kinds of violence associated with civil wars and world wars. But there is reason to believe that violence does not reveal its most essential and

168 Freedom Made Flesh
168   *Freedom Made Flesh*

distinctive character in these forms of violence, particularly when they have a highly individual character. They are manifestations of violence, but they are not violence itself in its core character. They reveal one of the most important aspects of violence, its daemonic force and power, but they do not reveal the total nucleus of violence as such.

Leaving aside the monstrous phenomenon of war and the equally horrendous phenomenon of political repression and torture, we can say that current theological reflection on violence took its cue from the violent reality of the Third World. It is there that violence has revealed its essentially ambiguous character. It is this very ambiguity that lays bare the true nature of violence.

The other forms of violence mentioned above are not ambiguous. All of them are wholly negative in character, even though certain positive features may be imbedded within them. That explains the repudiation of them which is fully deserved from a Christian standpoint. At the same time, however, classical thought has seen a positive aspect in certain kinds of violence: self-defense, the just war, the fight against oppression, and so forth. This has helped to stimulate reflection on the ambiguity of violence. But since these kinds of violence seemed to be relatively isolated instances, they did not offer sufficient motivation for thoroughgoing, serious reflection on violence.

In the Third World we find a very grave and serious kind of violence: institutionalized violence. It is this situation that highlights the urgency of defending ourselves against violence at all times. It is this situation that reveals the terrible ambiguity of violence. There are two forms of violence which are completely distinct. Even though both are terribly fraught with pain and sorrow because they arise in a context of sinfulness, though not necessarily from a sin as such, they are in fact completely distinct in theory. This immediately suggests that the innermost core of violence cannot be discovered by people who stay on the surface level and focus exclusively on violent means and the violent use of force.

Two Religious Analyses

Hence it is no accident that two recent religious gatherings of major importance focused much of their attention on the problem of violence in the context of the Third World.

The importance of the problem and reality of violence is stressed in the basic "draft document" that was prepared for the Medellín Conference. Many people felt it had exaggerated the issue in its statements. Here are a few selections from that document:

> The people of Latin America, who have silently endured poverty for a long time, are suddenly awakening to the realization that their dire needs are outstripping the pace of development. What had been unconscious poverty is now becoming conscious misery. And alongside these new unsatisfied expectations there is developing a sense of frustration, which is often the feeling underlying the desire for revolution, for a quick and total change of the existing structures.
>
> Our peoples see the unjust social differences that exist, and they now realize that they are not fated to live that way forever. If necessary, they are willing to use even violent means to overcome the present state of affairs and get beyond it.
>
> It cannot be denied that many parts of the continent are dominated by a revolutionary outlook.
>
> It should not be surprising, therefore, that the hallmarks of violence are rising here. For the aforementioned situations themselves are violent, since they violate human dignity and oppress liberty. What is really surprising is the patience of the people, who have put up with an intolerable situation for many years. Such a situation would hardly be accepted by anyone with a developed sense of human rights.
>
> The lack of technological development, the blindness of the class oligarchies, and the weight of foreign capitalist powers impede the transformations that are necessary. They also actively resist anything that might infringe on their own interests. Thus they constitute a situation of violence.

Faced with a situation that is so serious and that has such a dramatic impact on our peoples, we feel that it is not enough to describe the situation that underlies the "temptation to violence." We feel obliged to denounce the egotistical and selfish interests of capitalism as well.

[The Church] realizes that many features of the present situation are signs of the presence of "the mystery of iniquity," which must be overcome.

[The Church] is particularly obliged to join in solidarity with the poor who are left on the margin of society, thus bearing witness to authentic Christian love. The Church must come to the defense of justice in a way that denounces existing injustices and stresses the need for structural reforms. It must cooperate in the task of effecting rapid, urgent, and comprehensive changes. In particular, it must courageously defend the dignity of the human person and man's right to liberty. . . . By fighting for these values, the Church will be making an effective contribution to the establishment of peace on our continent.

I do not intend to analyze these paragraphs. The religious and Christian outlook which runs through them implicitly embodies the basic theological backdrop to any interpretation of violence in terms of its ambiguity. Clearly we are dealing here with two types of violence. The first is the root kind of violence, even though it may be less visible on the surface. It is presented as injustice, and it is immersed in the mystery of iniquity. The second type of violence is a corollary of the first. It is presented as resistance to situations which in themselves are violent because they violate human dignity and oppress man's liberty. Contrasting with this form of resistance is the active resistance of some people to the urgent and morally obligatory changes that are needed. This latter resistance, in turn, creates an authentic situation of violence, not so much because it instigates violence but because it is in itself violent. So the Latin American Church talks about defense, struggle, and denunciation. It should be obvious that it is not simply calling for armed rebellion and bloodshed. It is calling for a determined fight against violence with means that are Christian and adequate to the task.

A parallel outlook can be found in a meeting of the World Council of Churches which took place in Uppsala one month before the start of the Medellín Conference. At that convention (July 1968), the delegates tackled the same general topic as a part of their agenda.[1] They acknowledged that we live in a world where man exploits his fellow men. Because of the reality of sin, political and economic structures groan under the weight of deep-rooted injustice. We must move rapidly towards a complete change in these structures. In other words, we must move towards a revolution. There is no reason why revolution must be equated with violence, but the process of revolutionary change may be forced to take a violent form in countries where the oppressor groups are indifferent to the aspirations of the people and, on the pretext of maintaining law and order, use coercion to resist necessary changes. Social changes are desperately needed. Because of the sinful structure in which we live, the means used to effect these needed changes cannot help but be ambiguous. If the Church has an obligation to look for effective non-violent tactics that will abet this revolution, it has a prior and even more serious obligation to make every effort to liberate human beings from the terrible injustice in which they now live.

The Uppsala convention went on to say that the primordial task of the Church is to summon human beings and nations to repentence. It pointedly remarks that "to be complacent in the face of the world's need is to be guilty of practical heresy." As Visser't Hooft noted, a church member who refuses in practice to assume any responsibility towards the disinherited of the earth is as guilty of heresy as someone who rejects a particular article of faith.

The stances of the two conventions are very similar, and this fact of ecclesial community itself is of great Christian import; it

172   *Freedom Made Flesh*

opens the way for real and deep theological reflection. It is
clear, then, that the whole topic of violence is a religious and
Christian topic in the strict sense of those words. For it crops up
in a context where the urgency of the Christian vocation is
readily apparent. The Christian is summoned to work against
injustice and for development, for the establishment of a new
world where oppression and unjust inequities will be forever
blotted out.

If theological reflection is to prove fruitful, the whole topic of
violence must be framed in this basic context, which is more
social and religious than individual and political in nature. If we
are scared off by this truly Christian kind of reflection, or if we
feel the whole question is settled because we only consider
certain consequences of this critical revolutionary change, then
we are minimizing the question and failing to appreciate its
human and Christian import.

Before I explore the problem in strictly theological terms (see
Chapter 7), however, I feel it is most important to explore
aggression and aggressiveness in two other directions. This
exploration of aggressiveness, based on the viewpoints of biology and psychoanalysis, will help us to determine the "natural-
ness" of that which can be viewed as the natural foundation for
personal violence. Aggressiveness and violence are not the same
thing, particularly if we view violence in the social context
where its full import becomes apparent. We cannot overlook or
disregard the natural basis of violence, i.e., the aggressiveness
that is inscribed in biological life and man's psychic life.

Aggressiveness from a Biological Standpoint

Biography is not simply the linear continuation of biology, nor
is human history merely the linear prolongation of animal
evolution. But neither can we forget the biological and natural
roots of man as we study biography and history. The human
being is not just a subjectivity. Hence subjectivity cannot be

understood in idealistic terms—as if man's natural reality had no essential place in the real-life definition of humanity.

In concrete terms this means that we must take note of aggressiveness at the biological level in treating the topic of violence—violence as such being a specifically human phenomenon. At the biological level, the inherent animality of man presents itself to us as the factor that both causes and inhibits what rationality—not humanness strictly—converts into violence. Konrad Lorenz has worked out a masterful biological analysis of aggressiveness, and his book on the subject is already a classic.[2]

Here is what Lorenz proposes to us. Struggle is so omnipresent in nature, its weapons and operative mechanisms are so well developed, and it has so clearly appeared by virtue of the pressure of natural selection that it seems we must put positive value on it despite the risks it entails. Speaking in general terms, we can say that it is aggression which permits the survival and improvement of the species. The struggle for existence and survival, proclaimed by Darwin to be one of the major factors in the perfective process of evolution, is also one of the fundamental instincts of the animal. The most obvious results of aggression are the balanced distribution of animals, the selection of the strongest, and the defense of one's own offspring as well as the young of the group. But aggression also plays a major role in the structuring of society among the animals that are more highly developed biologically.

Hence one must say that aggression or aggressiveness, far from being the diabolic or destructive principle which many view it as, is an essential component in the vital organization of the instincts. Incidentally it can function poorly and be harmful, but the same holds true for other instinctual forces. And there is another point, which we shall consider more closely below: Mutation and selection, the two great pillars of evolution, have chosen intra-species aggression as the means to open the door to personal friendship and love.

If we wish to move on to theological reflection here, it is of the utmost importance that we recognize the spontaneous nature of aggression. The aggressive impulse is tied up with a primary and spontaneous instinct; it is not just a response or reaction to a hostile environment. Together with sex, hunger, and fear or flight, it is one of the major instincts of the animal. It may show up in many different forms, especially when it is transformed by the inhibiting mechanisms that are necessary to prevent it from being a wholly destructive force, but its spontaneity and utility are undeniable. If it were otherwise, aggression would have been eliminated in those animal species where social unification is necessary for survival. It has not been. Its undeniably dangerous potential has not justified its disappearance in evolutionary terms. The basic impulse, which is indispensable and generally beneficent, should remain unaltered. In those cases where it might cause harm, it is checked by a special inhibitory mechanism.

Among the more highly developed vertebrates we find countless examples of inhibitions which preclude harm vis-à-vis fellow members of the same species. Even a mother animal must be guarded against the dangers of aggressiveness directed against her own offspring. But this impulse ought only to be inhibited, not destroyed, because an animal who is suckling young must be especially aggressive towards any other living thing. So, for example, cannibalism is very rare among warm-blooded vertebrates and almost wholly unknown among mammals, probably because the members of the same species do not have much taste or talent for it.

Three general features of inhibitory mechanisms are worthy of careful consideration: 1) the correlation between the effectiveness of the armory at the animal's disposal and the strength of the inhibition which precludes use of this armory against members of the same species; 2) the special rites of pacification which set in motion the inhibitory mechanisms in the aggressive parties; 3) the fact that the link between the inhibitions and aggressiveness is not absolute or infallible. When an unexpected display of submissiveness inhibits an attack, we can conclude that an active form of inhibition has been produced by a specific stimulus-situation.

But it is not enough that aggressiveness not be suppressed. It should not simply be inhibited either. Aggressiveness should be redirected. The redirection of aggressive behavior is one of the most ingenious reversals of evolution, first and foremost because it is directed toward the individuality of the other members of the species. The aggression of a particular individual is withdrawn from another individual and discharged against the rest of the members of the species. In this way the distinction between "enemy" and "friend" arises. For the first time we see the rise of "personal" ties between individuals on the ladder of evolution; for now the role played by one individual in the life of another individual cannot be readily and easily filled by just any other member of the species.

Contrary to what one might think, the most primitive form of social organization is not the family group; the most primitive form of "society" is the anonymous herd. Personal friendship does not exist in the anonymous herd because friendship is always paired with aggression, and aggression is reduced to a minimum on the intraspecies level in animals who live a herd life. On the other side of the coin, we do not know of any animal capable of personal friendship that does not possess a large dose of aggressiveness.

It is through this process that a real group is constituted. Like the anonymous herd, the group is maintained by reactions aroused in some by others. But unlike the situation in an impersonal social order, reactions in a group are inextricably tied up with the individuality of the members. In the latter context, aggressiveness shows up in intimate relationship with sexuality. The sexual behavior of the female unleashes a typical form of aggression in the male; this aggression finds its target in another member of the species, and ordinarily in a territorial neighbor. Here we have a redirected activity. What was triggered by one object, the female, is discharged on another object, the territorial neighbor. Why is that the case? Because even though the female emits stimuli which are specifically responsible for the response, she simultaneously emits other stimuli which inhibit the male's response being directed at her. This behavior can be ritualized, in which case it becomes independent of the particular response of an individual. As a result of the process whereby aggression is unloaded on one's territorial neighbor, room is created for tenderness towards one's comrade and one's children. The nearness of the beings who are loved facilitates the intensification of aggression vis-à-vis one's territorial neighbor, and the proximity of one's enemy fortifies one's love for one's own. Thus aggression towards strangers and the bond with one's own interact and support each other. What is more, it is aggression that is the principle underlying the bond, even though aggression gradually takes on an autonomy of its own. That is why the object of love also remains an object of aggression to some extent. In cases of genuine love there is a great deal of latent aggression; when the bond is broken, it gives rise to the phenomenon of hate.

Considered from a purely biological perspective, this relationship between aggression and love is a highly significant datum; it points to the basic, radical ambiguity of *homo*. Animals in whom aggressiveness has been for the most part eliminated do remain united for life, but their association is purely anonymous. We find a personal tie and individual friendship only among animals with a highly developed degree of intraspecies aggression. The most aggressive mammal, the wolf is the most loyal of friends. Intraspecies aggression is millions of years older than personal friendship and love; it can and has existed without the latter. But love does not appear on the scene unless aggressiveness is present and operative.

There can be no doubt that these "animal" currents are present in man. It is also obvious that they are "distorted" by man's rationality—although the scope of this distortion still remains to be analyzed from many different points of view.

In discussing rationality, Lorenz does not use the term correctly; but we shall keep the term here with all its imprecision. Rationality, then, is the factor that jeopardized the human animal, who now was endowed with the faculty of conceptual thinking and with language. The knowledge that derived from conceptual thinking deprived man of the security which he had possessed by virtue of well-adapted instincts; this security had been put together long before any other type of secure adaptation appeared on the scene. The evolution of the social instincts, of the social inhibitions in particular, was not able to keep up with the new material culture of man. There is sufficient proof, for example, that the discoverers of the "pebble tools"—the African Australopithecines—used these new tools to kill each other; and it seems that Peking Man used fire to burn his fellows after he had learned how to make it and maintain it.

But rationality also enabled man to anticipate the future. While it posed new dangers for man, it also provided means for avoiding these dangers. Before rationality appeared in the process of human evolution, no inhibitory mechanism was required to forestall violent death. Since the human animal had very limited offensive potential, the would-be victim had time to awaken the kindness and goodness of the would-be aggressor with submissive gestures and pacifying attitudes. The invention of artificial arms destroyed the balance that had existed between destructive potential on the one hand and social inhibitions on the other hand. Humanity would have destroyed itself if it were not for the fact that the discoveries and a sense of responsibility stemmed from the same source: the capacity to ask questions and to anticipate the future.

Thus man was prepared for the task of overcoming his dangerous aggressiveness. In the struggle against his hostile environment, however, there was an increase in the quantity of his aggressiveness; and this aggressiveness does not find a ready or beneficent outlet in more advanced societies. There is no doubt that the process of intraspecies selection has led to an abnormal increase in aggression and hence to its repression. Today, for example, business competition threatens to give a permanent, hereditary fix to certain traits which are good in themselves but which would be fatal for humanity if they were to become excessive.

To counter these increasingly dangerous excesses, man relies on a system that has been promoted by the same forces that unleashed the danger in the first place. The overall system is shaped by the dynamics of instinctive impulses, by the models of phyletically and culturally ritualized behavior, and by the watchdog force of responsible morality.

At the same time, however, we should not rely on the "sublimations" which aggressiveness may assume. Thus "military enthusiasm" is a specialized form of communal aggression that is rooted in the most primitive forms of individual aggression. This military enthusiasm, which opens the way to militarism and what are called the military virtues, reveals its origins in the fact that the strength and force of conceptual thinking and moral responsibility are diminished as it grows in strength. Lorenz cites a Ukrainian proverb that sums up the process: When the banners are unfurled, the bugle takes the place of reason. According to Lorenz, anyone who has witnessed the behavior of a male chimpanzee defending his family will be inclined to have doubts about the spiritual character of human military enthusiasm. In the last analysis we are dealing with an instinctual response whose mechanism is conditioned phylogenetically. It is a real autonomous instinct that has a great influence on the social structure of the species. Humanity is not enthusiastically combative because it is divided into factions; it is divided into opposing camps because that is the situation which stimulates military enthusiasm.

In general, the stimulus situation which unleashes this autonomous instinct demands a social unity of some sort with which the individual, now threatened by some outside danger, identifies himself. It also entails the presence of an enemy who is threatening one's own set of values; the existence of a leader who welds these sentiments together; and, above all, the emotions shared by and with various members of one's own group.

Here we have another response of nature, one that is simultaneously worthwhile and dangerous. Its eradication would be fatal for the species. We must redirect it or channel it or, in some cases, sublimate it. Sports for example, in Lorenz's view, have as their chief function the healthy and cathartic discharging of the aggressive urge. But only love and friendship can properly control aggression. And this is particularly true with respect to its most indispensable and dangerous form: aggressive military enthusiasm.

Not all naturalists and biologists agree with Lorenz's view that man is an animal who is essentially and naturally aggressive. A substantial number of them disagree with his view, and with the view of Robert Ardrey who maintains that all animal groups, including man, instinctively fight to defend their own territory, possessions, and advantages.[3] Their opposing views have been presented in an anthology edited by one of their number, M.F. Ashley Montagu,[4] who maintains that human aggressiveness is the result of acquired behavior, which is exacerbated by the conditions surrounding present-day civilization. Carrighar, in particular, maintains that present-day patterns of aggressive behavior could be overcome in a few generations, but that there is little incentive to undertake the task so long as we continue to believe that aggressiveness is innate and instinctive in man.

His view is very much open to dispute. Why? Because it fails to recognize the positive value of aggressiveness, which should be given direction and sublimated but definitely not eliminated. Lorenz's critics regard aggressiveness as something that is both biologically and ethically evil rather than viewing it as an ambiguous reality. For the reasons presented by Lorenz, and for other reasons that will become clear later in this discussion, it seems more correct to me to talk in terms of ambiguity rather than in terms of absolute positiveness or negativeness.

Aggressiveness from a Psychoanalytical Standpoint

The psychoanalytic standpoint is equally significant for any theological reflection on this subject. Here again I am not going to go into an exhaustive analysis. I simply want to mention certain aspects of the Freudian standpoint which can be considered more important for our present purpose.

Initially Freud did not give autonomy to the instinct of aggression in man. He felt that the aggressive urge arose in relationship with the libidinous urge, that it was a reaction produced when the latter urge remained unsatisfied or was overlaid with guilt feelings. Thus he attributed bipolarity or ambivalence to the drive system: the aggressive drive, particularly its sado-masochistic aspects which were recognized as primitive, was viewed as being inextricably tied up with the erotic drive. The transition from bodily needs to desire in the development of the child inevitably led to frustration. This gave rise to aggressiveness which, poorly tolerated, led to a desire for self-punishment. That in turn increased the aggressiveness twofold, leading once again to a quest for chastisement. A vicious circle was thus set up between frustration and a continually increasing quantum of aggressiveness.[5]

After World War I, Freud modified his theory and accepted the death instinct as an autonomous reality. He now felt that the automatism in repetitive behavior lay outside the bounds of the pleasure principle; that it could only be explained in terms of a search for rest, that is to say, for death. He thus posited a force distinct from libido in man's instinctual reservoir—an instinct for destruction that he labelled the death instinct. To it he attributed sado-masochistic tendencies. These tendencies, incorporated in the super-ego, formed a system of unconscious aggressiveness that was opposed to the libido. Thus the unconscious became the locus of two kinds of drives: libidinal drives on the one hand and death-seeking aggressive drives on the other. The latter drives could be directed against oneself or against others.

In one of his last works, *Outline of Psychoanalysis*, Freud would tell us that after much doubt and hesitation he finally decided to accept only two instincts as basic: eros and the destructive instinct. Opposed to eros, the destructive instinct sought the dissolution of that which was organized and united. It sought a return to the inorganic level, to the primitive original state. Sometimes these two fundamental instincts were opposed to each other, sometimes they joined together. The whole range of vital manifestations could be reduced to the struggle or cooperation between these two fundamental forces. Thus the psychoanalytic viewpoint echoes a classical notion that Empedocles elevated to a philosophical category: Love and hate are the two primeval forces which give rise to movement, and hence to reality as it presents itself to us.

It is well worth noting that Freud regarded the destructive instinct as something necessary for the individual. While it operates in, and is directed towards, the interior of the individual, it does not show up for what it is. It takes on its specific profile when it is directed towards the world outside the individual. The problem lies in the fact that with the appearance of the super-ego something of the aggressive instinct is fixed in the interior of the ego, and there it causes grave havoc. The repressed aggressiveness turns into aggressiveness directed against the self. Even under the best conditions, when aggression is let loose towards the outside world for the most part, it is never completely discharged and it ends up by destroying the individual. Freud voices the suspicion that the individual dies from his own inner conflicts, whereas species die from their failure in the struggle against the outside world.

For Freud, then, that which we can regard as aggressiveness

is something characteristically human; it takes on its formal and essential character only in man. This point is particularly evident in his first view outlined above. It might seem that he sees it as a purely negative thing, insofar as he regards it as an instinct for destruction and death. But that is not the case. Freud's aggressive instinct is necessary to counteract and prevent an unrestrained development of the libido. If its presence in the human psychic apparatus is assumed, then it is not possible to repress it completely and push it down into the interior of the individual. Such repression would lead to destruction and psychic disorder—in short, to dehumanization. Though it is true that Freud's destructive instinct cannot be dovetailed point for point with what can be labelled aggressiveness, it is clear that there are substantive similarities between the two. These similarities offer us new light on the whole question of the precise nature of violence as a specifically human phenomenon.

Another point deserves emphasis here. While both eros and the destructive instinct do reside in the depths of the human psyche and hence are essential elements in any definition of the nature of man, man is not at the mercy of these two fundamental instincts in all his actions. For good or ill as the case may be, the ambivalent power of these two equally ambivalent basic instincts must reckon with the ego and the super-ego. Here again any would-be theological presentation is confronted with the essential ambiguity of aggression, which must be given adequate conceptual consideration. From both the biological and the psychoanalytic standpoints, aggressive and even violent features can be seen in very diverse behavior patterns in human beings. Some of these features are basically acceptable while others are basically unacceptable. There is sacrifice on the one hand, hatred on the other; or the thirst for justice on the one hand, and unbridled ambition on the other. This minimal amount of reflection suggests to us that the goodness or badness of aggressiveness, and of violence too, does not lie in these realities as such. Instead it lies in some other factor involving human liberty. Or, to put it in more general terms, it lies in a factor that is characteristically human.

As we shall note later on, there certainly are "violent" states to be found in man. There is a whole spectrum of pathological violence, whose specifically pathological aspect lies in the fact that these states exceed the capacities of the afflicted person's liberty. But this undeniable datum simply compels us to make a distinction between natural violence and violence that is specifically human and personal. It is only the latter that interests us in our reflections here. The normal human being is not simply at the mercy of his libidinous or aggressive impulses, though his life is ever grounded on them. There are two distinct aspects here, which suggest once again the ambiguous character of violence. The positive or negative worth of human violence is not determined at the unconscious level where aggressiveness resides; it is decided at the level of human behavior where freedom is operative.

There is another important datum to be considered in the framework on the psychoanalytic viewpoint. It calls our attention to the social—or at least conjoint—character of aggressiveness. Aggressiveness can sometimes appear to be solipsistic and wholly interiorized. In fact, however, there is always an original element of relatedness to others involved in it. It is man's entrance into society, into the human group, that alerts aggressiveness and makes it necessary. Even in the case of masochistic expressions of it, fundamentally we are dealing with a pattern of behavior aroused by real or assumed rejection by the human beings around us or by the lack of a desired response from them. We do well to keep this basic datum in mind as we proceed: even though aggressiveness—and hence violence —may be an innate force in the individual, it takes on its proper and full-fledged configuration only in terms of the environment that surrounds each individual.

Each human individual is placed in an ambiguous position

from the very start because two forces are intermingled in him. He draws closer to other human beings to seek personal fulfillment on the one hand, and he withdraws into himself for self-defense on the other hand. This originally ambiguous position will be given sense and meaning only through an authentic human growth in liberty. And this original ambiguity will also condition people's outlook, including their subjective interpretation of one and the same objective datum. What can be interpreted as a friendly approach may also be interpreted as an aggressive attack. It is only when these "natural" forces and this "natural" outlook come to be personalized that they can confront the surrounding environment in a personal and human way. Otherwise the surrounding environment will simply appear to be a "natural" one. It will awaken nothing more than "natural" reactions in the individual, making it impossible for real human communication to take place.

From a psychoanalytic standpoint one can propose various solutions for the curing of excess doses of aggressiveness. The point does not interest us here because it is aggressiveness as such, not its excesses, that is the object of our theological reflection. It cannot be denied that aggressiveness, by its very structure, calls for renunciation and ordered regulation. There is a constant danger that it will take on a destructive momentum which can hardly be controlled, and which will create in man an attitude of persistent fury that rules our clearsightedness and self-control altogether. Here we have another one of the dimensions of aggressiveness that deserve special theological consideration: the daemonic power of aggressiveness. Aggressiveness in man is virtually always accompanied by strains of diabolic compulsiveness. This offers us a psychological explanation for the fact that in the gospels certain cases of manifest aggressiveness are viewed as cases of diabolic possession.

NOTES

1. See Luis Acebal Monfort, "Upsala, julio 1968: Asamblea general del Consejo Mundial de las Iglesias," *Sal Terrae*, October 1968, pp. 691–712.

2. Konrad Lorenz, *On Aggression* (New York: Harcourt, Brace, and World, 1966).

3. Robert Ardrey, *The Territorial Imperative* (New York: Atheneum, 1966).

4. *Man And Aggression* (Oxford University Press, 1968).

5. H. Ey. Y. Bertheret M. Debuyst, and S. Lebovici, "Psychanalyse de la violence," *Semaine des Intellectuels Catholiques*, 1967, pp. 39–71.

7

Violence and Aggressiveness: Theological Reflections

Biology and psychoanalysis offer proof of the natural and original roots of aggressiveness in man. They also offer proof of its necessity on the one hand and its dangerousness on the other hand. Finally, they show that agressiveness in man, despite the many features it shares with that of other animals, takes on a special quality which paves the way for violence as a characteristically human phenomenon.

Theological reflection cannot help but express some surprise over the fact that man is naturally and originally aggressive, that this is true even before he personally decides to be violent or to let himself be carried away by an aggressiveness now converted into violence. But the fact is that man comes before us as a being who is aggressive by virtue of his very origins and from the very start. He is aggressive by nature. To put this another way: Man is "originally" aggressive. The allusion to original sin should be kept in mind, although the emphasis should be on original sin as "original" rather than as "sin." The point I would stress is that we are dealing here with something intrinsic to man's nature, not with something immediately or totally peculiar to man as a person involved in the full and free actualization of his personality.

By the same token, there is no reason to view aggressiveness as the result of some sin. It simply derives from the animal makeup of man and from his evolutionary origins. Whether these characteristics make man a being that is originally sinful is another question. And it is so because we can only talk about temptation to sin in the framework of the dialectic between his animality and his liberty. It is when man, possessing a certain animality, must work up the ethical shape of his personality that his being presents itself as a human potentiality on the one hand and an ethical problem on the other. And it is on this level that the original ambiguity of man's very roots are grounded.

In the previous chapter I repeatedly stressed the ambiguous character of aggressiveness. Without aggressiveness there is no evolution, no individualization, no love, no family tie. Without aggressiveness, a well directed aggressiveness, a normal psychic life is impossible; and it is no easy task to give proper direction to it. When the effort does not succeed, aggressiveness turns into a terrible force for destruction—both on the biological level of the individual and the species, and on the psychic level of the individual and society.

Because of its essential ambiguity, aggressiveness should be conceptualized theologically in terms of the category of concupiscence as understood and explained by Karl Rahner. We are dealing with a positive force in man, without which man could not fulfill himself in all his human dimensions. It is not something that should simply be suppressed. Its presence is indispensable if human life and liberty are to be what they should be. But aggressiveness is also a force that can strip man of his humanity, turning him into an animal who poses the most serious threat to the species and to the overall life of the planet.

It is worth stressing what I have chosen to call the "daemonic power" of aggressiveness and violence in certain cases. What does "daemonic power" mean in our present context?

In using that term, I am alluding to a force which is extraordinarily powerful and which, once unleashed, man finds almost impossible to control. It is one of those forces relied upon by man which are so powerful that they end up taking control of him and manipulating him at will. The presence and pressure of this force does not depend directly on human freedom. It can turn man into a being "possessed," an alienated being whose margin of personal liberty has been reduced to a minimum.

I am also alluding to an "obscure" force that wells up from "the depths." The psychoanalytic viewpoint has made this abundantly clear. Aggressiveness flows from the unconscious id, and it is subject to laws that consciousness and reason cannot clearly grasp. The biological point of view has also shown aggressiveness to be something rooted in the fact of animality, in something to which consciousness does not have direct access and over which it does not have direct control. In the perduring struggle between light and darkness, aggressiveness, at least in terms of its ultimate roots, wells up from darkness and is wholly mysterious.

In using the term "daemonic power," I am also alluding to the unbridled character of the destruction that aggressiveness carries in its wake. There is in it a destructive fury which takes delight in destruction for its own sake, which feeds on what it destroys, and which therefore can be understood as real hellfire. (I use the latter term here insofar as the basic concept may include an anthropological dimension, leaving aside any possible mythical explanations.)

But aggressiveness is not just an obscure and unbridled impulse. Its most terrible power, its authentically diabolical power, shows up when it is hominized without being humanized. Aggressiveness is common to man and animal. The specific aggressiveness of man is violence. Violence shows up as a rationalization of aggressiveness. By rationalization here, I do not mean that aggressiveness is made subject to reason and due measure. I mean that it is intensified and made worse by the cold calculation of reason. Insofar as it is hominized, aggressiveness acquires an infinitely dangerous character, unless it is also humanized—that is, made subject to ethical and truly human exigencies. If aggressiveness is hominized but not humanized, then it is no longer the "obscure" force that I described it as above. It now reveals its calculated character. Instead of being a "daemonic" power, it now becomes a "diabolic" power. Human·violence presents itself as a daemonic force when it has just gotten beyond the bounds of being pure aggressiveness; but when it becomes violence in the strict sense, it presents itself as a diabolic force. The greatest danger of destruction is posed to the human species and all other forms of life when the forces of nature are hominized. Hominization without humanization is not evolutionary construction; it is evolutionary destruction.

And so aggressiveness presents itself to us as radically ambiguous. It is undoubtedly a positive and necessary thing. But it is simultaneously a force that is ever in danger of going beyond its proper limits and dragging man down in its wake—either as a daemonic or a diabolic force.

This radical ambiguity launches us right into the middle of the whole problem of violence—in the strict sense of the term. Is this same ambiguity to be found in violence? Must we make a careful distinction between two different forms of violence? Is there one form of violence which embodies the positive value of an aggressiveness that has been sublimated on an ethical level, and another form of violence which embodies the negative side of aggressiveness insofar as the latter can be perverted into a willed dehumanization? If the answer is yes, then these two forms of violence would have nothing in common except the presence of an ambiguous reality called aggressiveness. It would be wise for us, then, to differentiate them completely from one another; for in reality they would embody two contrary attitudes even though the resultant actions might bear certain external resemblances. And we would have to ask ourselves: What basically differentiates the two forms of violence?

Before I tackle that question directly, I want to investigate a characteristic feature of all violence. Violence is always a symptom, but of what is it a symptom? Some consideration of the symptomatic character of violence will help us to find out what violence is as a reality.

Violence as a Symptom

If we consider violence as a bare and plain fact that needs no further specification, if we take it as a reality that is present and immediately recognizable, then we can say that it is present in every part of our human world today even as it was in the past. The omnipresence and universality of the phenomenon of violence is a symptomatic datum that merits and demands reflection. As I have already suggested, not all forms of violence have the same ethical and human stamp. But if we consider the reality of violence apart from any value judgment on it, it is obviously omnipresent and universal. We see individual violence, interpersonal violence, group violence, social violence, and international violence. We also see the violence of propaganda and, in more general terms, the violence of the communications media. We see the violence of socio-economic structures, the violence of oppressive power mechanisms, and the limitless violence of war.

One particular class of violence, which is also symptomatic, should be set aside immediately so that we might be able to get closer to violence in the strict and formal sense. It is what might be called the violence of nature. It cannot be denied that nature is violent in some sense. It unleashes the destructive violence of earthquakes, floods, and drought; of plagues and illnesses; of insanity and physical deformation. All these forms of violence can be attributed directly to nature itself; they are not due to personal culpability. There is the physical violence of the insane person against other people who are not directly responsible for his condition. There is the violence of the newborn child whose gestation or birth causes the death of its mother. Of what are these forms of violence symptoms?

One could say, with good reason, that none of these things is violence in the strict sense. But the very reality of such "violence" brings us to two conclusions: 1) Not every form of physical violence is strictly violence at all, however destructive and disordered it may be on the human level, however much suffering and pain it may cause to human beings. The specific character of violence does not lie in its seemingly cruel and destructive power. This becomes especially clear when we realize that these forms of "violence" are to be attributed directly to the Maker and Governor of nature. 2) Some form of violence, some force which is directed against man's will and which causes real havoc to him, seems to be indispensable and inevitable. The natural world in which man is immersed has an evolutionary character, and man himself seems to be a wayfarer moving progressively forward. This fact seems to compel us to accept a continuing process of "violence" exercised and endured, not in and for its own sake, but for the sake of the progressive journey itself.

This suggests that violence is clearly symptomatic, not only of our deficiencies but also of our proficiencies. We are faced with a new ambiguity. Violence implies struggle, but struggle seems to be indispensable for evolution and progressive development. So taken as a whole, it is something positive. But it also implies that something is wrong even though it leads to good.

Something is not right. Violence is always symptomatic of the fact that something is not all right. When signs of violence present themselves, they may well be signs of the fact that aggressiveness and struggle are at work in a positive sense; but they are also signs that something is wrong, that something is faulty. All the "violences" of an individual character have psychological implications of needed relief or escape or evasion or substitution or something else along those lines. As a symptom on the psychological level of the individual, violence calls for psychoanalytic or ethical reconversion. I choose the word "reconversion" deliberately to emphasize the need for a change, for a painful restructuring.

But we must proceed further here, for it is not on the level of the individual that violence shows itself for what it is. In instances of collective "violence" there may be a problem of personal catharsis on the individual level, but its collective character is symptomatic of something much more serious. Consider "revolutionary violence" insofar as it is really that rather than pure revenge or a mask for purely egotistical attitudes. Such violence is, at the very least, clearly symptomatic of an unjust and inhuman situation and of a growth in personal awareness that does not accord with the enormity of the injustice which is trying to hold truth in bondage (Rom 1:18). Here "violence" is symptomatic of an intolerable situation and a determined will for change.

Sometimes the symptom presents itself in a feeble form. But to concentrate on its feebleness rather than its symptomatic character is to give evidence of superficiality or bad faith.

The Specific Character of Evil Violence

I have been stressing the point that we must unmask certain attitudes that are now widespread in the face of the global phenomenon of violence. I have also been suggesting that we must make a distinction between the different forms which violence assumes; that such a distinction will enable us to talk about one kind of violence which is always evil and condemnable, and another kind of violence which on occasion may be absolutely necessary even though it undoubtedly entails evils. Given the existing circumstances, the latter kind of violence may be not only tolerable but even required.

The fact is that in many forms of violence we can see not only a real symptom of an intolerable situation but also an authentic moral denunciation of a prophetic cast. Whether it is in word or in deed is not the important thing; the important thing is that it be an authentic prophetic denunciation.

What is the aim of this prophetic denunciation? More concretely, against what exactly is it directed? To answer these questions, I shall begin by citing one of the most "violent" psalms:

> *Answer, you rulers: are your judgements just?*
> *Do you decide impartially between man and man?*
> *Never! Your hearts devise all kinds of wickedness*
> *and survey the violence that you have done on earth.*
>
> *Wicked men, from birth they have taken to devious ways;*
> *liars, no sooner born than they go astray,*
> *venomous with the venom of serpents,*
> *of the deaf asp which stops its ears*
> *and will not listen to the sound of the charmer,*
> *however skillful his spells may be.*
>
> *O God, break the teeth in their mouths.*
> *Break, O Lord, the jaws of the unbelievers.*
> *May they melt, may they vanish like water,*
> *may they wither like trodden grass,*
> *like an abortive birth which melts away*
> *or a still-born child which never sees the sun!*
> *All unawares, may they be rooted up like a thorn-bush,*
> *like weeds which a man angrily clears away!*
>
> *The righteous shall rejoice that he has seen vengeance done*
> *and shall wash his feet in the blood of the wicked,*
> *and men shall say,*
> *"There is after all a reward for the righteous;*
> *after all, there is a God that judges on earth."*
>
> Psalm 58

This is not an isolated strain or passage in the Old Testament. Such texts are abundant in the history of the Israelite nation. In dealing with such a passage, we must strip away the whole literary and environmental covering in which the word of God presents itself to us. We must illuminate it with the definitive light of the New Testament, without which we cannot discover the projected sense of many Old Testament texts. And even in the Old Testament itself we can find other passages and attitudes that condition the partial view presented in this psalm.

These and similar observations oblige us not to insist upon the definitive and literal validity of the transcribed biblical phrases. But even without going into the difficult task of trying to establish exegetical precision, we cannot help but recognize and admit two things: 1) The atmosphere of this psalm is pervasive in the Old Testament; 2) it has profound anthropological and religious import for a genuine interpretation of the true nature of violence. A bland conception of Christianity and of man, which ultimately leads to tolerance of unjust oppressors, has made us incapable of understanding such strong texts and attitudes. They seem "primitive," if you will, and they scandalize "civilized" Christians.

What permanent and perduring value might such biblical texts have with respect to the topic under discussion here? The theme of the text cited above centers around the notion of justice, the justice which the powerful carry out or fail to carry out. The powerful tip the scales in favor of the violent. Over against these men and their behavior stands God; it is he who works justice on the earth. They are wicked men whom God will have to chastise on this earth.

The reader of the Old Testament knows very well what goes into the injustice of the powerful. The psalmist does not spell it out in this particular psalm, but it is commonplace in the psalms and the writings of the prophets. They speak about the injustice of the powerful towards the poor, the lowly, the defenseless, the oppressed, the weak, the innocent, and so forth. The point needs no stress here.

The psalmist traces the misconduct of the wicked back to their mother's womb. They are born evildoers. The poison is part of their being even as it is of the serpent, and there is no ready remedy for it. All one can hope for in their case is that they will be chastised and destroyed.

The "violent" tenor of this chastisement is surprising to us. The words could hardly be more harsh or cruel. The psalmist asks God to impose the full weight, not of his justice, but of his wrath. An all-powerful and enraged God must stand for the oppressed and inflict punishment on the unjust oppressor. The punishment is not left to God because the oppressed should not do the job; it is left to God because the oppressed cannot in fact do the job in the concrete, so God is asked to do it for them.

The just man wants to bathe his feet in the blood of the wicked. Only then will he benefit from their chastisement. His pleasure will come when he sees the vengeance God exercises vis-à-vis the wickedness and injustice of the powerful.

I do not think for one moment that this psalm is God's final and definitive word on the whole subject of justice and violence. But I would emphasize the fact that it is not a unique or isolated passage in the Bible. And there is something else that also deserves to be emphasized. It may be true enough that much of the angry and violent language in both the Old and the New Testament has to be purified. At the same time, however, the sheer quantity and weight of such passages suggests that they must retain some modicum of real meaning; otherwise the words of the Bible would be erroneous and misleading.

This psalm makes it very clear that there are two forms of violence. One is the violence of the unjust oppressor; it is the original, aggressive violence. The other is the violence performed on behalf of the oppressed, the violence with which God punishes the unjust oppressor on this earth—whether that oppressor be an individual, a group, or a whole nation. In other words, good violence possesses not only the element of moral denunciation but also the elements of chastisement, punishment, and the rehabilitation of an order that has been put out of kilter by the abuses of the unjust people in power.

The point I want to stress here is the duality of this violence. Both types of violence, the evil violence and the good violence, resemble each other in their force and their destruction. From a theological standpoint, however, this resemblance has no meaning or value. The thing that distinguishes the two kinds of violence, the thing that defines evil violence as the real violence, is the fact that it is the violence wrought by the powerful on this earth who are acting unjustly. The psalmist does not regard the punishment of the unjust person in power as something violent. Thus violence is the injustice imposed by force on people by those in power. It is the injustice wrought against a whole group of people, against the defenseless and the oppressed. The physical force employed in the process is an element of lesser importance; hence it is not the thing that characterizes violence as such.

The second form of violence, which is not violence in the strict sense, has a twofold character. As I noted above, it involves both punishment and rehabilitation. But if people say that the punishment of unjust men in power, of what we today would call the structures of sin, ought not be performed by human hands—at least not by the hands of people who are not lawfully constituted authorities, then they do not really understand what theology means by the punishment of sin. Viewed in theological terms, such punishment is not a sanction imposed by a judge in accordance with the dictates of some positive law. That would be a legal, external punishment. This can indeed be justified, but it does not tackle the problem in all its seriousness. From the theological standpoint, the punishment must be regarded as the natural outcome of an unjust action, as the natural fruit of sin. It is the response—initially natural and only derivatively personal—triggered by the unjust structure or the unjust action.

This link between the term "violence" and injustice must be forcefully underlined. Why? Because people in power who claim to be the established authority try to center the notion of violence around the whole concept of legality. The use of violent force on people against their will, and derivatively its use against the things which they have made their own, is castigated as violence only when it falls outside the law or contravenes the law. In this outlook legalized violence is not violence; or, at the very least, it is justified violence.

To be sure, power cannot be exercised at all unless those subject to it renounce some of their potentially individualized liberties for the sake of the common good. This renunciation can be insisted upon, even by force, when it is refused for irrational or unjust reasons. But when this force is employed outside the control of the community, or even worse, when it is used to maintain oneself in power against the general will or to defend a legally established order that is substantially unjust, then such force is violence in the strict sense, however legal it may seem to be. Paradoxical as it may seem, authorized power—be it governmental, economic, or religious—has less justification for employing violent methods of a repressive nature. And one of the reasons is that it has recourse to many more indirect means. While these means may not be as effective in the short run, they help those in power to avoid one of the most serious and tempting sins open to them: the abuse of power. The abuse of power can take many different forms that are unjust and violent. Three forms deserve to be denounced as particularly grave: 1) legislation that tries to perpetuate an unjust situation in the political and socio-economic order; 2) political torture in all its forms; 3) falsehood propagated deliberately to misguide the consciences and conscious awareness of the people. This would be covert, legalized violence, but it remains the worst violence of all. It is unjust violence, or, the violence of injustice.

So violence in the strict sense is the injustice which deprives man of his personal rights by force and prevents him from giving shape to his own personal life on the basis of his own personal judgment. The thing which differentiates real violence is not the method used but the injustice committed. This differentiating factor is highlighted most clearly in those structures which make a truly human life impossible. Even though these structures are supra-individual, they do not cease to come under the responsibility of all, of those in power in particular. They constitute what is social injustice in the strict sense. They can be called social and established violence. When people become aware of their personal rights, social injustice gives rise to what is called revolutionary violence. This fact proves how closely and naturally violence is bound up with injustice.

The institutionalization of this social injustice is the highest magnification of violence. There we find the worst form of violence; there violence reveals its full theological and human maliciousness. If people truly want to repudiate violence, it is to this institutionalized social violence that they must turn their attention. They must not be led astray by sporadic violent reactions to it, for it is in the former that the mystery of iniquity infects man most gravely and that collective sin takes on its most serious form.

The Mystery of Iniquity and the Violence of Injustice

From a doctrinal standpoint, from the standpoint of the Church's magisterium today, it is easy to prove that the Christian conscience regards the sin of social injustice as a very grave one indeed. I do not mean to say that the magisterium has explicitly labelled this social injustice as the worst form of violence. The plain fact is that violence, as a new topic in our day, has not yet been given full and mature consideration at the level of the magisterium. But it will suffice here to highlight the prophetic denunciation by the magisterium of the concrete elements that go to make up the formal violence of social injustice. The statements of the magisterium clearly stress the sinful character of these elements.

The theme is familiar to everyone by now, and so I need only treat it cursorily. What should be noted, however, is the new tone and accent of Vatican II and the faithful at large, insofar as they choose to focus on these elements as most worthy of condemnation. Here are selected passages from *Gaudium et spes:*

> As a result very many persons are quite aggressively demanding those benefits of which with vivid awareness they judge themselves to be deprived either through injustice or unequal distribution. (no. 9)

> With respect to the fundamental rights of the person, every type of discrimination . . . is to be overcome and eradicated as contrary to God's intent. For in truth, it must still be regretted that fundamental personal rights are not yet being universally honored. . . . For excessive economic and social differences between the members of the one human family or population groups cause scandal, and militate against social justice, equity, the dignity of the human person, as well as social and international peace. (no. 29)

> Since economic activity is generally exercised through the combined labors of human beings, any way of organizing and directing that activity which would be detrimental to any worker would be wrong and inhuman. It too often happens, however, even in our day, that in one way or another workers are made slaves of their work. (no. 67)

> In many underdeveloped areas there are large or even gigantic rural estates which are only moderately cultivated or lie completely idle for the sake of profit. At the same time the majority of the people are either without land or have only very small holdings, and there is evident and urgent need to increase land productivity. It is not rare for those who are hired to work for the landowners, or who till a portion of the land as tenants, to receive a wage or income unworthy of human beings, to lack decent housing, and to be exploited by middlemen. Deprived of all security, they live under such personal servitude that almost every opportunity for acting on their own initiative and responsibility is denied to them, and all advancement in human culture and all sharing in social and political life are ruled out. (no. 71)

> In spite of the fact that recent wars have wrought physical and moral havoc on our world, conflicts still produce their devastating

effect day by day somewhere in the world. Indeed, now that every kind of weapon produced by modern science is used in war, the fierce character of warfare threatens to lead the combatants to a savagery far surpassing that of the past. . . . Among such must first be counted those actions designed for the methodical extermination of an entire people, nation, or ethnic minority. These actions must be vehemently condemned as horrendous crimes. The courage of those who openly and fearlessly resist men who issue such commands merits supreme commendation. (no. 79)

It must be said again: the arms race is an utterly treacherous trap for humanity, and one which injures the poor to an intolerable degree. (no. 81)

If peace is to be established, the primary requisite is to eradicate the causes of dissension between men. Wars thrive on these, especially on injustice. Many of these causes stem from excessive economic inequalities and from excessive slowness in applying the needed remedies. Other causes spring from a quest for power and from contempt for personal rights. If we are looking for deeper explanations, we can find them in human jealousy, distrust, pride, and other egotistic passions. . . . The world is ceaselessly infected with arguments between men and acts of violence, even when war is not raging. (no. 83)

The greater part of the world is still suffering from so much poverty that it is as if Christ Himself were crying out in these poor to beg the charity of the disciples. Some nations with a majority of citizens who are counted as Christians have an abundance of this world's goods, while others are deprived of the necessities of life and are tormented with hunger, disease, and every kind of misery. This situation must not be allowed to continue, to the scandal of humanity. (no. 88)

Whatever is opposed to life itself, such as any type of murder, genocide, abortion, euthanasia, or willful self-destruction, whatever violates the integrity of the human person, such as mutilation, torments inflicted on body or mind, attempts to coerce the will itself; whatever insults human dignity, such as subhuman living conditions, arbitrary imprisonment, deportation, slavery, prostitution, the selling of women and children; as well as disgraceful working conditions, where men are treated as mere tools for profit, rather than as free and responsible persons; all these things and others of their like are infamies indeed. (no. 27)

Many people, especially in economically advanced areas, seem to be hypnotized, as it were, by economics, so that almost their entire personal and social life is permeated with a certain economic outlook. These people can be found both in nations which favor a collective economy as well as in others. Again, we are at a moment in history when the development of economic life could diminish social inequalities if that development were guided and coordinated in a reasonable and human way. Yet all too often it serves only to intensify the inequalities. In some places it even results in a decline in the social status of the weak and in contempt for the poor. While an enormous mass of people still lack the absolute necessities of life, some, even in less advanced countries, live sumptuously or squander wealth. Luxury and misery rub shoulders. While the few enjoy very great freedom of choice, the many are deprived of almost all possibility of acting on their own initiative and responsibility, and often subsist in living and working conditions unworthy of human beings. (no. 63)

There is no dearth of similar texts in other documents of the magisterium published these days. *Populorum progressio* alludes to the injustice that cries out to heaven, and that pretty well sums up the state of violence in which the vast majority of human individuals and nations now live. As the conciliar message of the Third World bishops puts it, the people of the Third World form the proletariat of humanity today.

Here a brief synthesis is called for, one that takes its cue from such texts and focuses on the mystery of iniquity and the violence of injustice. The Church is clearly aware that the vast majority of humankind, and particularly those who live in the Third World, presently exist in an inhuman state of affairs. This cannot be attributed to their personal guilt or negligence; it is due to injustice and oppression. It is a degrading and scandalous situation because it destroys the human person and the very image of the Creator and Redeemer. It is the result of sin. However, it is not the result of some primeval, impersonal sin to which the powerful are wont to allude in order to assuage their bad consciences. It is the result of real human sin and of sinful attitudes: the desire to dominate, contempt for human beings, envy and overweening pride, egotism and everything else that directly opposes charity. It is the very incarnation of sin.

Faced with such a situation, the Christian cannot remain inactive. Every form of discrimination against the fundamental rights of the human person must be overcome and eliminated because they are contrary to God's plan. Vatican II called for the condemnation of every kind of action which led to the extermination of whole peoples. It also said that those who openly opposed such actions deserved the highest commendation, and that the implementation of needed solutions was proceeding much too slowly. It is Christ who is raising his voice in the cries of the poor, and it is not surprising that this voice would be less than calm after so many centuries of oppression.

But the mystery of iniquity continues to operate. It continues to nurture greed and selfishness. It continues to nurture the sense of a good conscience by granting concessions which allow for the maintenance of the existing inequities and structures. It makes people forget that the Christian message is not compatible with the existing situation of sin. It appeals to economic laws to justify its complete disregard for the spirit of the gospel message; that message sees the possession of worldly goods as the great temptation facing humankind.

In denouncing this situation, Vatican II was simply following in the footsteps of the Old and New Testament and reflecting their spirit. I do not want to cite a whole list of biblical passages because the Bible's denunciation of injustice is severe and repeated. But let me cite one passage from the Old Testament and one from the New Testament as typical of many. Here is the Old Testament text:

Shame on you! you who make unjust laws
and publish burdensome decrees,
depriving the poor of justice,
robbing the weakest of my people of their rights,
despoiling the widow and plundering the orphan.
What will you do when called to account,
when ruin from afar confronts you?
To whom will you flee for help
and where will you leave your children,
so that they do not cower before the gaoler
or fall by the executioner's hand?
For all this his anger has not turned back,
and his hand is stretched out still.

(Is 10:1-4)

It is the same line of thought: Iniquity and injustice are being wrought against the poor, and retribution will come from the outstretched hand of an angry God. And here are two passages from the Epistle of James which treat of this same sort of unjust oppression:

Listen, my friends. Has not God chosen those who are poor in the eyes of the world to be rich in faith and to inherit the kingdom he has promised to those who love him? And yet you have insulted the poor man. Moreover, are not the rich your oppressors? Is it not they who drag you into court and pour contempt on the honoured name by which God has claimed you? (Jas 2:5-7)

Next a word to you who have great possessions. Weep and wail over the miserable fate descending on you. Your riches have rotted; your fine clothes are moth-eaten; your silver and gold have rusted away, and their very rust will be evidence against you and consume your flesh like fire. You have piled up wealth in an age that is near its close. The wages you never paid to the men who mowed your fields are loud against you, and the outcry of the reapers has reached the ears of the Lord of hosts. You have lived on earth in wanton luxury, fattening yourselves like cattle—and the day for slaughter has come. You have condemned the innocent and murdered him; he offers no resistance. (Jas 5:1–6)

Here again we find the same central thought: The rich have been oppressing the poor and robbing them of their due; now they are doomed to perish. God's name is invoked on behalf of the poor; an offense against them is an offense against him. The cries of the oppressed have reached heaven, and the Lord of hosts is preparing to deal out punishment. The rust on the wealth of the rich is the sign that punishment is at hand. James asks patience of the just, but impatience of God.

I do not intend to explore the complete thinking of the Bible on the general relationship of oppressors and the oppressed. It will suffice to point out that this oppression is one of the sins most certain to enkindle God's wrath. It embodies the hatred of the evildoer, which is directed against the children of God since it cannot be directed against God himself. In the last analysis, it is the mystery of iniquity at work on earth. Faced with its presence, Christians and all those who hate injustice are obligated to fight it with every ounce of their strength. They must work for a new world in which greed and selfishness will finally be overcome.

8

The Christian Redemption
of Violence

The whole problem of violence is often posed poorly. Violence
is viewed solely or principally in terms of the physical force
which is used to resist oppression, that is, social oppression in
the concrete. It is said that the social problem cannot be re-
solved by violence understood in that sense. But what if the
social problem itself is the product of social violence? What if
the social problem itself is social sin and violence, however
much the force involved is hidden under more or less legalized
structures?

That is why I have insistently tried to show that the roots of
violence lie elsewhere and that its character as sin must be
emphasized. Viewing it in this light and seeing it as sin, the
Christian solution must be framed in terms of redemption.

The theology of development has been too quick to forget
that development often starts out from a basic structure that is
marked by sin and injustice. Directing its gaze towards the goal
which it seeks—well-being for all and an abundance of the
world's goods—the developmentalist outlook is often deluded;
it forgets the institutionalized sin at the root of the problem. How can we fashion a better future if we operate with

the same egotistical concerns and outlooks, if the craving to possess more goods is stronger than any other motive?

The theology of revolution, by contrast, looks at the existing sinful structure and frames the problem in terms of Christian redemption. Historically speaking, however, Christian redemption is presented to us under the sign of the cross. The cross is the Christian form of violence, though of course it is animated by love rather than by hatred. We are still left with the difficult job of determining exactly what this cross of violence is, but we cannot avoid framing the whole question in terms of redemption. This is the framework we must advocate vis-à-vis both extremes. We must advocate it over against those who think that we need only destroy the existing setup and fashion a new world without being concerned about the conversion of individual human beings. We must also advocate it over against those who think that there is no need for any important change, that the problem is merely one of good intention.

Over against both extremes we must assert that the present structures of injustice and oppression cannot be overcome without redemption and the cross—without bloodshed, according to the thinking of the Old Testament. To think otherwise is to fall into error from both the sociological and the theological point of view. Only by doing radical violence to themselves will those who wield unjust power be able to undergo conversion and fashion themselves into the new man of Christianity. We must remember that resistance to change almost always stems from those who possess wealth or power, and that the Christian message advocates the renunciation of greedy possessiveness. Hence it is easy to see that there is little Christian authenticity in many who staunchly defend the existing order. Unfortunately history shows us that if this conversion is difficult on the individual level, it is collectively impossible unless it is forced by the weight of circumstances. The violence of the cross is almost intolerable.

So we are presented with the necessity of exerting force

against the unjust will of those who hold power in the oppressive structural setup which crucifies the weak and does not leave room for a truly personal or Christian life. It is urgently necessary for us to frame the whole problem in a Christian perspective. What basically might be entailed in the Christian redemption of violence? The expression is ambiguous, to be sure, but we have already stressed the fundamental ambiguity of the phenomenon of violence. Violence must be redeemed, but the primary, sinful violence alluded to in the last chapter cannot be redeemed except by a certain form of violence. The latter is a distinct form of violence, to be sure, one which must be given a Christian configuration.

Hence we must insist forcefully on the concept of the "redemption of violence." It is the right concept to use in facing up to this difficult problem which has both an individual and a collective dimension. Here too, perhaps, an objective redemption will have to come first, so that it can then have an impact on the subjective life of each individual as history moves along. In any case I shall try to keep both aspects in mind as I attempt to tackle the notion of the redemption of violence and set it in biblical perspective.

We are dealing here with the redemption of sin. In discussing atheism, Zubiri[1] distinguishes an original sin, a personal sin, and a historical sin. The original sin is tied up with the very structure of human life. The personal sin stems from a personal decision, however much the latter may be conditioned by existing human structures and the historical context. The historical sin, the sin of the times, is connected with the essentially historical character that is man's; it is the "power of sin" as a theological factor of history, and its concrete form may vary from age to age. Now it is easy enough to see that we can use the same three notions in dealing with the problem of violence. We can talk about an original sin, insofar as violence wells up naturally from animal aggressiveness. We can talk about a personal sin, especially in the case of personalized forms of violence. And with even more reason we can talk about a historical sin, about an objectification in supra-individual structures which exercise real power over personal patterns of conduct.

The redemption of violence must also be framed in terms of these three dimensions. The redemption of original violence would include the task of bettering *homo* as such, of Christianizing the evolutionary process. The redemption of personal violence would entail the effort to raise people's consciousness and heighten their sense of personal responsibility—in short, to erase all the various forms of man's bad conscience. The redemption of historical violence should be viewed in terms of historical grace vis-à-vis historical sin. Historical violence has always been around, but today there is developing a real historical awareness of it. The redemptive process itself must take the form of revolution because we are confronted here with structures, not merely with personal decisions.

This is the reason why the Christian redemption of violence must be implemented in different ways and at different levels. Take the problem of historical violence, for example. The redemption of this violence must bring into play those forces that are capable of changing the sinful structures. In the framework of such structures we find that human behavior patterns, insofar as they are interrelated in and through these structures, are objectively unjust and anti-evangelical.

There is no doubt that sin is one of the major forces giving configuration to history. Two of the great driving forces behind history are greed for money, which is one of the causes of God's wrath (Col 3:5), and greed for power. Their outcome is injustice in general, and the oppression of the weak in particular. The latter sin is one that is castigated frequently in both the Old and the New Testament. In the New Testament its transcendent theological gravity becomes very clear. It is a sin against the first commandment and an offense against Christ himself, who is hidden under the concrete shape of the weak and the oppressed. The authenticity of this view of the matter is verified in Matthew's description of the last judgment (Mat

25:31–46). If failing to act on behalf of the oppressed merits such a clearcut condemnation, what would the Bible say about those who actively maintain a situation in which this oppression is institutionalized? How can we avoid talking about redemption in the face of such a situation?

Biblical Categories for a Redemption of Violence

Our theological reflection here cannot overlook the terms and categories in which biblical revelation frames the topic under discussion. Though it might not seem so at first glance, the sin of violence and its redemption is a major biblical theme—particularly in the Old Testament. It is up to biblical theologians to explore the subject in full detail. Here I shall merely suggest some of the biblical categories which ought to be considered in any study of our present problem.

The first set of categories would include: *Egypt, Babylon, the Beast, captivity,* and *persecution.* Though I shall only touch on them briefly here, they should give rise to a host of thoughts in the minds of those who are at all familiar with the thinking of the Bible.

Underlying the force of these categories is another notion: the idea of a chosen people. Initially it is a specific people, a specific racial and historical group: the people of Israel. But a new idea begins to show up in the idea of a *remnant.* This remnant is a persecuted people in need of liberation. Made up of the poor and lowly, the remnant grows more universal in scope as it loses its racial connotations. To some extent this group owes its unity to the oppressor in power, to whom it is subjected. In this context one can readily see the importance of the biblical interpretation of *Egypt.* At one point Egypt was a saving center of power for the Jewish people; it gave them asylum and protection during difficult times. Soon, however, it turned into an oppressor, into a center of power from which the Jewish people would have to be liberated. Egypt turned into

Babylon, that is, into the clearcut incarnation of abusive power
that would bring ruin to the religious, social, and political
character of the chosen people. The Hebrew nation is persecuted and enslaved by a diabolic power which the Bible describes under the image of *the Beast.*

Sociological and theological reflection on these biblical
categories enables us to draw up a social and religious picture of
what an oppressor power is. Against this power the people of
God react. Though this oppression is frequently pictured as a
punishment for the sin of infidelity, the nation is still called
upon to fight against the oppression to which it is subjected. We
find this line of thought in Psalm 137:

> *By the rivers of Babylon we sat down and wept*
> *when we remembered Zion.*
> *There on the willow-trees*
> *we hung up our harps,*
> *for there those who carried us off*
> *demanded music and singing,*
> *and our captors called on us to be merry:*
> *"Sing us one of the songs of Zion."*
> *How could we sing the Lord's song*
> *in a foreign land? . . .*
> *Remember, O Lord, against the people of Edom*
> *the day of Jerusalem's fall,*
> *when they said, "Down with it, down with it,*
> *down to its very foundations!"*
> *O Babylon, Babylon the destroyer,*
> *happy the man who repays you*
> *for all that you did to us!*
> *Happy is he who shall seize your children*
> *and dash them against the rock.*

The oppressed and exiled Jew is asked by his oppressors to
sing for his captors, but in such a situation he cannot sing the

Lord's song. As Muenzer would put it: "You cannot be called children of God while they (i.e., oppressive rulers) govern you."[2] Babylon cannot help but evoke waves of protest and of vengeance for its oppressive and violating deeds.

The apocalytic characterization of this oppressive power as *the Beast* sheds new light on our theme. There is no doubt, of course, that we cannot simply equate the political dimension or the human dimension with the religious and supernatural dimension of the revealed message. But even though they are not to be equated, these dimensions are not to be dissociated from each other either. And the persecution of the people of God, with whom Christ is identified in a special way, cannot help but be categorized and evaluated in religious terms. Moreover, while the apocalyptic complaints against the Beast can sometimes be interpreted as the result of religious persecution, we must not forget that this religious persecution is carried out in and from a political standpoint. Why? Because the new religious force represents a grave danger to the established order.

Another typically biblical category crops up in this sad chain of historical oppression and condemnation of it. It has to do with *hardening of heart*. The book of Exodus insistently stresses the hardening of heart that takes place in the pharaoh. He will not let the oppressed Hebrews have their liberty, and the hardening of his heart is viewed biblically as a punishment for his sin. The oppressor hardens in his sin, rationalizing it and offering justifications for it. The prophet speaks out in the name of the persecuted, protesting in the name of justice. But the light of his just protest blinds the oppressor rather than enlightens him. This gives rise to the worst sin of all: the sin against the light. The light of protest is wrongly interpreted; it is used by the oppressor to bolster his own position and to defend himself. Hardening of heart is thus the objectification of sin, punishment for sin, and the radicalization of sin. The situation now becomes intolerable. Redemption is no longer possible from within the situation because the potential elements of redemption have been turned into elements producing hardness of heart. Proper sociological and theological use of this category would shed much light on the sin of violence, for "hardening of heart" is deeply rooted in the message of revelation.

As we noted, hardness of heart itself is a divine punishment to some extent. But it also calls up *God's wrath*, which is another biblical category that is very pertinent to our present theme. We cannot set it aside, claiming that it is an ingenuous biblical anthropomorphism. It certainly is an anthropomorphism, as are most of the attributions that religious thought applies to God. But it certainly is not ingenuous, for several reasons. First, the oppression of man by man cannot help but incite wrath. Second, this divine wrath is viewed by the inspired writer as an authentically human and religious response to the injustice that surrounds him. God's wrath certainly should not be identified with human anger, lest the repression of violence lead to a new form of unjust and inhuman violence. But behind the manifestations of divine wrath, so frequently evoked in the Bible, we must see something serious and important.

At times God's wrath is directed against the chosen people, who also commit sins of their own. This shows us that God's wrath is unleashed because of sin. This wrath does not rule out mercy, but neither does mercy rule out divine wrath. God's wrath is aroused by sin, and its goal is to effect conversion from the sin (Is 9:7–21). It is aroused especially by the violent (Is 24:16), that is, by proud and ruthless rulers (Is 25:5). Even though the oppressor and the destroyer may incidentally be instruments of divine punishment, they themselves must be castigated. And their punishment is not meant for the sake of correction; it is meant to bring about the final and definitive elimination of all oppression (Is 33:1–5; 2:4).

The whole strain of prophetic thought in the Bible clearly underlines the theme of God's wrathful response to sin and oppression. Christian love should dwell upon the theme often, lest it grow soft in its fight against the sin of injustice which robs both the oppressor and the oppressed of their human character. Amos and Hosea, in particular, deserve to be read in this connection; but the whole history of salvation echoes the theme. The eschatological dimension of this divine wrath, embodied in the notion of the "day of the Lord," does not remove its historical character and its historical dimensions. The whole strain of apocalyptic thinking about God's wrath indicates that the definitive settling of accounts will come later, but that we must try to move towards that in every moment of history.

What is to be done in the face of this divine wrath? A second set of biblical categories comes to our aid here. They are the categories of *expiation*, *penance*, *conversion*, and *reconciliation*. The words speak for themselves, and it is easy enough to analyze them in biblical terms. So here I shall merely make a few observations that are pertinent to our present theme.

There is no doubt that the first response to be made to the sin of violence is that of conversion; it is the first step towards the redemption of violence on the subjective level. The burning words of the prophetic message call for a profound and radical conversion of heart. Man must move from a heart of stone to a heart of flesh; from a heart greedily seeking power and possessions to a heart living a life of humble love and service. There must be a complete conversion, a complete overthrow of our own ideas and the structures which objectify them. We must work for a complete change in structures (an objective revolution) and for a complete change of mind and heart (a subjective revolution). It is utopian to think that we can get one without the other.

This conversion requires expiation and penance. They are not to be considered directly and formally as a penalty or punishment for sin. Rather, they are a way of putting to death the whole way of living with which we had identified ourselves. Only then can we move on to a new life. To rise to new life we must die to the life we have been living. Here we find one more reason for asserting that development cannot be initiated without a process of painful reconversion.

There is no element of revenge in this requirement of conversion. This is evident from the fact that it is to end in reconciliation. There is to be a reconciliation with the once angry God, and this is not possible without a reconciliation between human beings.

But what is to be done when and if this conversion does not take place? Biblical thought presents us with another set of categories that are of singular importance in salvation history. They are the categories of *sacrifice*, *cross*, *bloodshed*, and other related ones.

There is no certainty to the view that we are to see the example of Christ as a bloody quest for the cross as such. Christ did not come to be crucified. He came to convert, to save people by offering them a message of conversion. This message was not accepted by those in power. Because Christ remained faithful to his mission, their repudiation transformed salvation into a bloody redemption that is embodied in the notions of sacrifice, cross, and bloodshed. Christ clearly shows us that the first duty of the redeemer is to incarnate himself among those whom one seeks to redeem and to flesh out a life at their level, paying heed to the dynamics of the real historical situation. The case of Christ and of many others reveals the underlying dynamic of much history and the tremendous effectiveness of established violence. As the letter to the Hebrews puts it: "Indeed, according to the Law, it might almost be said, everything is cleansed by blood and without the shedding of blood there is no forgiveness" (Heb 9:22).[3]

There is no reason to believe that we must take the bloodshed of the new covenant in completely literal terms. As an image, however, it does make clear to us the fact that the redemption of violence calls for a purification and a renewal that can only be regarded as a resurrection from the most painful of deaths.

Resurrection is the hopeful expectation in this redemptive death. It is a hope that looks towards not only a new heaven but also a new earth. The latter is one of the most classic desires to be found in the hearts of all religious human beings. If we simply project it beyond existence here on earth, then we are in fact denying it altogether. It is on earth that the painful process of birth to a new world must take place. It is on earth that peace and love founded on justice are to reign. It is on earth that we are to attain liberty through a painful process of liberation; without the latter, the former is nothing but an empty word. The new earth will render present the kingdom of God; and only in this kingdom will God's incarnation among human beings reach its culmination.

Here I shall conclude this brief overview of biblical categories that offer much food for thought in any attempt to spell out the Christian redemption of violence. The message of revelation is not a political message, but it is an incarnate message. If we live it truly and deeply, we will glimpse Christian solutions to the sin of violence that confronts us. These solutions cannot take refuge in complacent inactivity on the one hand or in the daemonic power of hate on the other hand. Along what general lines might such truly Christian solutions proceed?

Christian Approaches to the Redemption of Violence

Theological reflection should not offer a book of readymade recipes or practical techniques. It is not for me to define here the concrete means that are to be used in combatting and rooting out the sin of violence. But I do think it is proper to point out different Christian styles and approaches to the whole task of redeeming violence. Christianity is pluralistic, and it respects the differences that mark people's individual vocations. At this point, however, I think it would be useful to consider three different styles and approaches that have been used by Christians in trying to solve the conflict raised by violence. All three have been more practical than theoretical in nature.

Charles de Foucauld

The first approach rejects not only all violence, understood in the context of injustice, but also all use of physical force to achieve the gospel's objectives of peace and love among human beings. This approach is exemplified by Charles de Foucauld and the Little Brothers of the Gospel, the group which he established. They go out to live with the victims of violence, but not to fight on their behalf. Their aim is to bear witness to peace and universal love, to serve as the leaven in the dough and the condensation of those values that should be present in any Christian commitment.

According to René Voillaume,[4] three great realities underlie the attitude of the Little Brothers: 1) the immortality of man, who is a spiritual being waiting for the definitive establishment of a new order in and through Christ's resurrection; 2) the violent and sorrow-filled nature of man's brief existence; 3) the reality of universal love. This outlook should not be viewed as a dreamy disembodied idealism. It should be seen as the pursuit of an ideal of love which looks beyond this world towards the living, resurrected Christ, but which does not cease to be faithful to the human condition and its limitations.

Holding this outlook, what is one to do in the face of violence? The temptation is to repel force with force, but Charles de Foucauld chose another approach instead of active forceful resistance to violating force. He chose the silent witness of kindness, humility, and peace; one does not defend himself but rather hands himself over to death meekly for the sake of those whom he loves. Violence will not disappear from the world until its roots are eliminated, and the witness of Christ is directed against the roots of violence. In the face of the desire to

possess wealth, he preaches poverty. Against the concupiscence of power, he preaches humility. In the face of hatred, he
preaches kindness. Over against the strict rigor of an all too
human justice, he proposes mercy and respect for the most
lowly.

There is no hint of passive weakness in all this. It presupposes a firm and solid faith that the human dough desperately
needs the leaven of love and peace. It does assume, of course,
that one does choose to withdraw one's own life and vocation
from the web of pervasive earthly perspectives. One chooses
instead to frame one's whole life in the singular perspective of
God's kingdom, a kingdom which is to be foreshadowed and
anticipated by some of Christ's disciples. This is not a universal
vocation, the one vocation for every human being. Other Christians will have to perform other tasks aimed at establishing the
preconditions for authentic peace in the world.

Foucauld's aim is to seek out the level where divisions no
longer exist among human beings, where people share a common hope and are looking for the supreme good common to all.
And the one and only means to this end is Christ, his Gospel
and his cross. Such values as fatherland, ideology, or revolution
seem very relative to those who are devoted to one absolute and
supreme hope. Their vocation, motivated by love, is to share
the lot of those who suffer from violence; to bear silent witness
to the values for which Christ died, knowing full well that these
values cannot be fully attained except by a radical renewal of
humanity that will entail the second coming of Christ.

Martin Luther King, Jr.

There is a second Christian approach to the whole problem
of violence. It is alluded to in *Gaudium et spes:* "Motivated by this
same spirit, we cannot fail to praise those who renounce the use
of violence in the vindication of their rights and who resort to
methods of defense which are otherwise available to weaker
parties too, provided that this can be done without injury to the

rights and duties of others or of the community itself" (no. 78). The martyred Martin Luther King, Jr., stands as an admirable example of what this approach can achieve in theory and in practice. Here it will suffice to summarize the Christian interpretation that he himself put on his overall attitude towards violence.[5]

He tells us that we must move from passive conformity to direct action, but without falling into the snares of hatred and vengefulness. Effective action of nonviolent character lies between two extremes. One extreme is exemplified by those who are content with "tokenism," who for the most part let things go on as usual. The other extreme is represented by those who launch into action of a violent and uncontrolled nature.

Nonviolent action is born of two very powerful forces: the absolute and total rejection of injustice committed against human beings, and a love that impels one towards the construction of a new society. It transforms hatred into a constructive force. The process of Christian interpretation helps us to see that the real enemy is not another human being but the system that has made individuals evil. These individuals are the oppressors, who must be liberated from their active oppression. By dramatizing the injustice in a social context, one obliges consciences to face up to the injustice that is there. The oppressor is forced to recognize his injustice in an explicit and public way. The repression he uses to stifle nonviolent action makes clear his usual pattern of conduct, and nonviolent resistance reveals his own moral inferiority.

Martin Luther King, Jr. had no doubts about the efficacy of his approach in rooting out unjust violence from this world. If five percent of the world's oppressed were willing to go to jail for a just cause, victory would be assured. Furthermore, it is a line of behavior that attests to the maturity of those involved, for they demand a fair share in the goods and resources that belong to humanity in common.

There are four stages in this approach. First, one objectively ascertains that a situation of injustice exists. Second, one attempts to enter into negotiation on the subject, to resolve the critical issue by dialogue. Third, one undergoes a process of personal purification to prepare for the nonviolent action that is to be undertaken; one must be ready to accept the violence of others without responding in kind, and to go to jail if the authorities so decree. Fourth, one undertakes direct nonviolent action. The aim of this action is to bring irresistible moral force to bear on the process of negotiation by creating a tension that is morally intolerable. Dr. King was aware that privileged groups do not give up their privileges voluntarily because they, as groups, are more immoral and inhuman than individuals are. He realized that such groups would have to be forced to alter their stance—not by physical force but by moral pressure.

Dr. King was convinced that his approach represented the authentic Christian response to the violence of injustice. To begin with, he saw the need for a Christian response to the urgent summons of injustice. Of its very nature Christianity had to make some response to the outrages committed against human beings, convinced as it should be that the oppressed cannot go on being oppressed, that they must be liberated from such oppression, and that they themselves must do the work of self-liberation. Only extremism could resolve the situation; but over against the extremism of hatred, the Christian must implement the extremism of love.

This extremism of love has not exactly been the banner of the official white Church with regard to the problem of blacks. Indeed it has not been the slogan of the official white Church with regard to any problem of unjust violence. At most it has come up with belated and ineffective verbal declarations. It has become a defender of the institutionalized situation, thereby losing its sacrificial spirit and its prophetic sense.

The black Church, on the other hand, has looked for a truly Christian solution, for a way to confront unjust violence in Christian terms. This was possible because the black Church itself was incarnate among the oppressed. In and through this incarnation it realized that the authentic witness of Christian living calls for a social gospel, for a gospel that views the dignity and equality of human beings as an essential component of the Christian message. It has also realized that hatred and vengeance are a serious temptation for the black soul, one in which blacks could lose themselves completely. Finally, it has realized that the soul and human life of the black person and the black Church will be saved by a struggle for justice which combines love for all human beings with a willingness to pardon.

The theological thrust and import of this attitude is clear. Specifically, it says that there must be a confrontation with what is a structure of sin. Racial segregation is a most serious sin because it depersonalizes and dehumanizes. Moreover, it is the very embodiment of sin as a divisive force. People must be liberated from this sin. One must liberate oneself and one's oppressor from the personal sin and its social objectification. The tension activated by nonviolent direct action is the result of a salvific crisis which is seeking authentic justice as its goal. But justice is not to be equated with the legal order or with the seeming absence of tension. The law and the established order may really be impediments in the way of justice and social progress. In the face of legalized injustice, one can only offer an insistent demand and engage in a tireless struggle. Christian love must not diminish the vigor of this struggle.

Camilo Torres

A third approach has arisen from the Christian's painful experience of violence. Its most startling representative may well be Camilo Torres, the Colombian priest who died as a guerrilla fighter. Father Régamey has noted that the worst commitment that can be forced on the Christian is to see oneself forced to choose violence, and that was the case with Camilo Torres.[6] A staunch proponent of nonviolence himself, Father Régamey does not rule out the possibility that such an approach may not only be heroic but also holy. But he goes on to say that there is a terrible temptation to establish this as the rule for our time.

Camilo Torres was motivated by two fundamental "passions": a passion for justice and a passion for charity. These two passions were fleshed out in the real-life situation of the people of Colombia. They did not allow him to stay on the sidelines, to evade any sort of activity that was necessary to change the structures that had led the people into such dire straits. To stay on the sidelines would be to betray Christianity and his own personal vocation. The guiding principle behind his outlook and activity was clear to him: When existing circumstances prevent people from giving themselves to Christ, it is part of the proper function of a priest to combat those circumstances. Torres had opted for Christianity because he saw it as the purest form of rendering service to others. His analysis of the situation of Colombian society forced him to conclude that a revolution was necessary, that the revolutionary struggle was a Christian and priestly struggle. Given the real circumstances, the love that people were supposed to show to their neighbors could only be fleshed out in and through the revolutionary struggle. So he felt compelled to commit himself to that struggle as a way of bringing men to love of God.[7]

His ideas, his character, and the sociological conditions prevailing in his country drove him to specific means of political action, to the setting up of a political front and to dedicated efforts to make the masses more aware of their needs. He thus would help to create an authentic revolutionary spirit through his speeches, his writings, and his demonstrations. Eventually he joined the guerrillas and was slain in an encounter with the army. He did not see any way out of the problem by legal means. The only way left was recourse to arms.

An Evaluation

What are we to say about these three approaches, so briefly touched upon here? Do they correctly implement in practice what Christian redemption of violence is supposed to be? Leaving aside their actual working out in practice, let me try to reflect briefly on their thrust and import.

All three approaches recognize the reality of the sin of violence, of the mystery of iniquity which dominates so many political and socio-economic structures and which represents the very negation of a Christian order. All three feel that it is imperative for the Christian conscience to respond to this situation, and that this response involves a personal commitment of one's own life even to the extreme demanded by Christian love, that is, death. But the three approaches have different ideas about the concrete form that this Christian response should take. Does the distinctive character of each response rule out the Christian character of the other two responses?

The first response, exemplified by Charles de Foucauld and his followers, acknowledges that it is not the exclusive response from the Christian standpoint. But it also asserts that Christianity does have a spirit that is peculiarly its own, that this spirit may never be renounced in favor of some alleged terrestrial efficacy, that instead it should shine through in a positive way. It is the spirit that pervades the Sermon on the Mount. The Christian must bear witness to this spirit in a thorough and radical way; and those who have received the particular vocation and charism must bear witness to this spirit in an exclusive way. No single Christian can bear visible witness to the full richness of Christianity. Different groups of Christians must devote themselves to cultivating different important aspects of the gospel message and Christ's example. The Litte Brothers seek to bear witness to the transcendent aspect of Christianity as it is reflected in the patience of Christ, who silently submitted to death out of love for all and who nurtured the sure hope of a saving resurrection. In this outlook it does seem that the "struggle" for justice as an imperative of love, and the Christian character of earthly values, are somewhat obscured.

The approach represented by Martin Luther King, Jr., sees the gospel of Christ as essentially a social gospel. It realizes that the transcendence of Christianity is only made visible in the immanence of incarnation. If the kingdom of God does not commence here on earth, it will never commence at all. And the kingdom of God is justice, respect for human beings, and love. The struggle for justice and against social sin must be waged ceaselessly. At the same time, however, it must be motivated exclusively by Christian love; it must make every effort to avoid those means which, by their very nature, tend to unleash the daemonic power of violence. This approach is more combative and incarnate than the approach of the Little Brothers, and also more ambiguous. In the last analysis it may have a rather utopian confidence in those who hold the reins of power, and perhaps even in the very structures that gave rise to the situation in the first place. The situation of black people in the United States is morally intolerable but physically bearable, and this approach may not have taken due account of the radical sinfulness in the existing structures. It is a Christian option, however, and it certainly deserves a try at the start; for it is less dangerous in some ways and it is aimed directly at the liberation of the oppressed and the conversion of the oppressor.

The response embodied by Camilo Torres is frequently called the "temptation to violence" by Church authorities. It must be viewed and evaluated in terms of an existing situation that is very desperate. Such "limit situations" exist all too often. In trying to evaluate such an approach, we must try to explore its basic guiding principles. To that extent we can prescind from the concrete choice of means and its concrete understanding of "violence," for in theory a plurality of means and choices are available. It would seem that the motivating principles are an all-out battle against violence, a fundamental passion for justice, and a burning conviction that the existing political and socio-economic structures must be eliminated. Since these structures are the objective embodiment of the mystery of iniquity, they represent a real impediment to Christian love and Christian living. This approach stresses one of the fundamental aspects of the Christian message but obscures other aspects. It is akin to the approach of the Little Brothers in that respect, except that it stresses the other end of the spectrum. Does it deny those other aspects of the Christian message? It is a

226 Freedom Made Flesh

moot question, but I would suggest the following answer: The kind of solution exemplified by Camilo Torres does not necessarily deny basic Christian values although it runs the risk of doing precisely that. There is a temptation here, but it is not necessarily a sin. Certain temptations must be faced forthrightly even though it may entail great risks. Why? Because higher values are at stake and the situation is a limit situation. People who have defended the legitimacy of war should not be scandalized by solutions akin to the one chosen by Camilo Torres.[8]

At the start of this chapter I stressed that I was not going to try to offer practical solutions. My aim was to outline three different Christian approaches to the problem, three possible Christian ways of confronting and dealing with the tragic sin of violence in a redemptive spirit. I have briefly alluded to strong points and weak points in each of these approaches. The combination of strengths and weaknesses clearly highlights the inevitable ambiguity of any solution that attempts to tackle a sin incarnated in human persons and objectified in social structures. It also suggests that the Christian conscience must keep searching for a new solution to this urgent problem, for a solution that is fully Christian and completely efficacious.

Conclusion

Faced with the extensive and complex problem of violence, I have been forced to simplify and reduce its overall proportions. I have left many problems unconsidered, e. g., war, the existence of armies, the arms race, the use of propaganda at every level, and delinquency. Perhaps the basic perspective offered in these pages may help people to decide what the Christian should say about all these forms of violence which oppress human beings.

I have chosen a focus which may hopefully give us a clearer idea of what violence really is today. It is certainly not intended to provide a trigger for further violence; rather it is meant to be a summons to combat violence. I have discussed at length the reasons why the struggle against real violence should not itself be regarded as violence. No one can honestly say that I am preaching the use of violence to combat violence. And the social dimensions of the perspective presented here should help us to avoid those forms of struggle which are too strictly individualistic or too tainted with vengefulness. Violence is a sin which we all carry within ourselves, and we share responsibility for its objectified forms in societal life and structures. Advertence to these facts should dissuade us from entering the fray against violence for the sake of juvenile sport or mere political advantage.

Studying violence as a social phenomenon—be it revolutionary or counterrevolutionary violence—I began with its biological and psychic roots. Our analysis made it clear that agressiveness is not only a dimension of nature but also a necessary one for the equilibrium and betterment of both the individual and the species. Hence there can and must be aggressive patterns of behavior. A pattern of conduct is not wrong or evil simply because it is aggressive.

But aggressiveness is also an ambiguous reality, a natural force which is dangerous by its very nature. It is a positive, natural force; but it also includes a truly daemonic element which appears on the scene with the advent of personal rationality. It is from the combination of natural aggressiveness and personal rationality that violence arises as a typically human phenomenon.

On the human level, violence shows up at once as a symptom. It is in and through its symptomatic character that we draw closer to the real meaning and import of violence. Violence is symptomatic of the fact that something is wrong. It is symptomatic in the sense that force is used to maintain the disordered setup, and in the sense that force is used to change and improve the situation. The two uses are clearly opposed to one another, but they both signify that a situation of injustice exists.

The twofold form of violence forces us to look for the element that differentiates violence and makes it what it is. That element is injustice. All injustice is violent, and it is injustice that points up the true gravity of violence. When such injustice is not present, we cannot speak about violence in any strict sense, although we may be able to speak about force, or coercive force, or painful force. Viewed in the context of injustice, violence must always be regarded as sin. It is the sin of violence, intimately bound up with the whole mystery of iniquity, which prevents the establishment of conditions that will allow Christian love and salvific justice to flower.

The Christian response to the sin of violence must take a specific form, i. e., the redemption of violence. This redemption must be understood in Christian terms, but it must also take on flesh and blood in the very realities and at the very levels where the sin of violence itself is present. The biblical message offers us many concepts that will help us to evade the danger of disembodied solutions on the one hand and of excessively politicized solutions on the other hand.

If there is to be a Christian redemption of violence, we must find Christian approaches to that task. In the immediately preceding pages I outlined three such approaches. It may well be that we will have to look for another solution rather than trying to synthesize those three. It is easy enough to orient ourselves in the right direction; it is not so easy to implement our ideas in the concrete. The realm of implementation is strictly political in any case. Operating from a Christian outlook we must denounce every sin of violence unceasingly; but from that outlook we cannot calculate and spell out the concrete means and techniques that are to be used. What ought to be done and the actual doing are two different things; confusing the two could be catastrophic. Keeping the two things clear and distinct must remain a permanent concern of all those who rightfully wish to see the Church taking action vis-à-vis the sin of violence.

The prevailing violence, however, is strictly unjust in character. The injustice of it calls for extreme remedies. Any moral evaluation of these remedies cannot start from the assumption that the situation is normal, that it is not violent. The use of force will always be dangerous. It should be reduced to the minimum so long as we are not faced with a grave injustice. Under normal circumstances, however grave they may be, we ought to avoid any force that coerces, compels, or wounds. But in cases of established violence, whatever form it may take, we may be not only permitted but even required to use the force that is necessary to redeem the established violence. The good being sought does not justify the evil entailed in the means to achieve it. But if evil is an achieved and concrete fact already, it must be reduced and eventually eliminated. The obligation to reduce and eliminate evil compels us to use all those means that will help to reduce evil in the world. But now I am getting into the whole ethics of violence, and my purpose here was simply to provide some basic theological orientation.

That does not mean I am trying to be evasive. The reflections contained in this volume were prompted by reflection on the concrete reality of the world around us, and that of the Third World in particular. They are intended to provide a theoretical framework for concrete Christian action designed to combat the violence of injustice and the sin of violence. This combative action must keep in mind two points of the utmost importance: 1) Not everything in the existing structures is evil, neither as structure nor as personal achievement; 2) the Christian message demands that we move out of the whole schema of violence versus resistance to violence by the use of force as quickly as possible. Why? Because in that struggle, even when viewed simply as a means, there is great danger that we shall lose sight of the very essence of Christianity.[9] It is not just the sin of violence that is against the spirit of the gospel message. Resistance to violence is too, if it is adopted as a definitive attitude or if we allow ourselves to be taken over by its powerful dynamic. Christian redemption does not derive its power from hatred. It must derive its life from love, albeit a difficult love.[10]

Theological reflection on violence tends, of its very nature, to be extremist. It must be complemented and completed by reflection on related themes. But though it may be partial and incomplete, it is still urgent and pressing. The eradication of violence in all its forms is an urgent task that cannot be postponed. But stress must be placed on that form of violence which is protected by legal forms, which entails the permanent establishment of an unjust dis-order, which precludes the conditions required for the human growth of the person, and which therefore gives rise to strong reactions. Our rejection of violence must be absolute. The paradox is that the absolute character of this rejection calls for attitudes and lines of action that cannot help but be extreme.

NOTES

1. *Naturaleza, Historia, Dios* (Madrid, 1963), p. 394.

2. E. Bloch, *Tomás Munzer, teólogo de la revolución* (Madrid: Ciencia Nueva, 1968), p. 83.

3. I want to forestall two possible misinterpretations of my position here. One would reproach me for reducing the whole redemption of Christ to the problem of unjust violence. The problem is admittedly serious, someone might say, but it is not the whole story. The other misinterpretation would stress that Christ's redemptive work entails a cross on which he died voluntarily but passively; hence his example rules out any possibility of offering active resistance to violence. Both reproaches are unjust, and they are based on a false presupposition. They assume that I am completely equating the religious dimension with the human dimension. They do not choose to see my interpretation for what it claims to be, that is, an attempt to throw theological light on a problem that is not exclusively biblical and religious. I am not advocating a literal and complete carryover from religious conduct to political conduct, a one-to-one correlation. The whole matter calls for further clarification and treatment. Here I would simply enter a protest against such

misinterpretations, which overlook my intentions here and pigeonhole my thinking in terms of one extreme or another. My feeling is that the categories I employ here are valid and worthwhile in trying to tackle a problem that represents a difficult combination of the religious and the political. Polemical attempts to treat it in a disjointed way will serve no real purpose at all.

4. *La Violence*, Semaine des Intellectuels Catholiques 1967, Paris, 1967, pp. 205–11.

5. See *Stride Toward Freedom: The Montgomery Story* (New York: Harper & Row, 1958); *Strength to Love* (New York: Harper & Row, 1963); *Why We Can't Wait* (New York: Harper & Row, 1964).

6. *La Violence*, p. 219.

7. Various anthologies of Torres' writings are now available in English.

8. It is not my intention here to pass judgment on the subjective decision of Camilo Torres or on the soundness of his practical techniques and solutions. His personal case is treated in terms of a more general vision rather than in terms of its own concrete cast.

9. G. Lercaro, "Coscienza cristiana e violenza," *Aggiornamenti sociali*, September–October 1968, pp. 621–32.

10. Pope Paul VI, in *L'Osservatore Romano*, August 25 and 26–27, 1968.

Epilogue

9

Liturgy and Liberation

More and more the Latin American Church is coming to regard Christian salvation in terms of liberation. Since liturgy is an essential aspect of the salvation mission, the Christian cannot help but wonder how liberation and liturgy might be properly combined. This essay is an attempt to consider what the relationship between liturgy and liberation might be. If it manages to show how the liturgy can be enriched by a liberation perspective and how liberation can be christianized through the living forms of liturgy, then it will have accomplished its purpose.

The treatment here consists of three sections. The first attempts to make clear that liberation needs liturgy if it is not to be reduced to a purely political effort. The second section stresses the need for liturgical renewal if liturgy is to truly contribute to a liberative way of life. The third section will attempt to spell out some practical possibilities.

Redemptive Liberation and Liturgical Forms

There is more and more talk about liberation every day in Latin America. Some of it sees liberation in terms of the older liberal or neoliberal points of view, thus framing the topic in hackneyed concepts. Aside from this viewpoint, the term is usually used as a slogan against every form of repression and oppression—and particularly against those which seek to maintain the established order, the status quo. In that sense liberation is, and cannot help but be, a political task.

When we Christians talk about liberation, we are not trying to evade the political import of the term at all. Both the acceptance and the rejection of the established social and political order are political attitudes and perhaps even political activities. There is a basic political connotation in both. It is to be found when a person seeks to bring about change, and it is to be found equally when one simply chooses to let things go on as before. What more could the established centers of power ask than that the citizenry let them operate without interference!

Note what I mean here by the term "political" and "politics." I am not using them in the strictly technical sense of direct involvement in the running of the *res publica*. Here the terms refer to full-fledged activity on the part of the citizenry, which cannot help but entail involvement in the public and group life of a given society. Each and every one of us is involved with others, and no one can deny us the right and the obligation to be ourselves.

Thus we should not be alarmed that our Christian activity is political insofar as it is concerned with the present state of society and with the urgent task of societal transformation. When it has not been watered down by power, wealth, or indolence, the Christian spirit is always prepared to fight for urgently needed changes and radical transformations —whether they apply to itself or to the corporate self which we as a group constitute.

We should be alarmed, however, if Christian liberation were to be reduced to merely political liberation, if it were to be shaped more by political sources than by biblical ones. There is a real danger that our work on behalf of liberation might cease to be a totally Christian activity. Indeed we cannot say that we have always evaded the danger. So when we talk about liberation, we must always remember that we are talking about

Christian liberation. This is a redemptive liberation, and hence our actions must be shaped by the liberative exigencies of Christianity. Anything else is, at best, preliminary and incomplete.

Christian liberation loses its specific character when it is understood in a too restricted sense or purely negative sense, and also when it is deprived of any transcendent sense. It is taken in a too restricted sense when it is interpreted solely in terms of socio-political and economic oppression. It is taken in a purely negative sense when it is used solely to subvert existing structures without providing a basis for the construction of new structures. It is deprived of its transcendent sense when the note of sin is not pointed up in the existing situation of oppression and injustice. Christian liberation must stress that the truth of creation and of humankind is blocked by sin, that it is God our Father who liberates us in Christ, and that liberation activity should lead us towards the freedom of God's children.

Christian liberation can and should embody the fullness of Christianity, though it will be interpreted from within our concrete situation in salvation history. In so doing, it must not whittle down the Christian message or reduce it to a purely secular activity. Here I do not intend to discuss the dangers of reductionism and negativism. My intention is to point up how the liturgy can bring out the transcendent aspect and import of Christian liberation.

Authentic Christian liberation is discovered and fostered in the liturgy, and only in the liturgy. Insofar as it is Christian at all, liberation must be comprehended and lived in and through the summons of a saving divine word. This word finds expression and tone in the anguished utterances of people living today, and particularly in the utterances of the poor. But what we hear in their voices is the word of God, which speaks to us and imposes demands on us through their voices. Now the peculiar and proper place to listen to this divine word is, and ever remains, the Church, i.e., the ecclesial community brought together by God's word. And the vital community center for this saving word is undoubtedly the liturgical assembly, when this assembly truly is what it is supposed to be. The saving word of God becomes a living and vibrant appeal in the ecclesial community when the community evinces a vibrant and authentic liturgical way of life. The biblical message already has a vital place in the liturgical assembly, of course, but its aim in that assembly is to make the word of God present as light and life.

This saving word must be relived in the context of the actual historical situation, and it must be converted into here-and-now Christian experience. If it is not, it will find no listeners; it will be nothing more than a jumble of meaningless sounds, shedding no light on human lives and possessing no sacramental efficacy. The word of God must become light (the liturgy of the word) and life (the eucharistic liturgy) within the Christian assembly that has been convened by the Lord. There can be no Christian way of life without Christian light, and such light is meaningless if it is not transformed into a way of life. Faith and life come together as one in the action of the liturgy. If we separate them into distinct phases, that is only due to the human condition; it does not mean that we can really dissociate the two aspects of light and life. Since the light is also life, and vice-versa, we cannot interpret God's word in atemporal or purely individualistic terms. We must keep the two together at every moment; and we must keep them together in the liturgical assembly which is brought together in the Lord's name and has the promise of his special presence.

Only in this way can we get beyond the purely sociological and political realm of experience with regard to the process of liberation—without eliminating or neglecting this realm, of course. And only the liturgy can make liberation present as the plenitude of Christian salvation. From the Christian standpoint it is clear that we can and must get beyond a purely immanent conception of our work on behalf of liberation, though we cannot neglect that aspect. Insofar as that aspect is concerned, we must ever remember that the Church is in danger of forgetting and trying to evade the importance of fleshing out her salvific mission in the reality of this world, a reality which remains political and social for human beings. We can never stress too much the fact that the Church's understanding of Christian revelation must be enriched by her incarnation of that divine word in the flesh of a given time and place. But that is not all there is to the Christian message. The Christian message goes beyond merely profane reality. It has its own proper riches and its own proper autonomy. It has a priority of its own that sends out a summons to us. It is not a dead letter embodied in repetitious formulas. It is instead a summons to an integral Christian way of life, which is precisely what the liturgy seeks to bring about.

It is clear, then, that the Christian experience of liberation, of salvation as liberation, must be shared communally in and through the privileged locale for this sharing. In other words, it must be shared in the action of the liturgy. But if this is to happen, the liturgy itself must be liberated from the dangers that have all too often engulfed it.

The Liturgy and Alienation

One cannot deny the fact that the Church has contributed to the process of alienation. For our purposes here, two aspects deserve mention. The Church has abetted alienation by not doing all that it should have done to liberate people from the many serious forms of oppression that have existed in the world and still continue to exist. The Church has also abetted alienation by indirectly contributing to that oppression. It may be true that we must reject or tone down many of Marx's criticisms of religion, regarding them as superficial attacks that do not take due account of the historicity of man and society. At the same time, however, we must admit that the Church has contributed to the manifold forms of oppression both actively and passively.

Now the fact is that this negative influence of the Church has been wielded most strongly in and through the liturgy, in and through the very thing which we described above as the essential wellspring of Christian liberation. Let us admit that the liturgy has contributed historically to some forms of liberation. Let us also grant that in some instances where the liturgy has not done enough for the process of liberation this was due to basic historical limitations from which the Church could free herself only insofar as the history of divine revelation itself underwent change over the course of time. These explanations may be valid as far as they go, but that does not alter a fact of tremendous theoretical scope and significance. The fact is that the liturgy, if it truly is to be the acme of concrete Christian experience, must be vivified by the ongoing incarnation of God's word in the total reality of history.

The Christian liturgy should offer us the maximum possibility of salvation, yet the fact is that certain long-standing forms of the liturgy have contributed to man's alienation. Mere recognition of that fact should help us to preclude or obviate the ever-present danger. The root of the problem here is that all too often liberation has been equated with evasion. The liturgy has always sought salvation, even liberative salvation. But all too often it has jumped to the conclusion that authentic Christian liberation is to be found in flight and evasion.

First and foremost, the liturgy has been based too much on the *other* life, the life beyond this present one. Salvation supposedly lies in that other life, the life of eternity. We are saved here insofar as strains of the after-life pervade our life here and now. Thus the liturgy has focused our attention on the moral and religious realm, after reducing the dimensions of that realm. The important thing is the after-life; and it is the inner, secret, private aspect of our present life that is more directly related to the after-life. Hence we should withdraw from this world, living in anticipation of our entrance into the next life. The liturgy is more or less a pledge of that future life, and its whole apparatus is designed to give us a taste of, and a taste for, the celestial banquet. The ordinary liturgy has spiritually toned down the awesome social problems of poverty, love, and justice which are an essential part of the Christian message. It has intimated that one can do almost anything so long as one's intention is pure—even make war. And the exaggerated pleas of Isaiah, Amos, Hosea, Luke, and James are voices from another day. Once we spiritualize their content, we can reiterate their statements without losing our peace of mind even though our parish may be situated in the most affluent suburb in town.

That particular point need not be stressed greatly here, for it has already caught the attention of liturgists in Latin America. But there is another subtle mechanism at work which should be noted. It is all the more serious because it is grounded on a truth which post-Trent theology regards as of major importance in the interpretation of the sacramental life. It is the *ex opere operato* aspect of the liturgy. The Christian is obliged to accept and live the fact that the liturgy is based on an intrinsic sacramental efficacy. But it is a big step from there to the frame of mind which tends to minimize the role played by the active faith of the believer in the sacramental process. This step is taken all too often, so that our liturgy has been invaded by a whole set of factors which prevent it from carrying out its liberative mission.

The liturgy of *ex opere operato* tends to look at grace as a gratuitous gift which is caused directly by a sacrament once certain preconditions have been fulfilled. It tends to assume that grace can be received without one living the life of grace personally. The point is not to maintain that grace must be felt, but to point out that grace is not some tangible object we receive. Grace is a personal encounter, a personal communication. One line of Protestant exegesis goes overboard when it interprets the bread of life as the acceptance of Jesus Christ as savior in faith. But one line of Catholic dogmatic theology goes overboard in the opposite direction when it puts an overly physical interpretation on the Johannine texts which talk about eating the bread of life. This is clearly evident in the fact that the Catholic Mass has often slighted the liturgy of the word, and in the fact that many average Catholics see the liturgy of the word as so much time wasted prior to the eucharistic celebration itself. No real liturgical effort is made to make God's salvific word a living experience of the congregation, to turn it into a life-giving reality in and through the light of faith. It is a short step from there to turning the reception of the sacraments into an individualistic brand of magic. It is no longer concrete human beings living in a concrete historical situation who are to give life and breath to the Christian message in their context. As the liturgists of the "beyond" would have it, it is some universal and eternal humanity which remains the same in every time and place. Indeed if salvation, understood as liberation, were not something required for all human beings of every age and place, then it would not be a proper concern of liturgy at all.

Here we see one of the many dangers inherent in the liturgy of *ex opere operato*, and this particular danger is of prime importance to us here. The liturgy of *ex opere operato* downplays the changing historical situation which is part of the liturgy. If the crucial factor is the *ex opere operato* element, and if the grace of the sacrament is received passively without any regard for the personal encounter that is essentially a part of it, then one and the same liturgy can serve both the ancient Romans and modern Americans; and it can be expressed in exactly the same forms. The clearest evidence of this mentality is the fact that until quite recently the liturgy was couched in the ancient Latin language. Understanding the summons of the liturgical word was of secondary importance. If it happened at all, it happened on the level of the individual. The use of the vernacular today does suggest an advance, but we cannot stop with a translation of the language of the liturgy. It is really the liturgy itself that must be translated into all the languages and lifestyles of those who are supposed to live out the liturgy in their lives. Just to cite one example, how can we possibly use the same texts and signs in the Sunday liturgy addressed to a New York congregation as we might use in a Sunday liturgy addressed to some rural congregation in Latin America? Even if we could find some universal element shared by both, that would entail the suppression of the differences between them—the suppression of real life. But what is liturgy if it is not life? Of what use is a liturgy of *ex opere operato* that does not comprehend life in its totality?

In such a liturgy no real effort is made to make sure that the liturgy will carry out its specific mission of rendering the divine mystery present in living signs and making God's summoning word effectively present to the community. That word summons the community from within their real-life situation and calls them to act on behalf of that situation. But in the *ex opere operato* liturgy these important values are subordinated to some sort of uniform universality, as if this were the best way of maintaining the living unity of the Church.

Like the other areas of the Third World, Latin America has its own specific problem. It needs liberation on every level, from all sorts of oppression. But the forms of oppression existing in Latin America are very different from those which Marcuse has described in the context of the advanced industrial societies. This root problem must be tackled by the Latin American Church, and it must be tackled in terms which apply specifically to the Latin American situation. Yet the liturgy which we have experienced in Latin America has contributed more to oppression than to liberation, at least on the social front. There is a real danger that the new liturgy will be alienating too if it does not take seriously its mission to save the people of Latin America from oppression in all its forms. We cannot indulge in the luxury of elitist liturgies. For it is the whole people that is called upon to become the people of God.

Practical Suggestions

To begin with, we must get beyond a liturgy centered around *ex opere operato* efficacy and the after-life. We must fuse its elements with others, sublimating the whole into a unity that is

242 Freedom Made Flesh

much more incarnate in form. We must devise a new way of living the liturgical life, grounding ourselves on the gospel principle that "the truth shall make you free." We must come to experience the truth as a living force in the liturgy. We must treat this truth thematically and present it in such forms that it truly serves to enlighten our lives.

That does not mean we will have to put forced meanings on the texts, for in themselves they are perfectly suited to our situation of institutionalized violence. We need only read them in a truly vital way, relating them directly to our own context. But while this truth lies behind the efficaciousness promoted by the sacrament, there is no real efficaciousness unless this truth has been assimilated in and through faith. The truth must be fleshed out in concrete life. Its real purpose is to fashion human freedom, to move us from liberation to the freedom of the children of God. In his letter to the Romans (Rom. 8) Paul describes this process in predominantly physical terms, centering it around the notion of *physis*. Today we have every right to describe and interpret the same process in social and political terms, centering it around the notion of the *polis*. We are supposed to attain the freedom of God's children, and we cannot do that without effecting drastic forms of liberation. We must remember what Thomas Münzer told the German peasants at the time of the Reformation. Reacting against Luther's political conformism, he told them that they must not stop living as children of God and exercising the freedom which that status implied, for that was what grace demanded of them.

At this point I should like to offer some practical possibilities with regard to the Mass liturgy, showing how it might become a liberation liturgy. For the Mass is the culminating point of our liturgical activity, and remarks concerning it can be readily adapted to other liturgical ceremonies.

The Mass should begin with a penitential liturgy. What distinguishes Christian liberation at the outset is the fact that it interprets oppression as an active sin and the absence of true filial freedom as a passive sin. It sees sin in everything that

prevents the individual from attaining and exercising the freedom of the children of God. It sees sin in everything which
serves collectively to obscure God's loving presence within
existing social structures. Everything that poses obstacles to
true Christian community is also sin. Sin puts restraint on
everything, and we all are responsible for it in one way or
another. It is our offense against the God who is our Father, the
God who is Love, the God who has revealed his loving and
paternal nature in and through the sonship of Christ. This
sinfulness must be uprooted from the individual and from the
world. It must be uprooted from humanity as a whole and
created things as a whole.

The Christian community must focus its gaze on this fundamental sin when it wishes to call attention to the fact of redemptive salvation. We are all united in this sinfulness, and so we
should all be united in the redemption from it. The liturgy
should help the assembled community to see how this sinfulness pervades every sphere of life from the local community to
the realm of international affairs. We must accept our responsibility for it, especially for the sinfulness of our local community. Today there are many resources which can be used to get
the point across in the liturgy: films, pictorial displays, songs,
and so forth.

In accepting our responsibility for this sinfulness, our attention should be centered on conversion and change. Some aspects of our sinfulness will call for personal conversion first and
foremost. The "old man" must be put to death in us so that the
"new man" may be born. Other aspects of this sinfulness will
call for social change and a fight against the problems opposing
such change. It is in this area that we must heed the prophetic
strain in the biblical message, responding to its call for conversion and renewed hope in God. It is here that the people of God
must pay attention to the transcendent aspect of the Christian
message and its implications for their committed activity in the
world.

The penitential liturgy should be followed by the liturgy of the word. Frequently people's yearnings for liberation are nourished by sources that are not wholly Christian, and there is a danger that the authentic Christian sense of liberation will be given short shrift. The fact is that the Bible overflows with an authentic and original thrust towards liberation in all its forms, ranging from the innermost problems of the individual to the struggles of the chosen people as a whole and from the most critical obstacles facing the liberation process to the most positive ideals of total freedom. The full force and weight of the biblical word should be made clear in the liturgy of the word, so that it may become the concrete personal word of the individual and the people living today. The liturgy of the word must be more than a passive listening process. The biblical message must be not only understood but also assimilated so that it can help to shed light on everyday reality and open the way for active interpretation. Only in this way can the eucharistic sacrament be the source of freedom that it should be. Only in this way can we get human beings who are truly free in a Christian sense.

Finally we come to the sacrificial liturgy. Where there is sin, there must be redemption: and where sin has abounded, there death must also abound. The Christian interpretation of social disorder and oppression as sin must be consistent here and pursue its line of thought to its logical consequences. It must acknowledge that freedom can only come through death and subsequent resurrection. It is thus that the Christian interpretation of the situation evades the trap of developmentalism pure and simple. The latter outlook can point up a certain element of sacrifice insofar as it demonstrates the need for costly effort, but the Christian outlook is even more thoroughgoing and radical. Costly effort is not enough, it points out. If our existing societal reality is objective and collective sin, then it must go through a real death.

The sacrificial aspect of the Mass reminds us that Christian liberation must be a redemptive liberation in the strict sense. Proponents of liberation run a risk when they place too much emphasis on the positive aspect alone, on the attainment of freedom, leaving room for pain and death only insofar as liberation entails a struggle against the forces of oppression and domination. Too narrow a focus on structural change alone will impoverish and minimize the distinctive character of Christian liberation. For this puts great stress on the element of personal, individual dying to the old way of life so that one may rise to a new way of life. Quite apart from the fact and necessity of struggle, which is very real, one must enter into the Christian schema of death and resurrection. The individual must go through death, the people as a whole must go through death, and structures must go through death. Of course the hope of resurrection pervades this process, though we may only see it through a glass darkly in this life. There is only one redemptive sacrifice, it is true, but much is still wanting in the passion of Christ and in his resurrection as well.

The Mass, which is first and foremost a sacrifice, is the most obvious locale for living out this Christian reality. But there is a potential danger here too. We may place too much emphasis on its unbloody nature and on its intrinsic efficacy quite apart from the operative faith of the believer. Then we tend to take refuge in such notions as "purity of intention," "interior death," and a "poverty of spirit" wholly divorced from poverty in our life style. We tend to go in for purely secular and profane activities that are a far cry from the gospel message, excusing ourselves on the grounds that our motives are pure. We prefer to "die" at morning Mass than to die with the oppressed people around us, feeling disinclined to look for the dying Christ amid these people. But it is the ongoing passion and death of Christ in history that we should be living in the sacrifice of the Mass.

To be sure, the liturgical texts now in use in the Mass and the sacraments do not help us very much to grasp what dying and rising with Christ really means. Here professional liturgists could do a lot to help pastors find a way to give real-life efficacy to the liturgy without radically undermining its *ex opere operato* efficacy. People are dying in real life. We all are summoned to die in real life. That must somehow be brought out in the Mass. The mere repetition of a liturgical ritual will not do much to enhance either the Mass or those who stick to its fixed formulas.

This, then, is a brief outline of what a liberation liturgy might look like. It would have penitential, prophetic, and sacrificial features, culminating with the people's shared communion of the fruits of this sacrifice. Such a liturgy can do much to ensure the Christian liberation will truly be a redemptive liberation. By the same token, a liberation perspective can do much to ensure that the Mass will be lived out in a richer and deeper way, in the way it should be.